The Wheel of Rebirth

The Wheel of Rebirth

An Autobiography of Many Lifetimes

H.K. Challoner

A QUEST BOOK
Published under a grant from the Kern Foundation

THE THEOSOPHICAL PUBLISHING HOUSE
Wheaton, Ill., U.S.A.
Madras, India / London, England

© Copyright H. K. Challoner, 1969

All rights reserved

First Quest edition 1976 published by The Theosophical Publishing House, Wheaton, Illinois, a department of The Theosophical Society in America.

Mills, Janet Melanie Ailsa, 1894-
  The wheel of rebirth.

(A Quest book)
Bibliography: p.
1. Reincarnation.   I. Title.
BP573.R5M5   1976   133.9'013   75-26759
ISBN 0-8356-0468-3 pbk.

PRINTED IN THE UNITED STATES OF AMERICA

Dedicated
with affection and gratitude
to "A.N." and the other two

CONTENTS

Chapter		Page
	Introductory Note to the First Edition	9
	Introduction to the Second Edition	11
	Prologue	25
I.	Atlantis	45
II.	Egypt	59
III.	Persia	124
IV.	Greece	145
V.	Germany	169
VI.	Italy	206
VII.	England	218
	Epilogue	257

INTRODUCTORY NOTE TO THE FIRST EDITION BY CYRIL SCOTT

THE author of *Regents of the Seven Spheres* needs, I feel, but little introduction from me; nevertheless, I have been asked to make a few prefatory remarks with regard to the main object of this new book. In the previous work, pictures of the future were impressed by Devas; but *The Wheel of Rebirth* deals more specifically with the past, involving that fundamental truth of occultism, the theory of Karma and reincarnation which alone explains in a rational manner the inequalities of human character and destiny. Yet although occult students, and even laymen, may accept these doctrines as broad facts, they are frequently puzzled as to the rationale of their workings. What, indeed, are the particular effects produced by particular causes? Why *should* this particular effect result from that particular cause? The disquisitions on the subject to be found in theosophical literature have not by any means covered the whole of the ground. Now, for the first time, many of those enigmas and problems which perennially arise in connection with the idea of rebirth, and which perplex the minds of thinkers of all types, are answered in illuminating fashion.

Under the appropriate guidance, the author's higher consciousness was projected back through a series of lives which have been portrayed with the vividness of actual experience and are shown in their true relation to each other of cause and effect. Some of these lives, as such, may well appear grim and horrifying, notably those in which practices in black magic are described. But here I would remind the reader that many occult writers have implied in effect that the courage and strength of will thus acquired, albeit on the wrong lines, may prove an equally powerful force for good when transmuted into selfless service for humanity under the guidance of its Teachers; and that those who, throughout their lives, have lacked the initiative even to sin, may likewise be deficient in the corresponding qualities which would make them intrepid co-workers with the Higher Ones.

This, in short, is a book that may be taken as the life of Everyman, and if the sins and failures of his past are dispassionately revealed, so the potentialities opening out from the moment he has set his feet upon the Path are indicated by one who speaks with the authority of personal experience.

INTRODUCTION TO THE SECOND EDITION

THERE can be little doubt that from the moment man was intelligent enough to reason he asked himself the question: "Why has this happened to me?" "Why have sickness, disaster, tragedy befallen my family or friends?" "What have I done to deserve these cruel blows of fate?"

The more complex his existence has become, the greater his capacity for intellectual reasoning has developed, the more difficult it has been for him to find answers which satisfy heart and mind.

The breaking of taboos or the anger of the gods may satisfy primitive peoples, while the belief in chance or fate can be enough for the unthinking and the materialist; but they do not suffice for the man who is trying to discover truth. Nor is the Church's answer that it is the will of God any more convincing. Modern man quite reasonably rejects the concept of an apparently capricious and illogical deity who, while alleged to be a god of love, a father who cares for his children, permits the innocent to suffer from no fault of their own while the evil men and aggressors flourish exceedingly. Such gross injustice we, imperfect though we are, would not countenance for a moment.

But most of the Eastern religions as well as some systems of Western philosophy present us with another and more convincing hypothesis for the inequalities, the terrible and apparently fortuitous tragedies of the world, as well as for all the beauty and goodness which we can perceive around us, including our personal "good fortune".

Man, they insist, is basically the creator of his own fate, for good or ill. So far as the latter is concerned he is the victim of his ignorance of the spiritual laws which govern the universe. He breaks them and suffers the consequences. Thrust your hand into the fire and you will be burned; not because any "god" punishes you but because fire burns. It is as simple as that. We are told that the greatest law of all is love. So our mistakes, our crimes against others and against life itself are committed because, lacking love, we cannot see that in harming anything or anyone we are harming ourself and that in consequence sooner or later we shall have to redress the balance we have upset and pay the price for what we have done. At every level effect must follow cause, as night follows day. What happens to us now, either individually, as a group, or as a nation, be it good or ill, must be the result of earlier causes set in motion by acts made, often ages ago, the seeds of which have lain in the womb of time awaiting the appropriate conditions for germination.

It is obvious that, so far as the individual is concerned (although this is equally applicable to groups large or small), the effects of mistakes and misdeeds cannot possibly all be expiated or experienced in one short life or period of time; but by returning to earth we can pay our debts, perfect our relationships and finish what we have begun where the train of causation was initiated.

Interest in this hypothesis of reincarnation, or reembodiment of consciousness, the migration through time of the individual in many different bodies and sets of conditions down the ages has of recent years aroused increasing interest and attention. This seems to be because modern man is beginning to question and reject outworn dogmas and creeds which no longer satisfy his need to understand the deeper causes for the human condition.

But the fact that the concept is to be found in one form

or another in virtually every great religion and spiritual system of philosophy is still not generally known.

It must have been taken for granted at the time of Jesus since he asked his disciples: "Who do men say that I am?" and they replied: "Elijah or one of the prophets." Again Jesus was asked: "Did this man sin or his parents that he was *born* blind?"—the implication clearly being that he had sinned before his present birth. Jesus also bade his hearers to be "perfect even as your Father in heaven is perfect". He was not one to demand the impossible. So it is reasonable to ask how could ordinary people become perfect in one short life? The very best of men, even great saints, still have their imperfections. This saying makes no sense at all unless we postulate further opportunities for growth. But growth of an enduring nature is always slow, and the awakening from the darkness of ignorance to a true understanding of the meaning and purpose of life, with the conquest of the errors and weaknesses within us all, could hardly take place except by means of a long series of experiments in living which would gradually bring about an expansion of consciousness and develop the Christ spirit within us, the divine redemptive qualities of love, compassion and wisdom.

It was in order to exemplify and to explain the significance of the theory of reincarnation and of Karma—the Eastern term for the law of cause and effect—that this book was "given" to the author, from a higher level of consciousness, as is explained in the Prologue.

It illustrates the long journey through time of a group of people—and of one in particular—showing how the law of Karma operated in life after life and how effects were worked out from earlier causes. It is essentially the story of the interplay of relationships which in their inception were destructive and filled with hate but eventually through much suffering were transmuted into links of love and understanding.

Personally I am inclined to believe that the account is literally true, so far at least as I am concerned. But if this claim is considered by the reader to be too improbable or fantastic to be acceptable then this series of lives can still be taken as being symbolic of the lives of Everyman and his infinitely slow progress as he journeys upward from the miasmas of his own ignorance. It shows him passing through trial and more often error, through disasters and defeats, successes and periods of relative contentment; yet always possessed of an awareness, however faint and fleeting, of a perfection just beyond his reach; at moments even catching a glimpse of its bright face through the compassion and love in another traveller's eyes. Thus is he lured on from darkness to the first redemptive gleam of light and understanding of his real goal.

For no man is unique. Humanity is one; the journey is one; and so is the goal—liberation from our illusions about the real nature of life and death.

Although most of the questions and objections regarding this idea of rebirth which readers will certainly raise are dealt with in the text, I feel that some comments are necessary, together with a general broad outline of the basic principles involved, since many may never have considered the hypothesis seriously before and others, because of lack of understanding of the wider and deeper implications, may have been inclined to dismiss it out of hand.

Unfortunately, as happens with every religious and philosophical system of belief, distortions and misunderstandings have crept in and this concept has become further debased by all sorts of fantastic and romantic notions as well as superficial interpretations of the basic truths behind it.

But to begin with, there are two propositions which must at least be provisionally accepted if the account which follows is to make any sense at all.

The first is that man is perfectible. The second that there exists an aspect of our being of which we are not normally cognizant, called by Jung the superconscious and by religious teachings the Higher Self or Soul.

Unfortunately the teachings of the Christian Church never give us a clear idea of what the nature of the soul really is. We are told that our soul can be "saved" or "lost" if we do or do not believe in a set of creeds and dogmas or if we break the laws of God. But it remains no more than a kind of vague and shadowy appendage of our personality.

This is the cause of one of the primary misconceptions about reincarnation. We become hopelessly confused as to which aspect of what we think of as ourselves takes this long journey through time, passing from life to life.

Normally when we say "I" we associate the word with our personality, that which goes by our name, which suffers and rejoices, which makes links of love or of hate, which experiences all the emotions and events that are part of "our" life; so it is this personal self which automatically we think of as returning to earth in other bodies and in other times.

But the personality does not return; indeed it cannot do so, as a few moment's thought will soon make clear.

The word personality comes from *persona*—a mask, and what we know of ourselves here is literally a mask for our real self, "our" Soul, a centre of our consciousness at a higher level with which we can learn to make contact if we are prepared for the necessary effort.

But it is the expression "my" soul which is the real cause of so much misunderstanding. We are, in fact, each *a* soul which possesses, for its temporary use, a personality centred in the material world. This, even at best, is never more than a partial reflection of our total nature, cast forth for a short period into a material envelope so that certain processes of growth may take place, certain debts be paid, certain realizations achieved. For this aspect of our selves is also growing as is everything else in manifestation.

The soul might be thought of as the depository of all those memories of past experiences on earth valuable and important enough to have made a permanent contribution to its growth: a central power-house in which qualities and realizations acquired during these partial sojourns on earth are transformed into powers. Nothing of value is ever lost to us here, everything is used in the effort to create eventually a vehicle in dense matter through which we—soul and body at last united in consciousness can act as a channel for the transmission of energies from higher spiritual levels to mankind. For, as the Greeks taught, the soul is a bridge between heaven—that is the higher, spiritual realms—and the material world; an instrument for the hastening of that process called by Teilhard de Chardin the "divinization" of matter.

But because our consciousness is so deeply immersed in material existence and so completely identified with our personality, it is extraordinarily difficult for us to change our focus, as it were, and identify our human self with this higher and still unknown level of our being. And even more difficult to accept the fact that we, as we know ourselves here, our human "I", will probably not long survive death and that we ourselves will abandon it as a butterfly abandons the chrysalis when it has served its purpose.

It helps if occasionally we make the effort to stand back from our personality and consider *what* of this personality self we would wish to endure beyond death and return to continue the work we have begun; to perfect what we have left unfinished here, to re-embody those powers, qualities, talents we have been either deliberately or unconsciously developing during the course of a lifetime. This exercise might also give us a clearer understanding of what aspect of our being contains the seed of continuity and could effect this transmigration from one state or body to another; that is to say, wherein abides the nucleus of our consciousness of selfhood, that undying part which will move on after the pause for gestation called death to another experiment in living, even as a traveller crosses the sea to another country yet does not thereby lose his identity.

It would hardly be the child self—a creature of instincts, a little animal just opening its eyes to the world.

Nor presumably the adolescent, uncertainly experimenting, making endless mistakes, bewildered, half child half adult.

Would it be what we think of as the adult self, still in a halfway stage of development and usually too busy, too deeply involved in the essential activities of the material world to have had time to digest his experiences?

Or the old man, struggling with the difficulties and frustrations of failing powers and often resentful of their loss and of a growing disability to deal with life?

Each has represented our "I" of the moment, each is in some measure ourself, linked to our present "I" by memory; yet are we not more than all of them together? Is not this "I" which will survive in a sense a distillation of the essence of the totality of this latest series of new experiments from which all the while is being created a new aspect of individuality?

Another difficulty is to grasp the concept of karmic continuity, cause leading to effect, effect leading again to cause, operating through immense periods of time; for inevitably we see our lives broken by death into separate segments. Yet in reality there is no break. This long journey might be said to resemble a river, a single stream of consciousness flowing from the darkness of its primal source ever onward until it reaches the ocean of light and knows itself to be, what in truth it has always been, an aspect of the consciousness of the Infinite. Thus the soul's existence here on earth or in the afterlife is but one unbroken movement; ever changing its environment and quality, yet ever remaining in essence itself, each action, each choice contributing to the volume and quality of the stream, making it what it is.

Such a picture gives the pronouncement: "As ye sow, so also shall ye reap" a new reality. No part is dissociated from any other; the whole river is one, so what the personality may believe to be chance or a precipitation of Karma is part of the inevitable process of this onward sweep of the "living soul" towards the development of its own divine potentialities.

Behind this teaching there are deeper implications; for in essence all apparently separate "streams" are united in the basic unity of Life, each contributing to each and all to the All. But here we enter the realm of metaphysics.

It is obvious that we, whose vision and understanding are circumscribed by purely human conceptions of time and space cannot possibly discover how or when man developed the first gleam of individuality. Life manifests cyclically; therefore what we think of as beginnings may, in essence, be no more than the end of one cycle leading to the emergence of another with, again, no real break between, possibly with no beginning and to no end.

While every religion and tradition has its creation story, none of them can represent more than a symbolic picture of the Reality for which there would be no words in human language. Many, however, teach that at one "moment" in the cyclic ebb and flow of the One Life a divine spark of self-consciousness was implanted like a seed in animal man on this earth, and from this the first appearance of a "living soul" was born endowed with the potentiality of becoming a god-like being manifesting on earth divine qualities as did Jesus and the Buddha.

I mentioned above the distortions which have crept into the whole concept of reincarnation and which have made many people reject it out of hand.

INTRODUCTION TO SECOND EDITION 19

These have largely arisen from the very common tendency to take metaphysical or religious concepts literally, treating them as absolute realities instead of realizing that such realities can, in the main, only be expressed in symbolical form, by analogy or in metaphor. This applies as much to many Christian teachings as to any others.

One such distortion of the idea of rebirth is taught by a well-known school of what is loosely called "occultism".

The term "occult" is unfortunate and liable to create misunderstanding as its connotation in our day is almost wholly bad, being nearly always associated with dubious Orders, bogus claims in advertisements and the practice of primitive forms of magic. The word "occult" means "that which is hidden or unknown", therefore an "occultist" should indicate one who is searching for as yet undiscovered truths or facts either by scientific methods regarding the physical laws of the universe, or by the study and practice of the techniques to be found in the esoteric teachings of all the great religions which reveal the spiritual significance of these same laws and the use of their hidden powers in the service of God and mankind. When the word "occult" is used in this book it always relates to this line of research.

The idea held by the particular school mentioned above is, roughly, that if we fail in one life to make any real contact with the soul, do not meet our obligations or pay out debts, we shall have to re-live that life over and over again, exactly, in every detail, even meeting the same people and the same problems in the identical circumstances, until we do succeed in taking the vital step which will free us to move on.

No wonder the average person rejects it as either too terrible or too dreary to be contemplated. But how could such a fate be possible? How can we literally go back in time, into a past historical setting which no longer exists and into utterly changed social conditions? Moreover how can we re-meet the same people who will almost certainly themselves have changed in the interim and be quite different with different reactions? Even those of us—and they must be few—who have not profited from their experiences at all, must have still learned something, have absorbed new impressions even if only at subconscious levels, which would modify to some extent their thought and emotional patterns; so by this much they would have changed.

But as there can be no evasion of debts contracted in association with others or of the results of actions breaking moral laws, we shall almost inevitably find ourselves in similar, though *not* identical, circumstances and be presented with the same kind of problems until we do succeed in dealing with them from a higher level.

One of the ancient spiritual axioms declares that: *As it is in the inner, so it is in the outer.* If we are perceptive we can soon discover that indeed it is true that we make our "world" by what we are in ourselves. The psychiatrist has proved to us that indubitably:

> *The mind is its own place*
> *And of itself doth make a heaven of hell, a hell of heaven.*

The whole concept of Karma, the idea that causes from previous lives produce effects in others far removed in time, must continue to present many difficulties to the thoughtful, for it is obviously so profound, so subtle, so infinitely complex that we can only hope to recognize the more obvious and easily discernable repercussions. So it is always important to remind ourselves that we are seeking to understand spiritual laws and what we perceive here are only faint reflections of inner Realities.

This is exemplified by another misconception regarding reincarnation and Karma. Some people think that the idea of "an eye for an eye and a tooth for a tooth" is to be taken literally. Here again we are judging divine law by

INTRODUCTION TO SECOND EDITION

human standards and are thinking of Karma either as a punishment for wrong-doing, one that fits the crime, or as a reward for virtue. It is neither. There is no such thing as divine punishment. This is one of the most terrible and pernicious dogmas to be found in any religion. Nor are there any rewards. And we will get only one judge—our own Higher Self. It is said that after death there comes a stage when we see every forgotten detail of our lives, every act and thought and motive, freed from the delusions with which we guard ourselves from self-knowledge. This is the hour of judgement; the real "moment of truth".

We may punish ourselves here, as we often do, out of an exaggerated sense of guilt or punish others for even less admirable reasons. Virtue is literally its own reward for it builds into our being qualities and insights which will be our inheritance for all time.

Life is our school. We reincarnate in order to learn that love plus wisdom—so far as we are concerned the two are not, unfortunately, always synonymous—are the only keys to open the doors to a future of genuine happiness and inner peace. All the great teachers have repeated this over and over again, but only a few have listened.

There is one misapprehension which revolts people—and rightly. This is the belief that we can be reincarnated in animal form. As it stands it is nonsense. Once the spark of divinity has been lit in the darkness of the unself-conscious animal, it has become Man who can choose good or evil; who says "I am" and unlike the animal knows that he knows. So how can there be any turning back? However long it may take him, henceforth he is destined to become what, in the deepest sense, he IS, a son of God, a Light-bearer, a living soul. He may often appear to stand still, even sometimes to retrogress, but he will be expanding his higher consciousness all the time, whether, in his personality, he is aware of it or not.

But as with many such misapprehensions this one may well express a symbolical truth. Man remains an animal so far as his body and its functions are concerned and at an early stage he still possesses some animal attributes. These must eventually be transmuted into their higher counterparts; instinct, for instance, into intuition; the sex urge into pure love expressing compassion and sacrifice. To some extent these lower forces control and dominate the personality for long ages. But he who allows and even encourages them will inevitably become increasingly the slave of his animal nature in life after life. We know that there exist men and women who exhibit the worst forms of such retrogressive characteristics which, when conjoined with some measure of intellect, can make them a serious danger to their kind though most of all to themselves. In this sense only can human beings sink to almost subhuman levels. But the divine spark, however obscured, is still a part of their being; it *is* the source of their humanity. One day something may happen. Perhaps it will be an awakening of love for a bird or an animal which will stir within the hard carapace with which selfishness and blindness have imprisoned and stifled that eternal flame within; a turning-point will have been reached and its power will begin to operate. The tiny spark will slowly become a guiding beam increasing in strength in life after life, drawing the man up from the darkness and the slime, from among the "swine", towards liberation, glory and love in his Father's house.

One great obstacle to acceptance of the reincarnation hypothesis, particularly for the more scientifically minded, is that the demand for proof cannot so easily be satisfied. It is, of course, very difficult to obtain and there can be many other explanations for claims put forward by individuals who believe they remember past lives: although the appearance in very young children of what are normally acquired skills or even of genius, as with Mozart and very many others, is almost impossible to explain by any other means.

But of recent years much research has been carried out by numbers of unbiased people possessed of scientific training and integrity in an attempt to prove or disprove this proposition. They have examined hundreds of cases, sifting all available evidence, particularly when historical clues in the form of little known contemporary facts have been given. But the most convincing evidence comes from those few who claim to recall a very recent life, having obviously returned to a new body shortly after having quitted the old one. Here details of the past life in a specific country or district which the child—for it is nearly always a young person—can "remember", can be checked and have been found in a number of cases which have been rigorously investigated for fraud, conscious or unconscious, to be correct in every detail. Here again no other explanation except reincarnation seems possible.

An increasing number of books examining the whole case for the theory of rebirth and Karma are now appearing, many of which go very deeply into the subject in all its aspects.

This introduction is no more than a superficial review of the subject generally, but any readers who wish to know more of the whole vast field which the subject opens up will find a list of authors and titles in the bibliography at the end of this book.

PROLOGUE

It had been exceptionally hot that summer. Day after day the sun rose in a cloudless sky over the still sea and sank in roseate mists behind the blue of the distant hills. Day by day the heat increased. The marsh where cattle huddled in sparse shade by the dykes took on the same golden colour as the waste of sands and shingle and was half veiled by the same shimmering dance of fiery particles. Once there was a mirage over the distant headland; strange shapes like primeval giants walked the sea, ships hung in the void and a sense of unreality and menace brooded over the empty land.

Our bungalow stood on a ridge of shingle between the marsh and the sea. The older part was reputed to be haunted by a French sailor who appeared usually before some crisis. He was seen that year twice by one of our trio, but this did not trouble us for, owing perhaps to the extraordinary vitality of the air, we were filled with an almost reckless abandonment to the forces of nature and cared for nothing that might threaten us. We seemed, indeed, more and more to partake of the elements themselves, to be drawn ever closer, as day succeeded day in unbroken glory, into their very essence. The earth burned under our feet, vibrant with energy; at evening soft airs scented with hay, thyme, and seaweed whispered along the ridge; the water, advancing and receding in trance-like stillness, was so warm and buoyant that to float in it was like being suspended in liquid air. At night we would swim far out into a black and mysterious sea, afterwards running naked along the stretch of empty sands. We felt as if we had actually taken on once again the physical glory of some Greek incarnation; here the modern world was remote and the stress of living almost forgotten.

I had come to this place intending to start work seriously on a new novel, but so potent was the drive of sheer physical energy that I found I could do nothing. As the moon waxed, so did this sensation of strange unrest increase; it was almost as if one were being influenced by some elemental force.

At that time I was quite ignorant of astrology, else I might have realized that I was approaching some unusual crisis in my life. A similar event, we discovered later, was also mirrored in the horoscopes of my companions.

But of this we knew nothing; only as the days passed we became disturbed by a new factor which began to impinge upon our lives. Phenomena started to manifest all over the bungalow, and soon we realized that this mysterious force was becoming so powerful as almost to be inimical.

Now phenomena, as such, had never interested us. It seemed to me then—as it does now—a waste of valuable energy which should be turned to better account. We had none of us ever "sat for development", and I, at least, was perfectly convinced that I had no mediumistic abilities, being far more interested in the line of development which, through meditation and self-control, should bring discrimination and enhanced intuition, rather than what are loosely termed psychic powers. For to my mind the study of occultism, to be of any real use in this present age, should make men and women capable of dealing with the multitudinous problems of modern life from a spiritual point of view, rather than cause people to go off on mystic flights bearing little or no relation to the activities of the physical plane whereon they have been placed.

Before I speak further of the events which brought about the writing of this book I must explain that four of us were involved.

One had died several years previously. We had all been greatly attached to her, but we had never made any serious attempt to get in touch with her through mediums, as we none of us cared for this type of communication.

Of the others, one was the owner of the bungalow and had studied occultism with me for a considerable time, and the third was a very practical man of business who, although he knew very little of such subjects at that stage, was a natural psychic and occasionally passed out of his body in full consciousness at night. He had often seen our dead friend at these times and had brought back messages and instructions. In fact it was partly under her guidance that this bungalow had been built in a lonely place with a view to using it for spiritual study where higher energies might be tapped undiluted, as it were, by too many human contacts.

We were none of us of the type given to hysterical imaginings and were always on our guard against self-deception. Now, however, we found ourselves up against something we could neither control nor explain away.

For as the moon grew to its full, so did the phenomena increase.

Looking back with my present knowledge, I realize that the forces at work there must have been terrific. Even then, beginners though we were, we could sense Powers moving majestically over the wide stretches of marshland, brooding over the house, filling the air with their soundless voices. Since that time I have been permitted to visualize their shapes, to glimpse, however imperfectly, a faint shadow of their strength and their wisdom. Then I could only vaguely feel their presence. They were indeed gathering closer about us, forming a vortex of energy over this small centre, Powers of the air, the sea, and the earth; in their essence beneficent rather than malevolent; but to any who, like ourselves, had invoked them wrongly in past lives and were, through the mysterious compulsion of the Law, about to repay some of those ancient debts, they could represent a very real menace.

And as the vortex increased, the surplus of psychic energy began to take effect in physical matter. Its actual manifestations were trivial, but since we were all by this time unwittingly like small dynamos giving off power, objects in our immediate vicinity became affected by it.

Bedclothes were torn off the beds. Ink was thrown on to the wall. Messages were even found scribbled on any bit of paper which had been left lying about. Once a threatening sentence was written in the dust on a mirror in a disused room.

That room, indeed, soon became a focus for this alien influx of life. The dog refused absolutely to go into it and slunk miserably about, puzzled and alarmed.

The one clairvoyant member of our group occasionally caught glimpses of these activities; once he saw white figures marching round the little room which was always kept apart for meditation. He saw the sailor again. He saw the small garden full of moving lights and, what was more alarming, one evening he informed us that there was a gigantic toad seated on the back of a chair.

But we were not seriously worried; we treated it all rather as a joke, slightly irritated by the seeming irrelevancy of these occurrences, but not in the least aware of their real significance.

Then one night when the moon was almost full I had a dream; and from that dream dates the beginning of what was undoubtedly the turning-point of my own life.

Now I have found—and this has been confirmed for me by others, even by a practising psychotherapist—that there are two definite types of dreams. One is the ordinary mixture of symbols and images, nearly all arising from the activities of the subconscious mind, motivated by the desires, repressions, waking thoughts, and experiences of the personality; that happy hunting-ground, in fact, wherein the disciple of any of the innumerable schools of psychotherapy disports himself, without realizing that he is probing into that most illusive of all realms, the emotional or "astral" plane.

The other kind of dream, which I believe to be rare as yet with the majority of mankind, is so different that for one who has experienced it no confusion can arise.

Not only have such dreams a vividness, a logical sequence and an actuality lacking in the most logical even of the others, but they have another quality which, because of its very subtlety, is practically impossible to explain—just as it would be impossible to explain colour to a blind man, sound to a deaf one, or love to one who had never experienced it. These dreams inevitably have a powerful effect upon one's waking life and fill it with new significance, for they are actually memories of activities out of the body rather than anything connected with it during its conscious state.

Such a dream did I have that night. I found myself in Atlantis; I walked through the streets of the forgotten City of the Golden Gate, engaged in the consideration of a problem vital to my very existence; for I was at a crisis which was as clear and personal to me as my twentieth-century life is in my waking state. I woke before the problem was solved and slept again to find myself once more the same man. But now the scene had changed; my whole destiny had altered. I was engaged in the practice of a magical rite, the horror of which was such that I awoke abruptly as if afraid of being forced to re-enact that dead but still vivid episode of the past.

The next morning I took out my neglected typewriter and attempted to write the experience down in dramatic form. The words flowed with amazing ease. Every writer knows that rush of inspiration which carries him out of his normal self, surprising him often, using him when he fondly imagines that he is using it. But on that morning there was no doubt as to who had the upper hand. I felt myself to be no more than an instrument.

Scenes built themselves up magically, even the language was not my own. So for several hours I wrote, then abruptly the flow ceased like a river suddenly dammed, and I was left with a story only half finished. What intrigued me in this connection was that the black magic episode of my dream did not appear to fit in anywhere here, but obviously belonged to a later date in the life of this man who had, in these few hours, become somehow so intimately myself that I could almost feel his mind merging with my modern one.

I imagined I would get the rest of the story that night in sleep, but nothing of the sort happened. It then occurred to my friend that I should try what could be done with automatic writing. I was not hopeful. I had only once or twice attempted it, but the pencil had always remained motionless. Yet although I was actually in resistance to any such methods of communication, now I felt a strong urge to try what could be done.

One of our number had gone away for a few days on business, so the two of us who were left went that night into the sun-room, as the meditation room was called. We turned on the gramophone—it was César Franck's Symphony in D Minor, I remember—and I settled down with a pencil and block of paper in an extremely sceptical mood.

But to my amazement within a few minutes the pencil began to move. Like a thing possessed it rushed over the paper. I had deliberately not made myself too negative, and now I attempted to follow its movements with my mind, for the room was in darkness. After about half an hour I knocked off.

"Nothing," I said; "scribbles—pure waste of good time."

And so it was—not even an attempt at a word anywhere.

However, I thought I would give it one more trial, and the next night the same performance was repeated, except that this time it seemed to me that the pencil had formed, however crudely, the name of our dead friend.

This was found to be correct. The next evening a fragmentary message came through. Within four days I was writing fluently; but unlike the usual automatic writer, I always knew what was being written—hand and brain receiving the message simultaneously.

I am perfectly aware that to many this method will be dismissed as suspect, a mere projection from the subconscious mind or something of the sort. As a matter of fact, no one could have been more sceptical than I was myself. I had studied psychology too long to accept any such manifestations blindly. In any case I had always considered automatic writing more open to conscious or unconscious fraud than other forms of communication, and I think so still. I cannot even now prove that what I got then did not come from my subconscious mind—I can only say that in view of later events, of much careful investigation and proofs which satisfied me and others completely, I believe them to have been genuine messages.

An important point which should be taken into consideration is that they could have been due to no sort of wish fulfilment. Neither my emotions nor my desires were involved. As I have said, I had never wished to communicate with our dead friend. I had started writing fired by the extraordinary manner in which my Atlantean life had come through, and hoping to get some more information about that or other incarnations; I got nothing of the sort. My story remained incomplete, but instead, now, at any time of the day or night, whether alone or with my companions, information of all sorts poured through; some of it obviously of importance to our development, some of it merely mirroring the interest and affection of our dead friend for all of us.

About a week later she informed us that with her was a teacher from the other side who wished to get into touch with us. This, if true, was decidedly more interesting. We had, of course, no method of testing the veracity of this statement, save by sensing up to the best of our ability the utterances that the so-called teacher might think fit to put through; for in such a contingency judging a tree by its fruit is still, to my mind, the safest and only method of protection open to beings as limited as ourselves.

The teacher gave his message, and even as I wrote it, I sensed a change in the vibrations which flowed through my hand. There was immense power there, but also something more, something I cannot put into mere words.

I can only explain it by saying that I had an overwhelming sense of being flooded with protective calm, with love, austerity, and remoteness mingled. No masquerading spook, no one of the dark forces of illusion, could have evoked this change. Others have experienced this heightening of vibration, this supercharging of the atmosphere as with the essence of those great qualities which we may show forth feebly and in part, but which, when manifested so perfectly their contact alone results in an immediate amplification of one's own powers, so that for an instant one seems to participate in a superhuman consciousness.

This teacher was brief and to the point, as true teachers invariably are. They know the value of the economy of force; they obey a law which commands that no atom of energy may be wasted on any plane, no word used, no action performed, except in direct ratio to the value of the result to be achieved. Those whose work it is to teach humanity train their pupils with the same severity mingled with loving understanding that a competent teacher on the physical plane gives to the children under his charge. They have no time for idle talk and flattery, they look for results; if these results are not forthcoming in a specified time they will inevitably abandon the pupil to his own devices until he is ready to submit himself to that discipline which is necessary to all progress, spiritual as well as material.

This is not the place to give a detailed account of all he told us then, suffice it to say that, having informed us that through our efforts in this and in other lives we had reached a stage where it was possible to hasten our development, he proceeded to give us a very clear idea of the probable difficulties, dangers, and sacrifices which we, as pupils, would inevitably be called upon to face. We had freewill in the matter. It was for us to choose, but that choice once made, there could be no turning back save at great loss to ourselves. It were better, indeed, to struggle on quietly at our own pace and to leave any attempt to hasten forward until another incarnation. He left us to consider the matter at our leisure before he would accept any decision.

After he had gone, our friend spoke to us again and gave us a description of the teacher. What was my astonishment to find that it tallied with that of a guide who had been seen standing behind me by a medium some time previously. The medium had informed me that this particular individual was interested in my work and hoped to be able to impress me in the near future for various purposes. Since I did not think I had any mediumistic powers, I had entirely disbelieved the whole story and had forgotten it until that moment.

Two days later the third of our trio returned from town. He was very interested in all that had occurred. He, by his own methods, had also quite independently brought through a very curious episode in which the four of us were engaged again in some magical practices in Atlantis; and talking the matter over, we became convinced that this episode too must be another disjointed fragment of an Atlantean incarnation in which we had contacted each other and which was being re-projected into our consciousness. But at present it was like a jigsaw puzzle of which many of the most important parts were lacking. I felt, for some reason which I could not then define, that it was essential for us to get through the story complete—that in some strange way what we had done then bore a direct relationship to what we were attempting to do now, and that in all probability until this past was cleared up we would not be able to make the desired progress, on the same principle that in psychotherapy a patient's inhibitions and repressions must be brought up into the conscious mind before there can be any hope of a permanent cure.

We therefore determined to sit together in the sun-room and see if we could deliberately project ourselves back into this past. I realize now all the dangers involved in such an experiment. Fortunately, perhaps, we none of us had the slightest conception of the powers we were light-heartedly about to invoke. However, we did feel ourselves in some measure protected and under guidance—as indeed we were.

That night the moon was full. We bathed directly it was dark. The sea was phosphorescent; as our arms cleaved the black water, silver globules rolled from our fingers and washed round our heads. The warm night enfolded us; sea and sky and earth merged in one blue profundity, only the gold light from our bungalow hung in the void, marking for us the boundaries of earth. I swam far out, following the path of the moon—ancient goddess of magic; the water seemed to mingle with my very substance, cooling the fiery particles of the sun which had vitalized my limbs during the long August day.

I remember that, after our bathe, we put on the gramophone and sat for a while on the step looking towards the invisible sea over the little garden where the flowers glowed, dimly silver. The earth was so still that the tides of life might have all receded, leaving us in a dark void full of music. I think we must each have experienced the same feeling of expectancy of great events pending, but it was muted by a curious calm, as of something destined and inevitable.

Presently we went into the sun-room and put out the light. All the windows were wide open; the stillness was so intense one could hear, as if from infinite distances, the sibilant whisper of the little waves against the shingle. And as we sat there, so did the silence grow. It closed down on us now like a living presence. It became vibrant with unseen power. The power increased until it was as if every particle in the atmosphere, in our bodies, in our thoughts even, were supercharged, speeded up to an almost unbearable voltage.

Then suddenly, as if some alchemical process which had been long maturing were in that moment perfected, from one second to the next the process of time was reversed and we were back in an age dead thousands of years ago.

Of what followed I can speak but inadequately, and only from my personal point of view. Each man is the architect of his own edifice, no two have built alike, even though their acts may have appeared in essence similar. What my companions felt, I do not know; these things can seldom be described for they take place in a dimension for which mankind has as yet no words; but I make the attempt here because without some explanation all that follows will be meaningless.

Undoubtedly all four of us—for our dead friend was with us in this—each in a way peculiar to himself and his development, participated then, through some process of egoic memory which I do not pretend to understand, in the reflection of these ancient events.

Thus the past was recreated; we were back in that temple in Atlantis, engaged in a magical rite of which I have written more fully later on in this book.

As for me, I became at that moment dual. Half of me went back and took on the consciousness of this Atlantean, Cheor; but the other half, my modern self, remained all the while aloof and surveyed the scene with a detached, almost scientific interest.

However, I would have it clearly understood that I—for I identify myself solely with that part which stood aloof—never lost control of the personality which had rebecome Cheor, nor did I seek through any effort of will to evade the experience. I knew it had to be faced, that it was necessary and might not be avoided. I did not even fear it, for all the while I was conscious of that same exquisite and calm vibration which had enfolded us on the day the teacher had spoken. This was my anchorage despite the fact that on the physical and emotional planes where my body functioned the psychic turmoil increased with every moment and was gradually changing, so that at last it became the very quintessence of evil, corresponding to the nature of thost Atlanteans which we once had been. It grew; now it took on form. The room was filled with Presences which this black, evil rite had once evoked. They swarmed about us, personified forces of lust, of hatred, of satanic pride released at last from the prison-house in which they had been incarcerated until we had become strong enough consciously to contact them. They hurled themselves upon us, seeking in our present bodies any vibrations which, answering still to theirs, would allow them entry and offer them the opportunity of possession.

At that time, fortunately, I did not realize what was happening; I was aware only of tremendous conflict, unseen but vitally experienced and knew that, at all costs, I must retain control. But at last, when the horror of the experience reached its climax, when the converging forces broke with a shattering vibration over our heads, in extremity I called upon the teacher. Almost on the instant the tension lessened; like waves receding at the turn of the tide, the psychic forces grew weaker, gradually diminishing until they faded out and the room became like an empty shell.

We turned on the light. We were all considerably shaken. I remember my forehead was pearled with cold sweat, my teeth were chattering, and try as I might I was unable to control the occasional bursts of shivering which ran over me like jets of icy water. I would have given a lot for a stiff whisky at that moment, but drinks and smokes had already gone the way of meat diet and were strictly taboo, so we had to make the best of what seemed an extremely inadequate cup of tea.

I imagined that my night would be shattered by alarming dreams and visions, but I slept heavily and awoke quite fit and prepared for any other surprising events that might be waiting for us.

But that extraordinary experience seemed for the time being to have exhausted the psychic forces involved.

This last sitting had taken place just ten days before our party was due to break up, for I had to return to my work in London and another friend was coming down to stay at the bungalow instead of me. There was thus a short interim for readjustment, and looking back on these events, one marvels at the perfect timing of their activities by those on the other side. These ten days were absolutely essential in order that we should be enabled to settle down and prepare ourselves for renewed contacts with the outer world, since inevitably we were bewildered and shaken by the spectacular suddenness of these occurrences and still confused by contact with this new dimension into which we had all been hurled.

For, as I have said, the very foundations of our lives

had been affected; we none of us were, nor could we ever be, entirely the same as hitherto: and it was not going to be an easy matter to take up one's everyday existence from such a supercharged atmosphere of abnormality. Indeed it was a very long time before any of us came to view this episode with unbiased and wholly detached minds.

In those ten days the psychic forces slowly decreased. I still, however, received messages in automatic writing, but these were to continue for many months to come.

We were, as a matter of fact, rather disappointed at the return to normal conditions, for we were beginning to accept marvels almost as a commonplace; but had we not been extremely ignorant of the inner significance of such phenomena generally and indeed of all occult matters and the laws governing the subtler planes, we should have realized that we had already been subjected to a strain which was as great—or even greater—than most normal people could possibly stand.

No explanations were at that time forthcoming, but I have since been made to realize the danger of the experiment. No such probing, indeed, into previous lives should ever be undertaken except under the supervision of such a teacher as ours, one who can see every weakness and every potential danger-point in the make-up of the pupils in his charge, and who can gauge what their power of resistance is likely to be to those emotional forces which are bound to sweep in through this opening of doors which, in the majority of cases, had better remain closed. For these forces can be of such a nature as actually to destroy the rash experimenter.

Even under such supervision as we were given there remains still a strong element of danger; but as no rapid development is ever made without risks, the care and overshadowing of a wise teacher can mitigate them and keep them within the limits of the law of *past* Karma, so that no fresh karmic causes, due to ignorance, may be set in motion.

In our own case, for example, had there been in one of us if only for a second, what, for lack of a better word, I must call a short-circuit, so that the Higher Self or Soul lost contact with its vehicle of consciousness, those entities which our evil past had created might have swept in, seized upon the body and, once in possession, might never again have been dislodged, with the result that the person in question would have spent the rest of the incarnation in a mental home. Again, had there been some unsuspected or repressed vicious streak in our characters having a close affinity with the evil vibration of these entities, they could, once they had thus obtained a foothold, eventually have come to dominate the personality by playing upon and stimulating that weakness. This type of possession not infrequently occurs in connection with séances in which well-meaning but ignorant mediums, through succumbing to this intensification of some personal weakness, sink lower and lower, sometimes to end insane.

Later on it was explained to me that for the particular work we had each undertaken to do it was essential for us to make this close contact with our Atlantean incarnation; moreover, by thus permitting us to have so vivid and almost shattering an experience, our teachers were enabled to test our calibre, emotional, mental, and physical in order that they might correlate our future training to the result of the experiment upon our various bodies; for as no two persons react to a similar event in the same way, so for no two persons can the same method of training be applied.

It is for this reason that it would be of little value were I to speak in detail of my own training which began as soon as I returned to London and the comparative seclusion of my own flat. It was directed, of course, to the attainment of a certain sensitivity needed for the particular work I had to do. Almost immediately a series of drawings began to come through; some were pictures of Atlanteans and their ceremonies, some depicted nature spirits and devas and others were symbolical figures which I, who had had no artistic training, could not possibly have drawn by myself. But this, I was soon to learn, was only a preliminary. Gradually the more powerful type of automatic control lessened and was replaced by a type of mental clairaudience used in conjunction with different vibrations, so that in time I could differentiate between my teachers and could hear inwardly what I was to do or to write. It was then that I was told that my first task was to be shown certain past lives in order to write a book that would illustrate and explain that great fundamental law of Karma—of cause and effect—which governs men's lives and decides their fate in any incarnation.

These lives were later given to me and as I received them, so I have written them here, with some of the explanations which my teacher also gave to me at the time.

Unfortunately it has been necessary, through lack of space, to cut out one or two of these which were not so closely correlated with the Atlantean magic and its effects and to give a slighter sketch of several others.

It will no doubt be objected by many readers that these episodes sound too much like fiction or the result an overstimulated and unbalanced imagination to be taken seriously. It would be a reasonable criticism coming from anyone who had never had the experience of being precipitated back into past lives; yet those who, even momentarily, have stepped as it were out of time, will know that it is no more impossible to record the past than to record memories of one's present existence.

The ability to read the past or to cognize the future is latent in all human beings, since all living things must of necessity partake in every cell of their being of that all-pervading Mind from which manifestation is derived.

That few can as yet either remember or foresee beyond certain limits is due to the fact that they are not yet consciously aware of their unity with the Whole and have not, therefore, attempted to develop their potentialities. But undoubtedly this capacity to exercise greatly extended powers of more subtle sight and vision is increasing and one day will be universal.

It has been said that all things are "but thoughts in the Mind of God". If this is true it must follow that the entire past must still exist in some aspects of the divine mind. It then becomes a matter of knowing how to tune in to the dimension where this memory may be said to operate. We take for granted what once were considered to be the marvels of cinema and radio. One day perhaps we will take for granted the existence of this other dimension of consciousness which contains, or records—both words utterly inadequate and open to misconception—every event, thought and action from the beginning of creation to the end of manifestation.

There, for him who has learnt to perfect his own responsive apparatus so that he can evoke from, or tune in to, aspects of this universal record, lie all the answers to the questions and problems man is seeking so laboriously in the many branches of scientific research to wring from nature. There, in the past which might be called God's memory and the future which hides his intention, they await man's discovery. But how few must consciously have achieved even a modicum of the ability to do this. As for the majority, occasionally here and there are to be found men who, having developed intuition and the powers of creative imagination, are capable of receiving flashes of insight from this realm. Reading in the book of the past and the future, they make discoveries or accurate pronouncements while remaining unconscious of the true source of their inspiration.

But without having any access to these records a

student can if necessary be shown at second hand, as it were, events it is desirable that he should know by one who, at a higher level of consciousness, has perfected the ability to obtain information from this source at will.

This clearly is what must have happened in my case; my teacher adapting himself, of course, to my limitations and using whatever method was most suited to the occasion. Thus some of the episodes were revealed to me in dreams, some were shown in a friend's crystal, some were given clairaudiently, while others came in rushes of inspirational writing; but one and all were summarized for me in a brief outline which was put through by the same type of automatic writing of which I have spoken already.

In every case at the time of writing the episode I was so mentally attuned to it that my present life became almost unreal and I lived through those old distresses and emotions as vividly as if they had actually occurred within my present memory. It is for this reason that they appear here in so dramatic and vital a form. The past temporarily became my present, so that I was enabled to put down these lives much as a man writes his autobiography; to me they are no less than this. All the same a great deal has for obvious reasons been left out; only the chief event or events of each life—that event which in some way marked a crisis in my evolution—has been recalled; only the people closely connected with that event have been described.

Of my companions during this journey through time I cannot speak with any certainty. I believe that I and those three others who were with me in Atlantis met very often, usually in hate, but ultimately, as now, in love and companionship; but I do not pretend to be able to identify them throughout in the welter of personalities which crowd these visions of recollection. I only know that all through the particular lives I was shown, I was doing battle with the elemental forces I had evoked in Atlantis, and that in one form or another they will continue to return to me until they are utterly destroyed—or rather transmuted into beings of light.

Errors of course are inevitable in any attempt such as this to recreate the past, particularly when the instrument of transmission is necessarily still imperfect. Therefore if faults there be, they are not due to my teacher but to my own inadequacy in reporting his words and in recording the events I was shown.

Fortunately, since these events occurred some forty years ago, I have been brought into touch with a number of people possessing unusual occult gifts. One, an advanced student, P. G. Bowen, read the book before we met and tested it in his own way to see whether or not it was genuine. He came to the conclusion that it was, as others have also done. To him and all those who have helped me by "pointing the way" I owe sincere gratitude.

CHAPTER I

ATLANTIS

For many centuries the belief that there once existed a mighty continent which had been overwhelmed by the ocean remained in the racial memory merely as a legend and a dream, embodied in folklore and in the esoteric mysteries of the Temples of Egypt and Greece. It is only recently that the scientific researches of Donnelly, Lewis Spence and others have proved to the satisfaction of all but the most determinedly sceptical the existence of such a continent, the cradle of our own civilization.

Science cannot go much farther along the road of discovery by its usual methods, since so little remains to us of that mysterious land which has been called Atlantis; but there are other methods some of which I have already endeavoured to explain. From these men and women who have thus been enabled to evoke the past, we have learned much of the greatness and wonder of this dead civilization, which in some respects possessed knowledge now lost to us. This is actually borne out by those mighty monuments, the pyramids of Egypt and of South America—even, probably, the mysterious colossi of Easter Island—which were said to have been built by the various waves of colonists who left the continent at the time of the great catastrophes that ultimately destroyed it.

It was, then, to this lost land that the consciousness of out little group was projected during the experiences I have described. The events of the life which was revealed to us, partly at first in the bungalow, then later amplified through my hand, probably took place during the later stages of the Atlantean civilization when the forces of evil were gaining ascendancy and determined to undermine the influence of those who worked for progress.

The writing of this episode approximated more closely to the ordinary unconscious type of automatic writing than anything I did afterwards. Names were given which I could not have known or imagined—my mind not running to fantasy. The style was alien to mine and certainly I, who had never touched any books on magic in this life, having an instinctive aversion to it, could not possibly have invented such rites and ceremonies.

There are a number of reasons why it is undesirable to publish the script describing this life in detail; but it is necessary to give a summary of what happened to us there, since I believe that this apparently fortuitous gathering of friends in a small bungalow on the English coast was—fantastic though it may sound—undoubtedly the direct result of another gathering of those same individuals many thousands of years ago, and it is of its repercussions on them down the ages that I have to tell.

As I have said, in my first dream—and in several subsequent ones—I found myself in the streets of a great city, the fabled City of the Golden Gates; I walked among buildings so fantastic, yet so superbly designed and ornamented that, compared with them, our most advanced efforts today seem puny indeed.

But to a modern man visiting again this dead civilization, it would not be so much the buildings nor the great stature and beauty of the men and women he would find unfamiliar, as the mentality of this race which would be almost impossible to understand.

For their consciousness resembled that of very primitive folk today. They did not reason, rather they *felt* and "saw". What we now call extrasensory perception motivated nearly all their responses, for the reasoning mind as we know it was only just beginning to develop in the few. Therefore their whole code of behaviour, their aims and goals, were entirely different from those of modern civilized man who generally speaking is now endeavouring to control the emotional side of his nature and bring it under subjection to the mind.

Of course the more advanced of the Atlanteans—the governing classes who were all members of the priesthood—were being taught to become increasingly mentally polarized, while the Initiate Priests and the King had already attained the stage of those more advanced men of all ages who control the mental processes by the higher or spiritual consciousness.

This Priesthood of the Sun, as they were called, had been established in Atlantis for a long time. Their objective was to educate and lead the people from the instinctive, emotional phase to the development of intellect in order to be able to think for themselves, since without this freedom man can never grow to full stature. The final aim was that the Atlanteans as a race would themselves become the spiritual and cultural leaders and teachers of the nations yet to be.

I was one of the younger sons of the Ruler of Atlantis and as such was also an hereditary priest, brought up as a matter of course in the great Temple and taught those sacred mysteries which it was forbidden to divulge to any outside our caste. With me was closely associated my twin brother, Shahballazz. He had for me a very great affection which even I, degenerate and selfish as I was, returned in some degree.

As a younger son my position was an unimportant one, but I was proud and inordinately ambitious and in order to improve it began early to intrigue with a faction of malcontent led by a friend, Arion-Zat, and a renegade priestess who was his mistress, who were in secret communication with a traitor to the Royal House, Nazzaru. A man of immense ambition and power he had once been a high priest of the Sun in a provincial capital on the other side of the great mountains; but some years before had set himself up in opposition to the King and turned to the worship of Thlac-Shelaptha, Goddess of the Black Moon, ruler of the powers of death and destruction.

He had been joined by numbers of the more ambitious priests from all over Atlantis, for they had realized that once the aim of educating the masses of the people had been achieved and they began to think for themselves, they would inevitably break free from the guidance and dominance of the ruling Hierarchy. This, for such men as these, would mean the end of the absolute power wielded by all the priesthood, which they were determined not to relinquish.

As this process of education was already starting to affect the attitude of what might be called the middle classes, who were beginning to show an increasing degree of independence, they knew they must act quickly if they were to prevent it. Somehow the people must be forced back to the stage of mindless beings, utterly subservient and obedient to every command of their rulers, which they had been for so long.

Nazzaru was, in fact, the prototype of all the great dictators who were to plague, deceive, and enslave mankind, and it might even be suggested that the destructive and retrogressive forces he activated then in order to gain his objective, the ideas which became, in a sense, living entities, the devils of Mediaeval theology, are still ensouling those who are attuned to their wavelength.

My intrigues with this faction had, however, been quickly discovered, for unless one possessed very advanced powers and could guard one's thoughts, they could easily be read by the higher members of the priesthood. I was deprived of all the powers I had acquired and degraded from my caste, being condemned for the rest of my life to a menial office in one of the temples.

So, as I walked in this first dream between those shining buildings, the problem I was trying to resolve was whether or not, despite the prayers and warnings of Shahballazz, I should throw in my lot with Arion-Zat and Nazzaru. I was free to make my decision, to accept or reject the punishment I had brought upon myself. For there was no coercion exercised by our rulers upon those who had developed enough mentality to make their own decisions.

I learned from the script which was later given me that in the end I joined Nazzaru. I crossed the mountains to his palace and was initiated with what were, even to me then, the most terrifying and horrible rites into the Brotherhood of the Left Hand Path, as they were called. It was the path of involution, since its aims were to draw mankind backward into the dark past; the first step being the destruction of the Priests of the Sun and all they had so far achieved.

It was not as difficult then, as it would be now, to influence a whole race, so open to mental suggestion. Our first objective was therefore to encourage all the basest emotions and desires by directing upon the masses powerful, primitive, and retrogressive currents of thought—a form of magic even made full use of today.

I soon learned that Nazzaru's insane ambition did not stop at ruling Atlantis. Complete domination over mankind was not enough. It must continue, holding the entire human race in subservience for ages to come.

But how to circumvent the intervention of death which cut the thread of memory and consequently of continuity and of power? How leap that abyss between one life and the next, so that he and his followers would return with their immense fund of the secret knowledge intact and so be able to continue the work they had begun?

This was what we sought to discover in those dark

caverns beneath the great mountains. There seemed to us but one way in which it might be achieved. Although our bodies must die, if we could create beings on another, more subtle level of matter, not limited to man's short span of life, they could be made depositories of our knowledge and await the return of us, their masters. For we had learned enough to realize that thought, powerfully enough projected, is not subject to the laws of matter and can remain for immense periods in the mental atmosphere of the earth. If, then, we could create such entities and attach them to ourselves, even in the afterdeath state, then in life after life we should retain our powers and thus become rulers of the world for all time.

That was the dream, based, had we but known it, on complete ignorance of that spiritual law which the true rulers of Atlantis could have taught us had we not been too proud to submit long enough to the disciplines of their temples.

We set to work. There must have been many attempts, many failures, each and all costing untold sufferings and agonizing death to animals and human beings alike. For only through the shedding of blood could such shapes of darkness be created; only by a release of the life-force could they be charged with this primitive form of life.

A glimpse of one moment of the final effort, the climax of the most terrible rite hitherto attempted, accompanied by sacrifices beyond measure, was revealed to us, precipitated into the crystal and into our consciousness during that unforgettable night in the bungalow by the sea.

This was the moment when Nazzaru, Arion-Zat, and I, together with the priestess who had fled from the temple with us, perceived these artificial elemental shapes rising from the smoking altars, filling the great cavern with their baleful forms; when we, intoning the forbidden Words of Power, bound them to ourselves for ever.

Even that fleeting glimpse was enough. We could certainly not have endured a greater revelation of these abominations; so utterly alien to our twentieth-century mental equipment were these ancient rites. Much of what we did see could not be described. Even so, as I have explained earlier, we were guarded against their full impact. Had it not been so the experience might even have driven us mad.

The script which was given me later unfolded the sequel to this act of dedication to the powers of evil.

When the four of us had perfected our plans and were satisfied that the powers to which we had given form were securely harnessed, we gathered our followers together and marched upon the City of the Golden Gates. The fight was hard and long. We invoked the very elements themselves, the energies of the internal fires of earth, the waters, the tempests of the air and the earthquake to aid us, even as man does today by means of what is no more than a different form of "magic" which in essence is the knowledge of how to command and use the powers of nature.

At last the great city, poisoned by sulphurous vapours, assailed by tidal waves and cyclones, shaken by earthquakes, collapsed.

In the ruins of the Temple of the Sun I met Shahballazz again. His abiding love for me stirred within me some faint echo of good. I tried to save his life, but failed. He perished with the King and all his priests.

But such a triumph as this could only be ephemeral. It carried with it the germ of its own disruption. The powers of the elements we had invoked to serve us could not so easily be banished and pacified. In our struggles to control the demons we had let loose upon the land fierce quarrels broke out between us, and soon we were each striving for supremacy using our magical powers one against the other.

Arion-Zat sacrificed the woman in order to trick me to

my death; but I slew him and Nazzaru and I were left in a grim contest of rivalry and hate. In the end he became conqueror and I, too, was slain. But his triumph was short-lived; alone he was not strong enough to quell the destructive forces we had unleashed and he was swept away by a Power of which none of us had ever begun to comprehend the unconquerable might.

And the final result? We can only guess. Probably the boiling ocean; fire leaping to heaven as the earth opened her mouth and in an explosion which seemed to shake the earth, the land sank beneath the sea. So it must have been. Man cannot control and direct energies which, in their ultimate nature are divine, for personal gain or glory or for purposes of destruction, save at his peril.

But so far as we and those who worked with us were concerned in that insane endeavour to usurp the ultimate power, our end is of minor importance. It is that ceremony in the underground temple of Thac-Shelaptha, the Black Moon, which was the act that decided our destinies for thousands upon thousands of years. In our satanic pride, blinded by our ambition, and confused by our traffic with those Powers of Illusion that have tricked mankind through the ages, whereas we thought to return again and again as rulers of the world, in actual fact it was they, the beings of evil we had ourselves created, who became our lords and were to rule us, using our wills and our bodies for their own purposes, dragging us down to the depths of degradation in life after life, and only releasing their hold when at last we had gained sufficient strength and wisdom through suffering and experience to cast them out by an act of conscious will.

It is of my own efforts, my struggles and setbacks down the centuries that this book is concerned; but although the narrative may appear to be a purely personal one, it is not so. Each man certainly creates his particular destiny in his own way, but to those who seek separation, those who through pride and vanity ally themselves with deliberate intent to the forces of destruction, the path of return is always similar. Some few it is said never take the path of return. They go backwards until the involutionary process absorbs them utterly, but these do not concern us. They have made their choice, and have made it—at least once—with open eyes; for there comes a time when every man must make that choice in some form or another, and on that choice depends his ultimate destiny.

This was made in my case thousands of years later in Egypt, after many lives of unutterable degradation and misery as a result of my deeds in Atlantis.

I knew nothing, however, of these later lives until some months after I had received these revelations of my Atlantean incarnation. When the automatic script clarifying and correlating all these scattered revelations had been completed, I was left for some time without any further explanation.

The experiences dating from that first dream had been, I need hardly say, shattering. I had no idea where they were leading or what actually was their purpose. I was merely left, as it were, with the picture of my iniquities before my eyes, with the imprint of my enormities indelibly stamped upon my mind.

No more memories came to me and no enlightenment. The water of oblivion which a merciful dispensation has decreed shall separate man as he is and man as he has been, having parted a little while, now flowed back into their bed; yet across that waste of darkness—a waste which it had taken me thousands of years to span—there did stretch a slender bridge, the bridge of action I myself had built and by which I had come. Until this present life the existence alike of river and of bridge had been blotted out together with that solitary wanderer who, scorn and loathe him as I might, I yet could not disown since he was my very self. But now that the searchlight of truth had revealed this past to me, I knew that there would be no evading it any more. I was called upon to face the pilgrim from Atlantis, his deeds and all their implications; there was no ignoring the law of Karma, which, however much we may prefer to forget it, nevertheless rules our lives, decreeing that man shall reap to the uttermost the harvest of each seed of action, aye even of thought, that he has ever sown.

These memories had brought the grim irrevocability of this home to me as never before, so that I looked back into the Stygian darkness of that gulf between the then and the now with no little trepidation. What did it hide? How many of those deeds had already been expiated? Had I already paid my debts, or must I begin now, in full consciousness of the appalling magnitude of the task?

Imagination failed me: what kind of payment would be exacted for any evil so deliberately sought and practised? These thoughts tormented me. I understood well, during those black days of foreboding why it is that on each return to earth we drink of the precious waters of Lethe. We would go mad were we to know what our past lives had been. Our shuddering minds would become paralysed by the weight of old infamies, grown already alien and incomprehensible. We should be for ever brooding upon that past and have neither the courage nor the desire to deal with the problems of our present state wherein our eyes are fixed upon a future goal and our hearts tuned to the note of our own time.

One day while I was considering the threatening possibilities which these insistent memories of Atlantis had conjured from the past, I became aware of that exquisite vibration which heralded the approach of the one who had called himself my teacher. I felt him standing by my side, and he seemed to me to be smiling, humorously yet with tenderness, as a father smiles at the terrors of a child.

"Well, my Cheor," he said, and the accursed Atlantean name took on a strange music so that it seemed now to be cleansed and blessed, "is the idea of punishment all you can extract from these revelations?"

"It seems to me all I deserve."

"Then begin by realizing that actually there is no such thing as punishment. It is a man-made term for what is, in truth, a law of profoundest love whereby humanity learns through experience to associate effects with their causes. Until we do so, our experiences may appear to do violence to the personality, but in reality they are benefiting it, since they teach the foolishness of attempting to break the laws of nature and lead us eventually to realize how, by applying the doctrine of causation to every activity of our life, we may come to eliminate anything that can have pernicious consequences and retard our progress towards complete self-realization."

"But such causes as those . . ." I stopped, unable even to formulate my thought.

"Brought you, through their effects upon your personalities, where you now stand."

"You mean I have worked off the evil related to that past? Is that possible?"

"Only in part; what is left to do can be undertaken only through a deliberate and self-conscious effort of will, strengthened by a return of some of that ancient power which you once developed and then abused and which must be attuned now to the higher octave of service."

"And how can I regain this knowledge," I asked eagerly; "how can I begin paying off these debts?" For I was still weighed down by the thought of what those debts must be.

"Be careful," he warned me, smiling. "People so glibly talk of desiring to pay their debts, but when the opportunity is afforded, as it inevitably is when a man thus challenges his Karma, they discover that the payment is very different from what they had anticipated and entirely lacking in all dramatic interest. For again I bid you remember that every atom of energy you have wasted or perverted from its proper channel of manifestation you must replace by your own effort; and since thought is as much a force as action, it follows that every injurious thought, every idle, destructive word about another will have to be made good. There is but one way, and one way only, by which what you have filched from Life may be restored and the injuries you have imposed upon the universal Substance through destroying or disintegrating any part of it, be remedied. That way is through humble service to mankind and an amount of selfless effort and love which people are seldom prepared to give.

"You need not think," he continued, "that, because I have been permitted to contact and train you, you will be shown any short cut whereby you may escape this obligation. No one escapes. In fact, because you have demanded on the inner planes to go forward more rapidly, to become self-conscious in Karma, inevitably more payment will be exacted from you in this life than would otherwise have been the case. One of the reasons is that you will be put in touch with many of your past incarnations, and directly that happens certain energies which have been held in suspension, as it were, until the time is propitious, will be released.

"These will sweep into your life any links from that past who may be incarnated now. The balance sheet will be presented, and if the debit is heavily on your side you will be instantly expected to square accounts. It will mean much sacrifice of your time and energy, but if you are prepared to take the risk, the opportunity will not be denied you."

"But supposing I fail?" I inquired rather apprehensively.

"If you fail," he replied, "you will be adding to the

burden, making it heavier next time; for circumstances may not be so propitious again. A wise man once spoke of that tide in the affairs of men which, taken at the flood, leads on to fortune. . . . Take then the flood tide and do not even think of failure; such thoughts but weaken your powers. Why, moreover, should the payment of a debt be, of necessity, a disagreeable undertaking? Paid willingly and with love, it can bring the greatest joy, for to the man who loves enough no task seems hard or impossible. But if you do not yet know how to love, you had best set about teaching yourself the art of it; believe me, it will facilitate the accomplishment of everything you may be called upon to do. You will need a great deal of the driving power which only love can give if you are to reach in this life the goal upon which you have set your eyes.

"Now meditate upon what you have been shown, for much can be revealed to modern man about his world by a study of life in Atlantis, since this age is, in some way, an overtone of it. Many conditions are analogous, for that, too, was the end of one phase of development and the beginning of the next, although then they worked through different centres and through a different system of development. This is one reason why many Atlanteans are being reincarnated now. By this I mean that they are returning with the what I must call, for want of a better word, ancient karmic currents or atoms built into their new vehicles of expression. These, tainted at their source, they have now to purify and transmute.

"Only when this work has been accomplished by a certain proportion of the race will it be safe for the world to recover much of its forgotten knowledge and powers. Enough harm is being done by what man has already recalled—or, as you would say—discovered. If more secrets are wrenched from out the past before mankind generally has developed sufficient spirituality to use them aright, the catastrophe of fire and water which destroyed

Atlantis could be re-enacted only on a far greater scale.

"Already powerful elements are abroad on your earth causing upheavals and disasters. Consider your times well in the light of occult knowledge and you will understand whereof I speak. It is for those who can realize the dread consequences of the misuse of natural forces to warn the world of what lies before it, if once again it turns the creative gifts of God to destructive ends."

CHAPTER II

EGYPT

ONE day, some time later, my attention was directed to a scarab ring which I had worn for many years. I had been given the choice of several and had selected this one by what then seemed an incomprehensible impulse; for besides being slightly damaged it was the plainest of the collection. The inscription read: "May Ra protect thy days." Later I discovered, engraved minutely upon the back, a small hawk—Horus, the Son of the Egyptian Trinity, the wings of which, incidentally, were part of the insignia of royalty.

I was now informed by my teacher that the ring had belonged to me in the past, when it had been specially magnetized through a magical process, a vibration from the soul being projected into it. This had been done in order that, when it again came into my possession—as such a magical amulet would be bound to do by the Law of Attraction which draws like to like—certain latent currents from that past life would be, as it were, re-stimulated through the contact. This is the reason, he told me, why it is dangerous for uninstructed people to wear ancient amulets, since the powers therein imprisoned may possibly be inimical to them.

"Some day you will return to Egypt," he said. "Certain work awaits you to be done in connection with that country. For remember, birth into a nation implies the recognition of certain responsibilities towards it. Nations are spiritual Entities, and when you become a part of that corporate being—a cell in its body—you draw upon certain forces and aspects of its life which it alone can give you; therefore you owe it an obligation and must pay back what you have taken from it at some time or another. Hence it is that men so often feel the ardent desire to work, aye, even to die, for some particular country. In a time when much of the present Karma of separativeness is being worked off and man's more balanced development will dispense with the necessity for such differentiations, national characteristics will become less marked and all men will draw nearer to each other until eventually the barriers now separating nation from nation die out. Already the more highly evolved—men who have incarnated into many lands and given generously of their best to all—are free of every country. Seek to develop through better understanding this feeling of close kinship with all, meanwhile serving the country to which you are now tied by your karmic needs with the highest wisdom that you can.

"As for this debt contracted in Egypt, you will meet several links from that past in this life and be given the opportunity of paying your debts to them. You have never previously been fitted to undertake this work, as it involves certain knowledge which has been hitherto cut off from your consciousness but which will soon be once more revealed to you. But it may take many years to accomplish."

He watched me, smiling. "You do not believe me?"

"I do not understand how it can be done," I admitted, "with all the difficulties I now see in my path."

"You will find there are more ways than one of returning to the lands of your past," he replied enigmatically. And with that I had perforce to be content.

One night, shortly after this, I found myself in sleep before two great pyramids. In front of my eyes was the scarab ring and as I looked upon it the hawk appeared to detach itself therefrom, growing to such gigantic proportions that soon it filled the sky. It hovered over my head, its wings stretching above me. I seemed to hear the words: "The hawk of thy protection," and to my mind was recalled the ancient text: "And the shadow of his wings over thee is love...."

. . . . .

Yet when at length I found myself projected back into that past there was no scarab upon my finger nor any love in my heart, and the only protection I possessed was my own indomitable will. I stood at an upper window gazing over the flat roofs of a palace towards the faint line which marked the beginning of the desert. A full moon floated in a sky so darkly blue, yet so luminous, it seemed like a great inverted, jewelled bowl. The stars were pale in comparison with that livid light. I looked at them. Ah, if a man might reach the stars . . . but I was tied to earth, an earth which seemed to have nothing more to offer me since I could find nothing any longer therein upon which I might with profit and amusement exercise my powers of will.

Despite the fact that I was Pharaoh I was aware of a weariness so profound that it cannot be described. At that moment anything would have been welcome to my jaded spirit, even death. No, not death—since that meant the relinquishing of power. Death was defeat; death was the annihilation of that which was Myself. Power, victory, and the sense of myself as the very source of Will, of Being—as indeed almost a god, these could not be relinquished.

I passed my hand across my forehead. My head was aching intolerably. Perhaps soon I would welcome even annihilation—there were worse things than that . . . I shuddered.

From below, the sound of music and of laughter floated up on the scented air. I had retired from the banqueting hall some hours before leaving the revellers to their orgy. I had lately found myself satiated with such amusements, as indeed with every sensation evoked by lust, by battle and by sheer delight in cruelty to which at the beginning of my career I had madly abandoned myself.

The Egyptians were not by nature cruel, but my mother had been a slave from one of those tribes of semi-savages worshipping a god called Javeh who loved blood sacrifice and whose priests inculcated cruelty and vengeance into their people's minds. Thus in my veins the more gentle blood of the culture-loving people of the Delta lands was mixed with the ruthless and passionate strain of a Hebrew woman.

It was this perhaps, which had helped me to the throne. While the rest of Pharaoh's sons were weak, effeminate, easily succumbing to intrigue, I was hard as steel. I soon rose to be one of my father's most trusted generals. At that time Egypt was passing through one of her periods of temporary obscuration. But I dreamed of a united and victorious land with myself at its head. I did not intrigue against Pharaoh, I was far-sighted enough to perceive that there was no need to run such risks for he was his own worst enemy. When at length he was assassinated by one of his elder sons I swept in with loyal troops, captured the usurper, had him done to death and placed the rightful heir upon the throne. The fates played into my hands, as I, with foreknowledge, had well known they would do. In three months he was dead of a disease from which he had suffered long. The people of Egypt urged on by the High Priest, Besiurt, who saw in me the one man who could save the land from the gathering hordes of enemies, clamoured that I should accept the crown. The height of my ambition was achieved.

Seven years I had been upon the throne. Egypt was at last at peace, her borders secure, her enemies terrified into acquiescence. But I was beset by subtler enemies. And since, by my very triumph, I had been condemned to comparative inaction, they had become more powerful and insidious. From a child I had been prone to strange seizures, to outbreaks of uncontrollable rage, to long periods of depression so profound that it was as if I were immersed in waves of darkness which cut me off from the light of the sun and from all contact with my kind. In these last years the symptoms had alarmingly increased. Seldom now did I sleep; and when I did my dreams were filled with such fearful visions that I was thankful to return to consciousness. In vain I had gone to priests and physicians; neither their craft nor their magical practices availed me anything.

Yet I could not believe myself condemned thus to drift helplessly down to madness and death. That part of me which had driven on through a thousand difficulties knew that there could be no defeat for the man who did not doubt himself or his destiny. If these were demons that attacked me, then they could be exorcized. If my illness was caused by the Gods, then its cure must also be known to them. If there was no priest in Egypt wise enough to discover its causes and its remedy, then must I seek elsewhere and make my demand for help to beings greater and wiser than they. It seemed to me but a matter of right knowledge. Perhaps, I thought, the answer to my problem would turn out to be also the key to the very meaning of Life itself—a meaning which I had always vainly sought. And faced now with this awful menace, the conviction was forced upon me that I must indeed find the answer to my enigma—or perish.

My hands gripping the ledge with such intensity that the knuckles gleamed white in the moonlight, I leant forward, sending a wordless cry out into the night where Nut spanned the firmament with her shining body.

A burst of music and laughter was my only reply. Rage swept me like a flame. I swung round, strode to the doorway and with one wrench tore the curtain from its hanging. A terrified sentry confronted me.

"Go down," I cried, "bid those fools cease. Clear the tables, throw them all out. And tell them that, by all the Gods of Egypt, if I hear one sound more from any man or woman, they will be flung into the lions' pit."

The man prostrated himself, trembling. "The good God is obeyed," he muttered, and fled down the passage to do my bidding.

I returned to the window. From one moment to the next the uproar ceased and I was left alone with the quiet night.

I was still shaking, but now it was with fear rather than with anger. Through my head I felt the drive as of fiery swords, forerunners of a fresh attack from my secret enemies. Ah, were all my triumphs to come to this? What avail my lifelong struggle for power if it was to end in a limbo of madness and satiety?

The silence now was more agonizing to me than the music and the laughter. I could endure it no more. I left the chamber and passing rapidly down the passages which connected the Palace with the Temple, came at length to the apartments of the High Priest, Besiurt.

He was working tonight upon the roof of the Temple in a small chamber built with twelve sides, each dedicated to one of the Signs of the Zodiac, through the windows of which, it was said, he had power to command the emanations from the Signs to flow.

He rose to greet me, bowing ceremoniously; but the eyes in the stern and emaciated face were cold.

"I was studying the movements of the planets," he announced, "but if Pharaoh desires speech with me, I will listen."

His arrogance nettled me. "Perchance the planets can answer my questions, since the Gods remain silent—or is it that the priests can no longer decipher the heavenly heiroglyphics?" I went to one of the embrasures and looked out over the sleeping city.

"Pharaoh stands beneath the Sign of the Fish," came Besiurt's quiet voice behind me. "It is the symbol of an age which is of the far future. Does Pharaoh wish me to tell him how he will incarnate then? But mayhap it is better not to know, he might be a beggar—or a woman...."

I swung round thrusting my face, as dark and stern as his own, close to him. "I do not come here for idle prognostications, but for truth; can you give it me?"

"Truth? I have known men killed for even hinting at truth in the presence of a king."

"You are more like to die if you withhold it." I pointed to the rolls of papyrus upon the table. "You were to study once more the chart of my Stars. Have they aught to tell me?"

He hesitated and his eyes slipped away from mine.

"I have been meditating long upon it," he muttered, "but the secret evades me still. There are strange aspects there, I know not what they may bring. They form from the houses of the higher and lower mind."

"The mind? Speak, I do not fear. Might that mean—madness?"

"I do not know. With some it might manifest as an expansion, a pouring down of spiritual force. But with you—" there was scarcely-veiled scorn in his voice, "how could it mean that with you, who are not one of Us?"

His words had stirred me so profoundly that I was hardly aware of his arrogance. I sank into a chair and sat for a little while brooding deeply. Could that mean then that I should receive some enlightenment through which I might be enabled to do battle with my fell disease? Understanding or madness—these seemed the alternatives.

Presently I looked up. "Besiurt," I said, "tonight I

would open my heart to you, not as Pharaoh to priest, but as man to man. I know that you still scorn me as an upstart, but I would remind you that, without the fear of my right hand, Egypt would swiftly fall into anarchy; should I die now there is not one general, not one prince of the royal line who could defend the land. Yet I am dying; I am rapidly being overwhelmed, destroyed. You know of this, but you do not know all. During the last three years I have been daily growing more afraid, I, who have never known what fear was; for I seem to myself now to be two persons; it is as if some terrible enemy had made his habitation in the citadel of my body who grows ever stronger, gradually conquering my will."

I sprang to my feet and began pacing up and down the chamber. "You, immersed in your ceremonies, brooding over your planets and your calculations, you do not know the burnings of lust, the torments of unsatisfied ambitions, the fierce passions of battle and of the chase; nor do you know the desolation of satiety, the weariness of inaction, the terror of realizing that one's will is weakening and that no more will one be master of all these manifestations of life. Ah, to look ahead and see. . . ."

I broke off and sank shuddering into the chair. "Of what use to be Pharaoh, to be the greatest power on earth, unless one has power over oneself? Yet how may a man discover this power? What is its essence?" I strode up to him clenching my hands over my head. "I tell you, Besiurt, there is more than my life at stake in this—aye more than my sanity. For I feel over me a menace greater than that of the mere destruction of the body. I cannot tell you what I mean, for I do not myself understand it. It is as if I were faced, not with death—that matters little since we live again—but with a greater death—the annihilation—if that were possible—of my whole self, my very soul. Could such a thing be, Besiurt? To be destroyed utterly and without hope, so that not all the magical texts, not all the skill of priests and embalmers, nothing—nothing could prevail. It is this I feel. What have I done to deserve such a fate?"

He had gone pale, as if he too felt the breath of doom; his eyes evaded mine. Looking at him I was seized once more with this abysmal despair. What did it mean? I controlled my rising sense of panic fear which threatened to overwhelm me and continued more calmly:

"You spoke of future ages—it is of this future that I must feel secure. I have power now, but I must know the secret of a power that will endure through all my lives—that will give me an eternity of power. What is Egypt? What is the present? A little strip of land—a few short years. There are vaster lands—there is the untold and unimaginable future! 'Tis of all this I must be master; I must hold everything, not in hands that will drop to dust, but by some other binding force, the strength of my will which must be imperishable. There is some secret—I know it; a secret of eternal life—the mystery of Ra, God of the Eternal Sun: I believe I might be cured, not only of my disease, not of the threat of madness, but of this—fear, could I but tear aside the veil which hides it from my knowledge." I drew my hand across my eyes. "To be powerless ... to be unable to do anything ... Yet it is within me, in my own heart that the canker hides, the germ of death—the destroyer; in me—and I must perish if I cannot cast it out! There must be some way of escape. Why should I, of all men, be denied this knowledge? Is there no GOD who will come down and give me the key to this enigma of my being?"

I ceased. I found I was shaking from head to foot. My body was filled with pain, my head stabbing fire; but I would not succumb. I drew close to him and saw that he shrank before the madness in my eyes. "I command you," I cried, "I, Pharaoh, that you reveal to me the truth, that you lay bare to me the secrets. For know them I will."

He stood immobile, his cold, snake-like eyes half closed. Between us was the table covered with rolls of papyrus, strange instruments and blocks inscribed with ancient Chaldean script; I looked at them idly but my mind was probing into his. Presently I saw his lips moving, he seemed unaware that he was murmuring his thoughts aloud.

"He would not permit it...." I heard. "He would not reveal anything to him...."

"Of whom do you speak?" I asked sharply.

Startled, as a man stirred from a trance, he opened his eyes.

"Of no man," he stammered, "I was communing with the Gods."

I laughed scornfully. "The Gods? No, no. You spoke of 'him.' Who is he who would dare to refuse my request?"

"I spoke of Ra, the Most High."

"You spoke of a man! Who is this who would set himself against me? Are you a traitor?" I drew my dagger and advanced upon him; he stepped back in alarm.

"Pharaoh," he cried, "I swear I am no traitor. Did I not set you upon the throne? Should I seek to pull you down?"

"You'll have no opportunity," I said grimly, "for unless you tell me who this man is, by Set and the two and forty gods of the Underworld I swear that you will die and all your priests with you." I felt within me rising now the red tide of passion, tearing at me with a very madness of rage. "Aye," I cried, "and I will raze every temple in Egypt to the ground, I will torture the priesthood man by man till I discover who it is of whom you speak as if he, and not I, were Ruler in Egypt."

He had retreated before me into one of the twelve embrasures; now I caught him by the throat and thrust him back against the sill.

"I will cast you hence," I said, smiling into his face. "Think you I fear priest or god or devil? I will destroy whatsoever cometh between me and my will."

I forced him further towards the void, until his choking voice reached me.

"Loose me, and I will speak."

I loosed him, and as he walked with what dignity he could muster towards the table, I saw his eyes were filled with sullen hatred and knew I had made a dangerous enemy; but this did not trouble me over much for I was well aware that he needed me more, if anything, than I needed him.

"If I speak," he said at length, "it is not, O, Pharaoh, because I am afraid of death, but rather because I fear what you in the madness of your rage may do to the land I love. I was indeed speaking of a man; but of one who is as far above me and you as we are above the peasant working in the field. Only the Initiate Kings and Priests may know even of his existence. You are not one of these, therefore were not considered fit to be allowed access to the Fount of Egypt's wisdom. He, the true Ruler of Egypt, the Great High Priest, of whom I am but a shadow reveals himself only to the pure, the hereditary Sons of the Sun—they who have been initiated by divine right into the most Sacred Mysteries. Without his will you would not be what you are. For know, O, upstart King, it was at his command we chose you. He knew that none but you could at that time bring peace to this sorely harassed land. When the Double Crown was placed upon your head and you were sanctified King and God, he, invisible to you, stood by your side and gave you his blessing. He spoke to your soul and laid upon you the task of ruling Egypt well and wisely until the time was ripe for one of the true royal blood, a priest and Initiate, to step into your place. You accepted that trust. Woe betide you if you break faith with him."

I sat for a while in silence. I knew that he spoke truth and was sobered by the knowledge; the madness had left me faint and exhausted.

"Could he tell me the secret of myself?" I asked presently.

"There is nothing he could not tell you," the priest replied.

I rose. "Then reveal to me his dwelling place; I will go to him there."

He looked startled. "It is impossible, O, Pharaoh."

I smiled and laid my hand upon my dagger. "Impossible? I do not know the word. Must I repeat my arguments of a few moments since?"

He raised his hand. "It is useless. I do not know it. No one knows it. He comes and goes at will, revealing himself only at times of need through priests and oracles. If you razed every temple and dwelling in Egypt to the ground, if you destroyed every rock and tomb, you would not find him if he did not so choose."

Once again I recognized the voice of truth. But his words had given me an inspiration. I pretended acquiescence. "So be it then; but remember, I cannot be expected to fulfil those vows if I be mad or dead, and again I tell you I cannot endure much longer. I am a man, although I be called a god. I need sleep, I need a respite from pain, from the fire which devours me. I have the will, if I but knew how to use it upon myself. It might be better for you all if you could prevail on him to show me the way."

I turned and left him, passing out through the main court of the Temple. I felt I must be alone to meditate upon this amazing revelation. I called no guards. I did not need them. I feared no robbers or assassins, for I was a full head taller than the majority of my subjects and so strong that once when roused I had slain a lion with my bare hands. Moreover I was plainly clad, only the narrow band of gold encircle by the uraeus upon my brow proclaiming my rank.

I passed through the flower gardens. It was nearly dawn. A few faint bird-notes fluted upon the air. Soon the boat of Ra would rise above the horizon flooding the world in the glory of his presence. I came out upon the banks of the Nile. Here were drawn up barges which had been used to transport a colossal statue of myself from the quarries. It rested now upon its runners, and as the light broke upon the world, the flaming rose was reflected upon the still face. I leant against it looking upward. This was myself. To unborn generations this would represent what I had been. I had bidden them make it life-like, and now the fierce face with its hawk-like nose, its narrow lips and drooping eyelids gazed remotely out upon the world. It would live, but as for me, what would become of my spirit? Once more the intolerable fear and depression descended, stifling thought, hope and life.

I turned away and with lagging footsteps returned to my own place.

When all the pressing business of the morning had been attended to I retired to my private apartments and called for the Queen.

To validate my claim to the throne when I was made King, I had married my half-sister, daughter of Pharaoh and the Royal wife, but on her death shortly afterwards, I made Re-shep-sut, daughter of my mother, Queen in her place despite much opposition from the priesthood and the people, who believed her to be a sorceress. She was the one being I felt I could trust, for besides being of use to me through her magical powers, there had always been a link of admiration between us.

I told her briefly what had occurred and outlined my plan to her. She sat for a little while in thought, and I contemplated her with pleasure, for she was beautiful and fierce like some half-tamed panther.

"I am afraid, I know not why," she admitted. "I feel even we, versed in magic as we are, may not be strong enough to accomplish this thing."

I smiled. "Not alone." I dropped my voice. "The moon is full tonight; gain access to Net-Ka's apartments, drug her guardians and bring her to me."

Net-Ka was another daughter of my father, and between her and Re-shep-sut there had always been an extraordinary bond of affection despite their differences in temperament. For from her birth Net-Ka had been the chosen mouthpiece of the gods, their Oracle and Seer. Brought up in the Temple, surrounded and guarded by a band of priestess virgins, she was used only upon solemn occasions when some important message was to be given to the High Priest, and on special feast days when she was consulted by the rulers and governors of the land. Delicate in body, with a childlike and gracious mind, she clung to Re-shep-sut with such passion that for the sake of her happiness and because her every whim was gratified, they were allowed often to see each other. Thus it had come about that once or twice I too had been enabled to avail myself of her unique mediumistic powers for my own purposes, for it had not been difficult through our secret arts to smuggle her out of her apartments to a small summer-house in the gardens where was the chamber we used for our magical invocations. No men, save sanctified priests, were ever allowed in her presence at ordinary times, but such was her blind love for Re-shep-sut, that she had been willing to risk the dreadful penalties which would have befallen her had her participation in our secret rites become known.

Now I saw Re-shep-sut hesitate and frown.

"Well what is amiss?" I said sharply.

"Net-Ka hath been sickly of late; I believe we overstrained her powers the last time we used her as mouthpiece of Set."

"That was a year ago," I objected.

"I know, yet it is said she hath never been the same since that day. The priests are growing suspicious. If it were discovered she would be killed. They watch her. I had it from Nep-heb."

"Nep-heb?" I leaned over and grasped her wrist. "I hear too much of Nep-heb; is he your lover?"

She looked at me with narrow eyes. "No; but I use him."

"Remember you are my wife; the Queen of Egypt is chaste."

She flung back her head, showing a gleam of pointed teeth. "Do not ask too much of me, my brother."

She would have drawn away, but I closed my hand upon her wrist, running my nails into her flesh until she screamed with pain. "You will be faithful to me, to my throne and to Egypt. If I can discover through the powers of Net-Ka where this man dwells, I may be forced to put you to the test. You are ambitious; would you sit for a while alone upon the throne of Pharaoh?"

She gave a gasp of delight. "You would leave me in your place?"

"There is none other I can trust. If I have to seek him out it will be necessary; but I will not have your loyalty divided."

She smiled. "Never fear. I will be loyal."

I gave her an amused glance and drew a ring from my finger. "Good; take this, give it to Mer-hetsu, captain of my guard, and bid him immediately have Nep-heb cast into the lions' pit."

She went white as death and gave a stifled scream. "Ah no, my brother—I beseech you." She controlled herself with an effort. "Would that be wise," she asked in a calmer voice, "he is very useful to us; he acts as a spy for us in the Temple of Ra, besides being secretly an initiate of the Mysteries of Set."

"That is my reason. I do not want men about us who are traitors to their God. I may worship whom I please, but not so a mere priestling. Moreover, I desire to stand well with the priesthood of Ra; no doubt they know him for what he is and it will be good policy to please them by his death." As she still crouched at my feet, staring blindly before her, I leant over and tipped up her chin, smiling into her eyes. "Do you go, my beloved wife, or must I place another upon my throne should I choose to leave it for awhile?"

She gave me one glance, then slowly rose and went from the room.

That night Re-shep-sut brought Net-Ka to the chamber we kept for the purposes of magic.

The girl sank wearily on the couch and when she removed her veil, revealing a pale and sorrowful face, with sunken eyes, I knew Re-shep-sut had spoken truth. Here was one sick, almost to death.

She stretched out her hand in greeting and said in a faint voice: "My brother, I have come as you commanded; but I grow weary. I have strange dreams. I feel as if something terrible were happening. Must you use me in this way which I know is forbidden? I do not understand what you do—I have no memory when I return to my body, but," her lips trembled, "the last time I would have spoken in the Holy Place of the Temple, I could not. The God did not possess my body; they say I babbled strange words. Can it be that by visiting you here I am displeasing the High Gods?" She covered her face with small, blue-veined hands, "I dare not think upon such a possibility. My life is theirs. I beg you, by all the love I have for you, bid me do nothing contrary to my holy vows."

I comforted her with idle words, but I had no intention of sparing her, nor did I care who spoke through her or what happened to her afterwards, so long as I learned the secret I now sought.

"Do not be afraid, sweet sister," I said, "you shall not be used beyond your strength. It is for the good of Egypt that I would invoke the Gods."

Obedient, she stretched herself upon the couch. About it we drew the magic signs, and stripping off our garments, annointed our bodies with the unguents and placed upon them the symbols of Set. Then we began to recite charms above her still body with a low, rhythmic humming, The room became gradually shadowed by the increasing smoke from the great brazier and now about me I felt the great forms of power drawing ever closer. I invoked them by their secret names. The light fluttered like a dying moth and expired. Net-Ka moved, her body began to sway; she fell sideways, foaming at the mouth; her features twisted and grimaced. Re-shep-sut, rigid, hands upraised, intoned, moving in a mystic dance upon the figures drawn on the floor. Suddenly Net-Ka stiffened, sat upright, eyes wide. A deep voice boomed from her mouth:

"Greeting, my servants! I am here, I—the Eye, the Ear, the Voice. Greeting. What are your desires?"

I stood above Net-Ka. I steeled my will. The atmosphere pulsated as if alive with fiery particles. Re-shep-sut had fallen upon her face and was still.

"I will to know where is the abode of him who is the Secret Ruler of Egypt. I will to be shown where I may find him. I will to be brought face to face with him alone."

A tremor convulsed the entranced girl. When the voice at last replied, it had weakened, as if broken by some force greater than itself.

"Do not ask me. I warn thee, leave this man alone; he will be thy destruction."

"I do not care; I would rather be destroyed than continue to live in ignorance and fear. I must know his secret. All power, all knowledge lie hidden there for those who can wield these unknown forces aright. I have oft-times invoked you with the secret names, but never have you granted my desire, nor have you revealed to me the existence of this man. Now I demand...."

"Be silent!" cried the voice. And now the air grew thick about me, the pressure became terrible as if a disembodied will were combating my resolve.

"I will not be silent! If you are indeed Set the Mighty One, great in knowledge and power, if you be a God, then you must know. I demand this secret! I conjure you, God, spirit, demon whatso'er you are, give me truth. Deny my demand, and by my enchantments I shall shake the very earth, raise the dead from their tombs. I will to know how I may cure myself; I will to unfold the mystery of life. I will to be Lord of life and death."

I stood above the Oracle, my arms upraised. With the whole force of my being I sent forth to the uttermost part of the earth, to the confines of the heavens, to the furthest stars my cry. With all my force and knowledge I projected my power to combat this unknown, opposing mind which seemed to struggle with me as if seeking to keep from me the knowledge I desired. I might die but I would first conquer it. This was surely my enemy at last face to face.

My limbs were flame; power flowed into them; more power, a million particles vibrating to my will. Only one thing more was needful now to complete the invocation, the great forbidden Word, which it can be death to speak —which can by its note disintegrate the body of him who dares to utter the sacred syllables. I had learned it; but even I, hitherto, had never dared to project its shattering vibration upon the air. Now I paused, my whole being taut for this last act. I drew in a mighty breath; the Word waited; it grew—immense, expanding; slowly, every nerve tense, with breath controlled, I gave it forth. . . .

The great reverberation died. There followed a stillness so awful that it was as if all things had ceased to be.

I waited as the dead might wait—drained, empty.

I looked and saw Net-Ka writhing in the throes of a terrible convulsion; it was as if she were being torn by two opposing forces. Suddenly a change came over her. She raised herself upright until she was standing lightly like one poised for flight. Her eyes were wide, her face transfigured by a radiant smile.

"He comes," she cried; "He, the Master, our Lord." And with a long sigh collapsed upon the couch and lay still.

Then I knew fear. Always heretofore in my magical practices I had felt myself master. But now, gathering slowly about me was a force of which I knew nothing—against which I might strive with all my powers in vain. It grew; insidiously it invaded the structure of my body, sapped my will. It was like a pure, yet disintegrating note of music, like a white, yet icy flame. Beautiful as it was, to me it was discord and death. My limbs melted in agony, each cell, each nerve quivered and dissolved. I sank upon my knees, then upon my face, yet in this agony of dissolution I still strove to retain a hold upon myself, to keep my desire unwavering.

Then while I battled feebly there I heard a voice of such wondrous sweetness and of such power and beauty that I broke before it and lay as one dead.

"You called upon me," it said, "you invoked me. The means you used were wrongful and for that you will pay the price, but I, who can read the heart of man, know from what source the desire which drove you to this act was generated, so I am here."

I could not speak, but something deep within me, the last living particle, perhaps, must have responded.

"It is well," said the voice. "Since you have chosen, you cannot be denied. When the time is ripe I will bid you come to me."

Then the voice ceased and darkness enfolded my spirit.

When I awoke I found Re-shep-sut kneeling over me.

"What happened?" she asked, "I remember nothing. Did you learn the secret?"

I rose slowly, my limbs were like lead, my head was dizzy. "I do not know—yet." I pointed to Net-Ka. "Look to the child. We must get her back to the Temple."

Net-Ka was still entranced. Nothing we could do would rouse her. But I think some spell must have been laid that night by One more powerful than ourselves upon the Temple servants, for, although we had to support her between us, none met us upon the way, nor had any of her guardians stirred from their drugged slumbers.

Two day later Re-shep-sut came to me where I sat in the garden with my scribes.

"I have been told that Net-Ka is sick even unto death," she whispered when we were alone. "She lies for long hours without consciousness, and when she awakes, cries and screams as one possessed." Her eyes were wide with terror. "It is we who have done this," she said in a strangled voice, "if she dies, it will be we who have killed her."

But my thoughts were far off. Since receiving that strange message I had been occupied day and night in making plans for the protection of the country in case I was forced to be away from the throne for long. Men of doubtful fidelity had to be replaced at the frontiers by generals I could trust. Garrisons had to be strengthened. Secret schemes and negotiations perfected. I had no time to waste on women's chatter. I stared at her coldly.

"What of it? I shall not need her again."

She clasped her hands. "Can you not understand? Are you made of stone? I love her; she is the only being I have ever loved."

"Then you had best see to it that you are quickly cured of the disease," I sneered. "If you are to take my throne, for however short a while, I must know you above such weakness. Learn once and for all that those who are no longer needed for our policies are best out of our way—they are less likely to indulge in idle and dangerous speech. Let Net-Ka go and cease to be a fool. I have given out that you are with child. Although it is not yet true the Egyptians are more likely to treat you with respect and remain loyal if they imagine that you carry the future Pharaoh in your womb. I have much of importance to discuss with you. One thing I command: keep away from Net-Ka's apartments; do not see her even if she asks for you. I do not want it to seem as if we are involved in her affairs. It is essential that you should remain on good terms with Besiurt. You will obey him in every particular, for he will be the actual head of the nation while I am gone. He will dictate your actions and your words. Woe betide you if I find you have been unfaithful, or if through foolishness you let slip the reins of power."

A dark, stubborn look settled on her face. "If Net-Ka is dying and asks for me, I shall go," she said.

I leaned forward and fixed her with narrowed eyes.

"Re-shep-sut, if you do not hearken to my voice, if you do not swear upon the sacred symbol of Set which I wear upon my hand, that you will be faithful, that you will obey my merest breath, I swear to you by the Names which may not be uttered that I will cast you down and raise another in your place, that your hands will not grasp the sceptre, nor ever your body bear a child of the god."

At my words she flung herself upon her knees, clasping her hands about my feet. "O Pharaoh, O great God, have you no pity? At your word I sent Nep-heb to his death; now would you have me sacrifice my sister also? For I know that I alone may be enabled to cure her sickness. If I refuse her call she will surely die of grief."

I struck her with my foot. "Pah, you are like all the others at heart, ridden by emotion and weak sentiment." I leant back in my chair, smiling softly. "You have the choice. On one hand, O, Re-shep-sut, is the throne of

Egypt, unlimited power, great glory and honour—and this oath; on the other a half-witted girl, who is better dead—and oblivion, obscurity, death perhaps. Which is it to be?"

For a moment she remained motionless, her head bent, her hands twisting together; then slowly she looked up. "I will take the oath," she whispered.

I thrust out my clenched right hand at her. She stooped forward, pressed her forehead to the great ring, and muttered after me the magic formula of this most dread and binding of invocations.

"And now," I said, as I motioned to my scribes to return, "remember the penalty if that oath is broken. Neither in this world nor in the next will you have peace; neither in this life nor in any other. You have invoked the power which lies within this ring, the spirit of ambition and of will. While you obey me, it will be your slave; disobey, and it will become your master. Keep that in mind and forget it never, my sister—and Queen."

Since that night in the summer-house, the voice and the words I had heard had been seldom out of my mind. My own attitude suprised myself, for I found I was filled with a continual yearning to hear the voice again and to contact the man who had spoken. I could not recall ever in my life having experienced such a sensation as those tones had roused within me; the nearest, perhaps, had been the hungry passion I had sometimes felt for some woman, when I could neither sleep nor eat until I had possessed her; yet that had been ephemeral, this endured. It seemed to have affected me also in other ways, since now, for the first time for many years, I slept night after night; nor did I have any recurrence of my illness, until the evening of the day that Re-shep-sut came to me with her request. That night I was seized with an attack more violent than any I had ever experienced; it continued for two days at a pitch of madness, leaving me at last utterly exhausted. The third evening, while I lay semi-conscious on my bed, suddenly I was aware that I was not alone and turning my head, beheld the cloaked figure of a man standing beside me and heard again the accents of the voice for which my spirit yearned.

"O Pharaoh," he said, "art thou still determined to brave the secrets of thy destiny? For three days thou hast been in torment, but I warn thee, if thou wouldst know Truth thou will have to face worse than this."

"I am determined," I answered.

"So be it. Tomorrow at midnight thou wilt find a beggar seated by the outer gate of the Temple. Follow him."

Next day I called for Besiurt and received him alone lying upon my couch, for I was still weak.

"I rejoice to see your Majesty recovered," he said in a voice which belied his words; "they told me that the light of your countenance was darkened and that you were sick almost unto death; I and my priests have therefore been seeking to cure you by drawing your sickness into our unworthy bodies."

I smiled grimly. "I can see no sign of it in you, my friend; and let me assure you that it is not owing to your spells and remedies that I have recovered. The Gods be thanked, I will in future not be dependent upon the priestly College of Physicians for my health, spiritual or physical."

He raised his brows.

"I have found," I continued, relishing the prospect of his discomfiture, "another physician, greater than you all. And to him I go—tonight."

"There is no one in Egypt . . ." he began.

"There is." I quoted his own words at him. "One of whom you are but the shadow. . . ."

He was moved at last, "You will never find him! Here is madness indeed."

I laughed softly. "No, here is sanity—at last. Perchance it has been you, my friend, who have been a little mad, mad with your pride. I would recall to your mind that when first I took the throne I came and asked you humbly enough that I might be instructed in the Mysteries. I believed that through them I might come to the understanding I sought. I was even prepared to be a novice, to sit at your feet if you would teach me. You refused. You barred to me the gates of truth. You told me that I was unworthy, that my blood was impure, that I had touched the black arts and was befouled. I wonder, did you, in your pride and purity, consult your Master who put me upon the throne? I do not think so." I leant forward, thrusting my face close to his. "You wished to retain the ultimate power in your own hands, O Besiurt; you wished me to remain ignorant so that you and your priests could lord it over me. But you did not know me. I was not to be baulked. If Ra-Hermachis would not let me pollute his temple, then there remained Set, who is not so bigoted. I learned from his priests, I was initiated into the Mysteries of his cult, but I will admit that soon I found they could not give me this thing I desired, without which I could find no rest nor happiness. I did not know what it was, I do not know it yet—but I will know; and when that hour comes I shall make this knowledge forever mine. Not you, nor any priest on earth, can stop me."

He would have spoken, but I raised my hand.

"No, not even you, Besiurt. I do not think one appeals ever to the High Gods in vain, even though their priests would make them dumb if they could. I believe I was meant to overhear the words you spoke which revealed to me the existence of One in Egypt higher than you. I made my appeal to him—and he has answered."

The high priest sprang to his feet. "You are deluded; it is not possible. He would never speak to one who is not of Us."

"Perchance I am deluded; that I will soon discover, for I go to him tonight."

"Go to him? But you do not know..."

"I am to be shown his dwelling-place. I shall find it, if it be across the world."

"You cannot—you are Pharaoh. You have no right to leave Egypt!"

"Be seated," I said impatiently, for he was stamping round the chamber, waving his arms to high heaven. "I am still sick. Your voice is loud. Subdue it."

Without more ado I told him my plans. He demurred, cried aloud that I was a traitor; that the throne was a sacred trust I had no right to relinquish; appealed in turn to my ambition, my pride, my love of Egypt, but without avail. My mind was set, nothing touched me any more, for life had given me everything and I had found its best gifts but ashes in my mouth. My will was my only law, and before it at length he had perforce to bow.

I left him the royal signet; I left him with instructions to explain my sudden absence as he would—I did not care.

That night, clad as a peasant with a rough cloak to hide my face and a staff in my hand, I went to the outer gate of the Temple of Ra. A man in rags rose at my approach and without giving me a greeting turned down the street, walking towards the Nile. I followed him. Our feet made no sound upon the sand. We were as shadows moving in darkness, for there was no moon. Morning found us in the desert. All day beneath the burning sun we went without rest. Despite my great strength my feet faltered. He seemed untiring. Once by a well he stopped and gave me to drink, but did not speak. By evening my head was swimming so that I could scarcely see his form as it strode ever like a gaunt shade before me. Perchance I had grown soft with the life at court, or perchance my illness had sapped my strength more than I knew, but towards dawn

I sank down, unable to drag my body farther. He came back and stood over me.

"You have done well, O Prince," he said.

"Give me but an hour's rest and I will go on," I replied.

"There is no need; we are almost at our journey's end." Stooping he picked me up as if I had been a child, and walked on lightly despite my protestations. I know not how far we went, for I think I must have fainted. When I awoke I was stretched upon a bed in a quiet chamber where an oil light burned.

For three days and nights I remained there, attendants bringing me food and drink, then I was brought into the presence of him who was Egypt's Ruler.

He was seated at a table studying ancient rolls of papyrus and although he was dressed in a plain white robe with no sign of rank, when he raised his head and looked at me I knew myself in the presence of one before whom even Pharaoh of Egypt was of small account. I had an incomprehensible impulse to prostrate myself but suppressed it with an effort.

He bade me draw nearer. I stood on the other side of the table. A sensation of calm resolution emanated from him.

"Why have you come to me?" he asked.

"To learn how a man may gain dominion over all things."

"This is revealed in the Holy Mysteries of Ra-Hermachis."

"His priests refused me; they said I was unworthy. So I turned to Set."

He raised his brows. "Were you not afraid?"

"I am afraid of nothing."

"You speak truth; it is of nothing that you are the most afraid."

I started; he had struck the mark.

"You are afraid," he continued, "of the forces of annihilation you feel to be within yourself."

I shuddered at his words; I could not deny them. I raised my head and looked him in the face. "It is so; it is this fear indeed that has brought me to you." I leant towards him, striking my clenched fist upon the table. "I will not be destroyed! I will live—live!" After a pause I added, more to myself than to him, "I dare not die—it would be defeat...."

"Yet all must die," came his quiet voice.

I shook my head. "Nay; it is not death I actually fear; I have faced it too often, unafraid. It is something vaster, slower.... Disintegration? Yet what is that?" I flung out my hands to him in sudden despair. "You who must be more wise than other men, can you not tell me what would assuage this unending discontent, this restless yearning, this despair, this insidious poison which saps my strength, ruins my successes, and renders all my triumphs barren? Can you not show me how I may be freed from this suffering, this sickness of mind and body which I know to be the forerunner of madness, these moods of blackest melancholy that make all things appear as vain shadows? Why am I, alone of all men, so cursed? Why am I thrust apart? They know not these agonies, this perpetual menace, this fear of emptiness—of more than death. I am Pharaoh: Egypt and all her riches are mine—yet verily fools and slaves are happier than I."

"They have love," he answered.

"Love? Bah, I am weary of women and their ways."

"Do you know what love is?" he asked gently.

"I know it is weakness, not strength," I answered scornfully; "I know that to most men it brings disaster, not fulfilment. It is not love I need, it is knowledge, power, the secret of Life, for I know full well that until I hold these I shall never be cured of my disease. Love cannot serve me here."

"No, love cannot serve you until you serve it, my friend." His eyes narrowed until they flashed at me like points of fire. "So you come to me for power, to learn the mysteries of Life? My answer is that until you have first learned to love we cannot teach you anything. Of what use to you would be our inestimable gifts, while you are still incapable of understanding their true nature, much less of utilizing them? A seed, unless it is quickened, will remain unfruitful. So it is with this knowledge you seek: until it be impregnated with the vitalizing energy of love, it is of no use to you or to any man."

I listened to him, frowning with irritation and some bewilderment. To be told that the answer to my question was merely that I should love seemed preposterous; yet some instinct assured me that this priest knew of what he spoke. I felt drawn towards him and already respected his intellect, for he obviously could do many things that I, with all my knowledge of magic, could not. There was some mystery here that I must fathom, by guile if I could do so by no other means.

"Well, well," I said with a smile, simulating an attitude of humility, "if you can persuade me that what you say is true and to love is the key to the Temple of Wisdom, then I am willing to attempt it. What more is there for me to accomplish before I be permitted to learn the inner Mysteries?"

"You will have to break down the barriers which your own crimes have raised between you and the holy portals, you will have to love and serve mankind, paying thus the debts you have contracted through hatred and ignorance."

"You speak in riddles," I replied half scornfully, "but I accept your conditions. I will do this. Show me these barriers of which you speak that I may break them down and the debts that they may be paid in full. My power is great, my treasuries are overflowing, my will is Law in Egypt."

He rose; tall though I was, he seemed to tower above me.

"Vain man," he exclaimed, "you know not what you ask, your very words prove your utter unfitness even to attempt this undertaking. Your mind is of the earth. You talk of power, your power is less than a babe's. Did you not admit that you cannot drive the madness from you when it descends like a cloud? Can you conquer your own moods, your own despairs? As for this will of which you boast, you are ruled by vanity, pride and egotism—you are a slave, not a master." He turned and strode towards the door. "Follow me," he commanded.

We passed down many passages until at last we entered a small circular chamber in the centre of which was a great crystal globe that gave out a soft effulgence. Apart from this green glow, the room was in darkness. He bade me stand before the globe, then, coming behind me, he placed his hands across my forehead.

"Look into the depths," he said, "and see."

I looked; at first it was like gazing into the Nile clear green, deep yet full of light, then the light caught me, drawing me down. I forgot my present; I went back; I stood again in Atlantis; I became once more Cheor. Nothing was hidden from me of what I had done until the end. Then I found myself standing before an empty globe.

His voice recalled me to myself. "Tell me," he said, "what do you feel now about this past life?"

I frowned and hesitated, seeking to disentangle the confused threads of that memory. "I think," I said slowly at last, "that it has made me realize that I am not now as great as I imagined. I have always considered myself powerful, something of an adept in magic, but the magic we practise here is as a child's game compared with that. Ah, what have I not forgotten? Why, we held then the true secrets of the elements, we were as gods; not this earth alone was our plaything, but the hosts of heaven and the powers thereof. Our minds have indeed become like those of pygmies; everything was greater then, Egypt seems to us a mighty domain, and behold! I see now that it is but a speck upon the surface of a tiny world. I have much to learn."

I looked up to find his eyes piercing me as if searching my inmost heart, and there was an expression of wonder and sorrow on his face. "So you feel nothing but this regret—no shame for what you did, no horror?"

I laughed; so exhilarated was I by what I had seen that for a while all my forebodings were forgotten. "Why should I feel shame save perhaps for this man that I am now become, a man so misnamed a god? Ah, if I could know again what then I knew...."

"Does it leave no impression upon you but this desire for increased knowledge?"

I remained silent for a little while, attempting to identify myself even more closely with that past. As the pictures came back to me, one face stood out more clearly than the others, arousing within me an indefinable emotion.

"This Shahballazz," I said at length, "does he live now?"

"Why would you know?"

"I feel drawn to him; if he could be found I would have him in my councils, he is a man I could trust...." I hesitated. "It is foolish, perhaps, but the thought of him stirs in me a strange longing, a desire...." I shrugged my shoulders helplessly, incapable of expressing what I felt.

While I had been speaking the Ruler had seated himself upon the stone bench which encircled the chamber and remained for a little while sunk in thought. Yet in the strange and intense silence I felt as if his mind were, in some mysterious way, probing mine.

Presently he looked up and his stern mouth relaxed into a smile.

"Perhaps this is love you feel?" he suggested.

"It is possible," I admitted; "I have certainly never in

my life felt the need of anyone so much." Suddenly I strode across the chamber and stood before him. "You have spoken much of love today; you have told me that I can only gain my ends by serving all men and loving them. To me this sounds absurd. How can I love all men? All the fools I scorn and the enemies I hate? Now this man I could love perhaps, I might even serve him if I had to, yes, and you also, but the others ... In any case, I do not see how loving can have any connection with the powers that I would gain, unless, indeed, you use the word 'love' as a symbol for something else, some mighty creative force, or for some God who must remain hidden and unknown. That which men call love is of no use to me. What *is* this secret that you hide?"

He raised his head and looked at me.

Then something happened for which I can find no name. It was as if a blinding light shot from him and enveloped me, drawing me, for one fleeting instant, into his consciousness.

For an instant only—then the divine sensation passed. It was gone. I stood there dazed, empty, defeated, like a prisoner who has escaped into the light of day only to be thrust down into a darker dungeon.

Bewildered, I turned to him who had given me this ineffable glimpse into a state of being of which I could never have conceived, and which was already receding, becoming unreal—incomprehensible.

I found myself trembling; I leant against the wall for support. "What magic is this? What did you do to me?" I asked slowly.

He did not answer at once, but sat with his gaze fixed upon me. At last he seemed satisfied with his scrutiny.

"You imagined," he replied at length, "that you could come here, learn our secrets and depart to use them hereafter for your own ends. To do so would be impossible, but that you could not know. Yet since such a thought had even found entrance into your mind it became necessary for me to learn if this apparent passion for truth and understanding arose from lust for power or from fear alone, or whether there were not some deeper motive underlying these appearances. I therefore tested you by recalling to you the memory of Shahballazz. You were immediately drawn to him, responding to that note of love which memory caused to vibrate within your heart again. But this was not enough, for your love might have been a manifestation of selfish desire and nothing more; therefore I flooded you for an instant with the white flame of that higher love in which all that is evil must eventually be transmuted. Because you were not shattered by that clear note resounding through your aura, because you did not recoil from me in terror and revolt, this experiment has proved to me that within you the spark of love does burn, although it is not outwardly to be perceived. Therefore it will be permitted me to disclose to you certain matters that would otherwise have remained hidden for many lives. For know that if you had rejected him and me, I would have had no alternative but to send you back as you came, and you would have soon been overwhelmed by those evil forces to which you are still in bondage."

"I am ready to believe now," I replied, "that this mighty magical power which you call 'love' can indeed work miracles and could even heal me; but I still do not understand what part this man has to play therein, unless it be to help me gain insight into these mysteries. For now, more than ever, am I determined to learn how such a power can be acquired."

"He will teach you," he answered, "but not, perhaps, in the way you think. Tell me, would your life not be happier were he by your side?"

I considered his words for a little while in silence. It was strange indeed how this man's image had seized upon my imagination, how it had revealed to me a lack in my life of which I had hitherto been unconscious. I had never had a friend, had never loved nor trusted anyone. Re-shep-sut was perhaps the human being who had come nearest to me—other women had meant nothing, a burning lust and a forgetfulness—yet I had never trusted her. I had always been alone, on the defensive, holding men faithful by fear, by force, knowing full well that they would desert me the moment I weakened or they perceived that their advantage lay elsewhere; many of my fears were rooted in this knowledge. Had there been but one man whom I could trust to remain loyal when the sickness smote me; one man who, in these increasing periods of helplessness would defend me from the enemies of my own household, one man to whom I might speak my heart . . . one man who would love me enough—Yes, that was my need, I saw it in a flash—security. Security? Everywhere was conflict within and without, everywhere was uncertainty, now and hereafter. I wanted something or someone more stable, more enduring, greater than myself. Security . . . love . . . was this the answer to my problem? Were these two synonymous?

I raised my head. To desire a thing had ever meant for me the instant pursuit of its attainment.

"It is true," I said; "I need this man as an ally. He must be found."

"Nothing can be found unless it is sought in the right way," he remarked quietly.

I stopped in my swift pacing. "What is the right way?"

He remained silent. I frowned. "You say nothing? Do you know where he is? Show me the way to him!"

"I have already told you: the way is the way of love."

I made an impatient gesture. "But what I feel *is* love, what else should it be? I need him; I see that I cannot live without him. If you do not tell me where he is I will destroy the world to find him."

"Love?" he repeated, and smiled bitterly. "My son

you do not know what true love is, but yours is the best that you can contrive, therefore not to be wholly condemned." He shook his head. "O Pharaoh, how blind, how self-deceived you are in your arrogance and vanity! If it were not that I can see the point of development at which you stand, and can read in the faint gleam of that little spark of which I spoke hope for your future, I might well send you whence you came."

As I stared at him angry and baffled, he pointed to the seat at his side. "Come hither and I will endeavour to lighten the darkness of your understanding by showing you what love means and what gulfs lie between you and its attainment."

I came, feeling rather like a scolded child. Lassitude had followed the exhilaration of a few moments since; I began to feel again the old fiery pains through my head, forerunners of an attack, but for the first time I was not afraid. I had no enemy here who would take advantage of my weakness. I leant my head against the wall and closed my eyes. Slowly the pains grew less and I was soon enveloped in a great peace such as I had never before experienced.

"Throughout all your lives," he began, "you have had this passion for power; blinded by overweening vanity you have striven for nought but self-aggrandizement at all and any cost. As you saw, in order to attain these ends, you allied yourself in Atlantis with demonaic powers, separative in their nature, and therefore essentially inimical to man. He who persists in using such destructive energies is engaged, did he but know it, in slowly killing the flow of the universal Life force within him, whereas his true task is to make himself increasingly open to it at ever higher levels. With each incarnation, therefore, his vitality as well as his ability to respond to any higher vibrations becomes less, his powers generally weaken and his possibility of growing in mind and emotional response becomes more remote. Only one blinded, as such men inevitably are, by the illusory fantasies and hopes these contacts create, could fail to perceive that, by continuing upon this left hand path he could eventually condemn himself to suffering and degradation in life after life for untold ages."

I sat up with a swift indrawn breath.

He looked at me. "Yes," he said, "the fear which has haunted you all your life is a memory. Happy for you that this memory which is of the result of your early instruction in the temple of the Sun, has persisted despite all your efforts to crush it. Happy for you—else you might never have experienced even a faint desire to free yourself from the thrall of your self-inflicted blindness; you might not have become aware of your danger. For without this germ of truth sown by those who loved you, I tell you that you would not in this life have felt the stirring of that sense of imminent danger and that unease which is the first faint whisper of the inner voice of your soul and which gives you still, despite everything you have done, a hope of reaching eventually that height where the true source of power can be apprehended, the creative, unifying power of love. You have always despised it yet in one life it saved you, brought you back from the very edge of the pit.

He paused so long that at length I was forced into speech. "How did it save me?" I asked. "What is this memory? What happened in those lives between then—and now?"

"I could show you," he replied, "but what would it profit you to see again those wasted and ruined lives? Lives of slavery and degradation, lives in which, obsessed by the worship of yourself and blinded by vanity to your true condition, you sank lower and lower until, incarnating into ever more debased and savage forms, you at length became hardly more than a mindless personification of all those evil and destructive lusts you had created in Atlantis.

"Those who, by reason of certain links which you would not yet understand, were bound to you and love you still, watched you slip into the abyss but were powerless to help you since there was nothing in you that responded to the vibrations of love and truth they poured upon you. But no man is ever abandoned until all hope is dead and at last Shahballazz, whom you had once loved truly in a past more remote than this life in Atlantis, was permitted to make the supreme sacrifice and willed to be born in a body so coarse that he could contact you on your own level. So he descended into the slime with you and slowly through a long and weary incarnation, from that miserable outcast's shell which he had taken, played a perpetual stream of love upon you seeking thus to break through that crust of dense matter which enclosed you so that the light might enter in. As one blows upon the dying spark and at last brings it to flame, so did he blow upon an ember which all who saw not with the eye of love would have called dead. And he succeeded; for in that incarnation, obeying an almost blind instinct you sacrificed your life for his and had you but known it, for your own. Because of that one act when you passed over, instead of sinking instantly to the lowest level there to dwell, as had previously been your fate, among the hideous forms you yourself had created by your thoughts, it was possible to raise you to a higher plane. You returned to earth with some memory of a finer state. This memory haunted you even in the body of a black savage slave. The upward struggle had begun. Again and again you were hurled back into form in your search for fresh understanding until at last you reached a stage where once again you could be given some measure of responsibility. Powers hitherto cut off were therefore permitted you in order to test you and see how much you had learned. So you reincarnated into the household of Pharaoh, but through a woman who gave you that fierce and ruthless heredity which was still a part of your nature, for man is always what he makes himself. But there were great dangers, for the Law demands that when an opportunity for the use of ancient powers is given to a man, there are released at the same time any forces of retribution connected therewith from the past. Therefore all those destructive energies which you had deliberately attached to yourself have accompanied this opportunity for power. These are the enemies that attack you now and have come so near to destroying your body and your mind. These are they who will stand between you and all your soul's desires, love, happiness, security, any hope of progress, of capacity for usefulness in the world, until you control and redeem them, for until a man can rule himself and his own passions he is not fit to be anything but a servant."

When he ceased I sat for a long while motionless my arm over my eyes, seeking some way out of this abyss of darkness into which his revelations had plunged me. Now I understood my hitherto incomprehensible fears, but understanding only increased them a hundredfold. More than ever now I needed the solace and the strength of which Shahballazz had become the symbol.

The Ruler must have read my thoughts. "You had best know at once that Shahballazz is not here," he said, "and if he were, any meeting between you would be impossible while your vibrations remain as coarse and impure as at present. They would only injure him and interfere with his own work. Not more than once can such a sacrifice as his be permitted. It is for you now to reach him by purifying yourself until you are fit to stand by his side again. That day can only come when you have defeated the enemies in your own being. They are very real, very strong. You may be too weak to attempt any such conquest in this life —they may overthrow you."

His words struck at my pride and instantly all my being was in arms. What! They dared to stand in my way, these forces, these intangible enemies? They would separate me from this man I desired—they would hound me to my death, lonely, mad perhaps? ... And even beyond this life, ever denying me happiness, power, love? Pictures passed before my eyes. I saw them tangible, with mocking faces; they took on the shapes of all the people I had hated and despised. And as inevitably happened at the prospect of battle or when my will was thwarted in any way I felt rising within me that fierce passion of destructive energy which had swept and driven me all my life, the red anger which broke down every barrier, crushed every resistance. My head began to throb, my heart to choke me, force poured up until my limbs seemed inflated and the power of ten men animated my body; but now this fiery indignation was not directed outward, but turned inward against myself, against my own weakness, against these mysterious Powers that had dared to seize upon my mind, my body. Was I not master, I, Lord of my being? I sprang to my feet, forebodings and fears had vanished at this incentive to action. Here was a new world to conquer, here a greater and more potent adversary than the warring tribes about Egypt, or even red Set himself.

"I will defeat them," I cried, "only tell me how it may be done, how I may break these barriers down that separate me from my desires."

"I can only show you how to prepare yourself for the battle," he replied; "none can do the fighting but yourself. Before I do so, however, I would have you consider what you are about to undertake, coolly in the sane light of reason, in full knowledge, not in a haze of passion."

I would have spoken, but he raised his hand and leaning forward, proceeded to speak with such grave impressiveness that I felt the turmoil slowly die within me as fire dies under water.

"There are two paths by which men journey towards their goal," he said. "The slow way upon which the majority are travelling is safe and comparatively easy; it takes hundreds of lives, but also necessitates long rests in the intermediate worlds as it entails a very gradual expansion through the slow changing of the subtle matter of the bodies. There is a good measure of happiness, since payments are exacted slowly, but also a great deal of unnecessary suffering as protracted ignorance inevitably brings error and pain. But the second way, which must always be chosen deliberately with open eyes and by an act of will, is very different. Upon this steep path the man undertakes to hasten the normal processes of evolution; he is allowed no idle lingering, his debts are thrust upon him at every turn, his lives are crowded with bitter experience so that he may learn the more swiftly. Moreover, he calls down upon himself in life after life any elemental forces he may have created by magic in his past, and is forced to do battle with them continually until they are conquered. He is more self-conscious than other men, more sensitive to evil as well as good. Also, once having placed his feet upon this path a fall, if fall there be, has more terrible consequences."

"I will do it," I said defiantly, "not for me will these forces stand in the way life after life; I will soon deal with them now that my mind is set upon their destruction."

He gave me a glance half amused, half pitiful, but I was so exalted by the thought of all the marvels and feats of strength that I was about to accomplish and the power to be gained thereby, so roused by the sense of danger and adventure, that I hardly noticed it.

"Let me begin today," I added. "What is demanded of me?"

"The first essential is that you should see your enemies face to face, since no man can combat the unknown."

I smiled grimly. "Show them to me, I am not afraid."

"My son," he said, "do not forget that these enemies are within—they are yourself, you have made them one with you. You have no conception of the terrible power of the forces which vanity and selfishness create, particularly when, through black magic, the elemental energies of nature have been deliberately invoked to strengthen them. If I showed them to you unprepared as you now are, you would be instantly destroyed."

"What then? . . ." I asked at a loss.

"If you agree to undergo certain purificatory rites and penances which will probably last about nine months, it may then be possible to do so. But I warn you that these, in themselves, will constitute an ordeal which few men as undisciplined and unstable as yourself could hope successfully to undergo."

"And if I refuse?"

"Then you must straightway return to the world. You will be armed with the knowledge that you have already gained here, and can seek to govern the rest of your life in accordance with it."

"And remain ignorant of the nature of these powers that attack me and of how to combat them?" I shook my head. "No, no; I have already gone too far, I know too much—I must know all—and conquer."

"You may not conquer. I do not promise conquest; only fuller knowledge of the enemy and perhaps arms for the battle."

I shrugged my shoulders. "If I must perish in any case then let me die facing my enemy"—I smiled—"but I will not die."

"The choice is yours," he observed rather grimly. "But there is one thing you have overlooked. I said it would take nine months; during that time you will not have any contact with the outside world. Yet you have definite obligations there. You are Pharaoh; there is your throne —and Egypt."

"Oh, Egypt . . ." I waved it aside. "What do I care for Egypt? It can await my return. In any case, what has that life given me? I was weary of it long since. Indeed I have found little satisfaction there save in the original joy of conquest."

He sighed. At that time I wondered why. "So be it then, if such is your decision. Yet your servants may betray you and Egypt be torn by strife; the people may suffer—many may be destroyed."

"Better them than I," I said roughly. "Is not my soul more important than Egypt? If I can regain my health, my old energy, I can soon bring order again out of any chaos my absence may have caused. I made all my plans before I came here, and woe betide my servants if I find they have disobeyed me! It is my own weakness I fear, not the strength of my enemies."

"You have free will," he said non-committally. "Tomorrow then your discipline will begin."

For nine months I stayed in the Temple of the Rocks. My time was passed in those dark underground caves wherein the Mysteries are enacted. The Secret Ruler had spoken truly when he warned me what was to come. I, who had never known discipline or self-restraint, was very often on the verge of capitulation, but a stubborn pride kept me to my word. I soon discovered that whenever I faltered or rebelled my hesitations were reinforced by insidious attacks of my secret enemies seeking to undermine my resolution. Often, indeed, they seized my body rending it by paroxysms of madness; yet even of this madness, which so often casts men into the merciful pit of oblivion, I was a conscious and horror-stricken spectator; for never completely was I driven from my body as of old, there was always enough of me to watch, to struggle and often to despair.

At last he who had taught me all this while, and for whom I had developed a feeling which certainly must have come near at times to love, so admirable did I find his wisdom, his patience and his strength, called me once more to the Cave of the Sacred Light, where the great crystal stood.

"The probationary term is over," he said; "you have done all that it is possible for you to accomplish here and now. You must return to the world. But before doing so you may, if you so desire, see these enemies who yet hold you in bondage, face to face. But I warn you again, you still may not survive it."

"And must I return in any case?" I asked slowly.

He bowed his head.

"And until I see the truth about myself there is no chance of my reaching my goal?"

"No; eventually every man must see the Dweller on the Threshold who bars him the way. In this age, mankind is not ready to be brought thus face to face with his true self, the image of his past; it will only become more generally possible in an age removed by thousands of years from now. Until then man will combat his evil nature more or less blindly, following the slow path. You may still do this if you choose; you are not yet committed to the other. But should you desire to anticipate the future method of training I warn you now, as I did then, that it can only be done by a tremendous effort and at great cost. Some men are doing so, but *you* will do well to hesitate before you thus challenge the Law."

"I must know the truth," I said.

His expression became strangely tender. "It is well, my son. It will not be denied you. Now go to your chamber and rest yourself before the ordeal."

I do not know how long I slept, but awoke as if brought back with a violent shock. I was ice-cold and found to my horror I was unable to move hand or foot nor could I close my eyes which were fixed before me upon the darkness which had taken on a strange quality of translucence as if it were a great mirror. I struggled to free myself from the trance-like grip which held me; and as I lay there helpless an uncontrollable terror seized me, for reflected in this depth of darkness I became aware of a shape slowly materializing. It rose above me, its height so great that it reached the ceiling. At first it was merely a blur, lit with a faint, reddish glare, but soon it began to glow at the edges with a phosphorescent light and I perceived therein the semblance of a human face. At the same time I became conscious of a terrible stench which almost suffocated me and which grew with the apparition, pouring out from it like a putrescent stream. The features grew clearer and suddenly I realized that this face looking down into mine with dead eyes was my own. My own, yet not mine, for this was a mask so evil that it made me faint and sick, and from its eyes and nostrils and parted lips oozed a viscous stream of corruption hideous beyond imagining. Then I saw that it had no body, only an infinite darkness which seemed to go backwards and outwards into unfathomable spaces. Moreover, it appeared to be blind, deaf and dumb. Soon I realized that it was animated only from one centre, the lowest of all, which churned in a slimy, inverted circle, yet so powerfully that the whole simulacrum was directed by its force. With each moment the Shape grew clearer. Now I perceived that from every particle minute filaments of some blood-like substance floated out and connected it with—me. No longer could I evade the truth. My own breath flowed through that turgid centre of life; the foul stench which enveloped me was the emanation by which it and I existed; the dull humming which had tormented my ears since my awakening was its note—and mine. It was myself, part of my very being. Nor was this all, for as I lay there paralysed I became aware that the chamber was filled with lesser shapes, if shapes they could be called, for many were formless, mere sanguinary blobs animated by a slow-pulsing life; crawling things which reeked of stagnant marshes; wavering streams of grey light with evil eyes; blood-elementals with a semblance of human form;

a great, pale crab with tentacles stretched out to seize me, which I knew with a dreadful certainty in some life I must absorb. There were other forms which were perhaps the worst, for they were the shapes of men and women and animals whom by magic I had slain and whose subtler bodies I had enslaved. These seemed to cry aloud to me to give them back a physical form, to furnish them with the focus for experience of which I had ruthlessly deprived them. To them, as to that dread Shape, I was also bound. I understood at last what the Secret Ruler had meant when he told me to pause before committing myself upon the Path of Return. For these stood in my way; these barred the first gate. I knew that I must acknowledge, accept, and be prepared to pay my debts to these Dwellers of the Threshold before I could hope to go far upon my way.

And as this thought came into my mind, the great Shape began to sway and, like a turgid cloud, descended towards me.

Stark terror seized me. Not such fear as a man may know in battle or even the fear of disease, pain, or death; but a fear so vast and all-encompassing that it cannot be described. I screamed, but the scream was frozen in my throat; I struggled, but it was in vain. Closer it came; now it was above me, now it had descended, and I felt a loathsome warmth creep up my frozen limbs. The face looked into mine, the dead eyes grew larger, closer; the humming deafened me, the stench overpowered me. I knew what was about to happen, but was powerless to avert it. The Shape was returning whence it came—it was re-becoming —me. I think I must have fainted; when I recovered consciousness my limbs were free from the icy grip—I was re-animated—but by what? I lay supine, exhausted. Yet the mad terror in my brain urged me still to escape. But how could I escape from this that was myself? Did I fly to the outermost bounds of earth, to the furthest star, this would be with me. Unconsciousness, oblivion, annihilation must be mine; to go down into darkness, to be no more known and to know no more ...

With a tremendous effort I raised myself from my bed and turned to the seat upon which my garments lay. I caught up my dagger. To blot out memory, that was my one blind hope; for to remember, even for another second what I knew, would be for me the way of madness.

Then, even as I set the dagger at my throat, a hand was laid upon mine and I saw the Secret Ruler standing by my side. All pride forgotten now, I fell at his feet, grasping his robe in an extremity of supplication.

"Let me die," I gasped; "give me oblivion! This is more than I can bear."

"You desired to know—to see," he reminded me.

"I was a fool, a blind, vainglorious fool; let me go, let me die. I have no weapons wherewith I can combat this. I—I ... If I am this, then it were best that I be left to encompass my own doom. Let me be extinguished, let me be destroyed."

He touched my bowed head with compassionate fingers.

"Have you so soon forgotten that other thing you are, the glory which you experienced when first we spoke together?"

I shook my head. "Both I cannot be; that light shone not from my heart, but from yours."

"Nay, you *are* both; that light was the answer of your soul to mine, for all souls partake of the same essence of love. What you felt and saw tonight is the illusion, yet these illusions are real enough upon the lower planes and until they are destroyed, there is no escaping their ascendancy. Death would not help you, since death is but a door to another and wider aspect of life where much is revealed that is hidden from man in his physical form. If you left your body by your own will you would deprive yourself for a long time of the help of those who watch over the newly dead and you would merely be precipitated in full consciousness into the realm where those evil and distorted forms hold sway."

"What then?" I cried. "I am willing to fight then, but how can I, since they are myself? And far more myself than that other part of me you call my soul, but which I cannot see or feel or know, and which is therefore useless to me. What does it profit a man who is dying of thirst in a dungeon to be told that there are wells of water beyond the walls at which he could drink?" I leant back, exhausted by my emotions. "I am bound, I am helpless! If I do struggle with this that is myself, if I do suffer my errors during countless lives, what will it profit me?" I struck myself on the chest. "What do I gain—now? Bliss? In a thousand years of torture and agony? Perhaps it might be worth the struggle, for what I felt when you used your magic on me was wonderful—although already it is faded like a dream—but it was a state of mind alone; what I desire are tangible things...." I continued to stare at him heavily. I was trapped. I could think of nothing else. Lives of struggle, ages of suffering, and no way of putting any end to it at all. At least there was a way: more struggle and more suffering.... It was enough indeed to send a man mad! "Cease to struggle," something said; "defy the Law; seek annihilation, you have gone already too far, no bliss is worth the price." Annihilation ... once again the word roused those legions of fears within my mind. I remembered all I had learned in these past months, and why I was here. No, there was no escape. I laughed aloud, pressing my shaking hand against my brow. "... and I expected you to give me knowledge, to place the key to power, to happiness, in my hands...."

"I have given you knowledge," he said. "I have shown you the path to that place where the key of true power is hid."

"You have destroyed me," I answered.

For a little while there was silence, and in that silence

the memory of Atlantis returned to me. I had spoken those words before to the priests of the Sun who had condemned me. Yes, verily, the wheel had turned full circle. Would it be ever so? Was a man brought always back to the same point, the same problem, until by an effort he had freed himself from it? Cheor had listened to the insidious voices of the dark powers; he had defied the Law. . . .

Idly I picked up my dagger, turning it round in my hand. No escape. I looked up. "Well, what now?" I asked.

He laid his hand on my arm. "My son," he said, "do you not realize that the old must ever be destroyed to make room for the new?"

I smiled grimly and shook my head. "I do not complain. You have indeed kept your promise. I have fallen into mine own snare. What now, I say?"

"You return to your throne."

I shrugged my shoulders wearily. "What would that profit me, since I have failed in my search? I may as well be destroyed here as there."

Keeping his hand still upon my arm, he drew me towards the door. "Come with me," he said; "there is more for you to see before you go."

We stood again in the Cave of the Crystal. I glanced at it apprehensively, wondering what fresh terrors that mysterious surface would reveal.

He turned to me and spoke gravely.

"I perceive that you have not yet understood all that you came here to learn. O Pharaoh, when you accepted the throne of Egypt you took a solem oath to guard and protect the sacred land of the most high Gods. Look!" and he flung out his hand towards the crystal.

I looked, and behold, the surface was troubled. At first I saw only clouds of dust and rivers of blood, then slowly, out of the confusion I saw footmen advancing, falling beneath showers of arrows. I saw great temples going up in flame. Faces passed in confusion, faces I knew; my commanders, bloodstained and in despair, my generals and captains fleeing before hordes of barbarians. I saw Egypt in ruins and all my work undone. Then the pictures became clearer, more precise. I saw Re-shep-sut and knew that all the oaths by which I had bound her had proved unavailing. Net-Ka had died, and she, seeking to call up her sister's spirit and learn from her the secrets which may not be revealed, had sought the aid of the evil sorceresses who dwelt in the temple of Set.

I saw her falling more and more under their sway, ceasing to obey the voice of Besiurt, rejecting his counsel, mocking at his prognostications. I saw her taking lovers from among the lowest slaves and bringing shame upon the holy throne of Pharaoh by her riotous living and the abominations she practised openly. I saw the people, stirred at last to revolt, appealing to the priests of Ra, and Re-shep-sut making secret overtures to my most bitter enemies. Then did I see how Besiurt cursed her from the highest step of the Temple; I saw her fleeing, a broken outcast; I saw, for an instant, her despairing face sinking beneath dark waters.

I stepped back in fury, roused to the realities of a life I had almost forgotten. "I have been betrayed," I cried, "the barbarians have broken the frontiers!"

"There is no traitor but yourself," came his calm voice. "What right had you to put your responsibilities upon shoulders too weak to bear their weight? You alone precipitated this disaster. You had two ways of choice—it was not for me to force you to either, but I recall that, in your blind pride you said: *is not my soul worth more than Egypt?*" He stood before me now, tall and stern; at that moment he seemed like Thoth, the terrible God of justice. "What is the welfare of one man's soul compared to that of thousands of men and women who trust him? Upon you is the curse of duty unfulfilled. You desired power, you saw it slipping from you and came here, hoping to learn how you might keep your dominion. Now you have seen Egypt, you have looked upon yourself as you truly are. Do you still dare to say that you are fit for lordship? Do you consider that the destinies of men should be entrusted to one such as you, a man who abandons his country so as to save himself from his own passions which he cannot control?"

"What then?" I returned, angry and bewildered, "should I not have sought to strengthen myself and learn how I might gain this control?"

"To perform one's duty is more often than not the sole way to gain both strength and control," he remarked dryly. "Had you been willing to sacrifice your own welfare for your country you would have taken such a step forward in your evolution that you would have merited far greater help and enlightenment than I have been allowed to give you now. As it is, you have merely started fresh causes of retribution for which you will at some time have to pay the price."

I made a gesture of despair. "It seems that whatsoever I choose is wrong."

"Because your mind is still dominated by the powers of your lower self, my son, and you cannot understand the voice of wisdom even when it speaks."

And suddenly the full implication of his words swept over me. Previously my mind had indeed been confused, now in a flash of insight I saw clear. Perhaps it was because the barriers I had raised against my secret fears had been shaken that night as never before, and this fresh proof of my own blindness and inadequacy finished the work the ordeal had begun. But in that moment I recognized myself at last for what I was, no longer strong, terrible, self-sufficient, but weak, helpless, and alone. Wave upon wave of terror broke upon me, submerging me. Fear of the past, of the present, but chiefly fear of that unimaginable future. On and on, circling in the trap, ignorance leading to error, error barring me from wisdom; no escape. To be sent forth thus, to attempt to fight on haunted by this knowledge, that was impossible.

"I cannot return," I cried, "it is true, I am not fit to lead, to rule, nor to conquer. Let another take my place, I shall go mad indeed and all go down into ruin."

"You must return: no man but yourself can right the wrongs you have done."

I looked into his eyes and suddenly found myself at his feet: "Guide me, help me, show me the way! Alone I can do nothing; without you, O my Master, I am utterly lost."

He laid his hand upon my shoulder. "My son," he said in a voice full of compassion, "fear nothing, you will never be alone. For the first time in all your lives you have shown that humility which is the pre-requisite to all true progress and by this change of heart you have given us the right to be your guides and your mentors, for we can give no man the help he needs until he has freely acknowledged that need. From henceforth we will be ever by your side. Although still blinded by your limitations, you may, for many incarnations, be ignorant of our protection, it will never fail you. You have opened your mind to us; henceforth our voices, at all the great crises of your development, will be able to make themselves heard. No man who thus invokes us in humility is ever refused or abandoned. You will conquer."

He moved away and seated himself upon the bench, and I, still dazed and shaken, stumbled to my feet and sank down by his side.

Yet despite the shattering emotions I had experienced I felt curiously calm; I had given myself into his hands, henceforth let him direct me.

"Conquer?" I echoed, "you mean that I can be freed from these Shapes of Amenti?"

"I know it," he said, "just as I know that you will attain your goal." Was it my imagination or did a brightness flow from him? I sighed, abandoning myself to this mysterious influence. He was sure, then I too could have confidence.

"I know it," he repeated, "because the destiny of every individual is the destiny of Life itself; you can no more eventually escape love than you can escape the fruits of your deeds of hate. Love is stronger than hate. Even the annihilation you feared could only be a temporary passing into obscuration of that primeval spark of the One Flame which dwells within every form. In some scheme or another every unit will work out its destiny, be that never so long delayed, for nothing lives to itself alone, all are part of that mighty Being who is beyond all human comprehension. But delay means suffering, for it is resisting the stream of Life which bears all creation irresistibly onward towards the consummation of the Divine Will."

He paused and answered my unspoken thoughts.

"My son, do not imagine that either your struggle or your search is unique. Yours is the struggle of all men, yours their search, and also their goal. For an instant, when you came here, I gave you a foretaste—a reflection only—of that rightful heritage of mankind; that state of permanent love you must some day reach. I showed you, but it has faded now; I speak of it, but I know my words mean nought to you. You cannot even hope to understand them yet.

"But always at certain stages in the evolution of every man a vision is vouchsafed and a goal is shown to him so that the impression remains ineradicable. It is then for him to work towards that goal until he is ready for a further and still greater revelation. So he goes on from stage to stage and as he progresses so the vision changes, becoming ever more vivid and more real as he learns wisdom and comes to a clearer understanding of this deeply buried purpose of the soul."

"It is true," I said—"I cannot indeed understand how man could be content with such a state for ever—nor even with a goal so vague and unsubstantial. As for your promise, we forget; death will draw down the curtain and when I awake to a new life, I will find myself beset by these old enemies again—for I see now that it will take me more than this life to conquer them. But I shall be once more blind and lost, I may not even remember that there *is* a goal. I will not know that you stand upon my right hand to aid me. In this life, yes, your assurance may give me the courage to fight on—but how shall I fare then?"

He shook his head. "You will not forget. The circumstances in which the revelation has been given will certainly fade and be obscured by all the shifting forms of the illusory world in which you must dwell; but a dream, a vision, as of some lost perfection, will remain. All men, dear son, remember some shadow of their lost estate, that joy and perfection which is the eternal nature of their souls. But in those who, at some time or another, have faced their lower nature, this realization is ever more vivid, the struggle between higher and lower more acute, the yearning for freedom greater. Thus, realizing their lack, do they seek the ideal through life after life.

"They call it by many names according to their stage of enlightenment, their nature and capacities. Some call it happiness, some security, some union with the beloved, some knowledge, some success. The name matters not—all ideals are but a shadow of that final perfection; experience only will teach them to discern the dross from the gold, to discriminate between the ephemeral and the enduring. What matters is that somehow the man shall be driven on towards the final consummation. You will be so driven, for you have demanded Truth, you have challenged your destiny, it awaits you in the world outside these walls, to which you must now return. Wise deeds bear fruit even as do foolish ones and the memory of what you have faced here will follow you, it will haunt you, inspire you, like a mirage lure you on until that day when, having pierced, however small a rift in the barrier which separates you from the Truth which is indeed yourself, you will realize in yourself the Truth that will set you free.

"Now you must go forward along the road of life towards that distant goal; but do not forget that you make your own road. You *are* the road. All forces, both good and evil, wait to serve you if you invoke them aright, but you must learn the magic formulae of invocation. Nothing is denied you but what you deny yourself. Do you desire friends and lovers, then give friendship and love, and they will crowd around you. Give service and you will be served; heal others and your own diseases will be cured. If anything ever seems to be denied you, give of that thing freely and eventually through giving, you will receive. If the world appears to ill-treat you, look well, my son, into your own heart; you will surely find hidden therein something that is inimical to the world.

"Do not complain at experience however bitter it may seem; use it rather, turn it to account, for nothing comes to man but can be made to benefit him. See how fortunate for you your present sickness has been. Had you been healthy and strong, self-satisfied, unafraid, you would never have sought me out, never have learned what now you will always, in your innermost being, know. It is often the contented, relatively happy man who gains the least out of his life, for he is inclined to remain static; cultivate rather within you that divine discontent which ever reaches forwards towards fresh achievements.

"Strive therefore towards an ideal, towards the best you can conceive. One day your eyes will be opened; one day through manifold experiences you will be brought to understand. When you reach that high place, when you find within your own heart this truth, this serenity, this fount of perennial inspiration, of joy, of bliss; when, that is, you have cast down the final barrier and have united yourself by an act of willing sacrifice to That which in very truth you are—the Spirit of Love, which some men call God and others know to be beyond any name—then you will acknowledge that no striving has been in vain, no mistake to be deplored, no experience valueless, no suffering a waste of time.

"For the man who has cast aside his fetters and has tasted this blissful union with all things, suffers no longer from the limitations imposed upon lesser men. He knows no fear, for fear implies menace, and how can he be menaced who is one with all Life? Pain and calamity do not touch him, the joy which wells up perpetually in him from that great fountain-head of Love of which he has made himself a part, sustains him in whatsoever situation he may find himself. As a man looks back upon the necessary disciplines of his childhood, so will you, in that day, my son, look back on the many lives behind you and, grown to the full stature of a man, you will go forward strong and secure at last, fit to play your part either in this world or beyond it; it matters not which, for all worlds and all states are one to the man who has found himself."

Next morning before sunrise he brought me to the mouth of the great cave which led into the desert. And now that the parting had come, I realized to the full what this man meant to me. I felt like a lost child. We stood side by side looking out towards the distant horizon. He raised his arm.

"Yonder is your city, O Pharaoh."

I dropped on my knees before him, lifting the hem of his garment to my lips. "O my Master, yonder is death—here is all my life. Do not send me alone into this exile. Grant me at least that I may see and speak with thee again."

"My son," he said and the music of his voice and the joy of his presence brought a great peace upon me, "it is not death—it is life, for it is the Path of Return; there is no exile for the man who walks in Truth, and no separation for those who are bound together in the bonds of love. Between our souls there will be no separation any more. It is for you to become one with that soul of yours, for until you have learned to listen in the silence for its voice, until you can catch, if but an echo, of what is both yours and mine, you must indeed walk seemingly in exile and alone. You will not see me again until you have completed another stage of your journey; and when you have reached that stage there will be no need for you to invoke me—I shall be there. But before you are ready for what I will have to give you then, it is essential that you shall have at least broken the full power which these elementals of Atlantis have over your body and your mind, and cleared to some extent from your emotion and your mind their influence and their emanations. Now go forth. Heavy is the task upon you; I see darkness and blood over Egypt; you will have need of all your strength if you are to prevail. By yonder palm trees you will find a company of bowmen and a litter. Take up the sceptre which you laid down and bring peace to Egypt before your life ends."

I stood up slowly. "That will not be long," I said.

He held out his hand and in the palm was a small brown scarab set in a ring. "This I have magnetized for you. Wear it always—let it be buried upon your heart when you enter the tomb. There will come a day when your mummy will be despoiled and through this despoilation eventually the scarab will return to you; that time is far away, but when once more you set it upon your finger you will be re-linked with this moment. When that happens you will know me again."

He blessed me. I looked into his eyes, and now the stream of love which flowed into me from him brought with it a sense of exhilaration, of power, of glorious certainty.

A few steps away I turned and raised my arm in salutation, as I did so the first rays of the rising sun shot up from the rim of the desert and illuminated his tall figure till it seemed lost in a golden flame.

I pressed the ring upon my finger. It gave me hope. I faced the sun and went forward towards the Path of Return. . . .

. . . . .

The Path of Return. . . . Long after this vision of the past had faded, these words and their implication remained in my mind. I did not know at what date in the immense ranges of Egypt's history this life had taken place, but assuming it to have been during one of the later periods of dynastic change and unrest, it must still have happened thousands of years ago.

What then could I have been doing in the interval to have lingered so long upon that Path? My progress must have been appallingly slow. But at least I could comfort myself a little by the thought that some of those Atlantean forces must have been transmuted in that long interval, some of the barriers broken down, since the scarab was now upon my finger and once more a teacher stood by my side.

However, when I considered those thousands of years, filled no doubt with endless mistakes and backslidings, I was overwhelmed with regrets not only for the waste of time involved but for the poor return I must have given for those efforts made on my most unworthy behalf in the Temple of the Rocks. But also I was filled with humility and gratitude at the realization that beings such as my teacher should trouble about people as little evolved as I had then been and indeed still was.

My bitter self-revilings were answered for me when at length I was once more allowed access to his mind; and caught in the rhythm of those dearly-remembered vibrations, even my rage against myself was somewhat assuaged. No anger nor hatred could long survive that profound calm which he radiated.

"Do not waste time and energy regretting the past," he said, "seek rather to understand it; study it if you are granted the opportunity, not emotionally, but as a scientist studies the ingredients necessary for some experiment. That is, after all, what experience really represents: the material used by the soul in attempting to make for itself a perfect body of manifestation. Once the man has understood this he will realize that his work lies in preparing himself much more self-consciously for the future than he has ever done before. This is actually what is happening in the world today.

"More people are beginning to understand some of the fundamental laws of nature and are recognizing the immense powers of mind; they are, in fact, rediscovering magic. Man is inclined to look back upon the magic of Atlantis, of Egypt, even of the Middle Ages as crude superstition, or something legendary and fantastic which humanity has outgrown; it can never be outgrown for magic is simply the ancient name given to the ability to use aspects of the great creative energies through which manifestation has been brought into being and which can be invoked, manipulated and controlled by knowledge of their secrets combined with the power of the will.

"People forget that each age must express itself in its own terms. Every man who thinks forcibly is a magician, either black or white, according to the motive and purpose behind his thought.

"In the past he achieved control over matter through the use of sound, ceremonial and various rituals; now he does so mainly by scientific means, psychological knowledge and organization. The first method calls into being certain energies generated by intense, concentrated emotion and desire; the second by concentrated thought, although combination of both are used today. The written word and pictured image are primarily the magical weapons of this age. Consider for a moment the influence of the Press, advertising, cinema and radio which mould the plastic minds of the masses. These methods of exercising control may not be so spectacular as the ancient ceremonies and incantations but, since all men are more closely linked in this age than ever before, the new magic is infinitely more potent and can be more sinister.

"Those who use these powers to cheat, deceive and manipulate the unwary in order to gain their personal ends and further their selfish interests are every bit as dangerous black magicians in their way as the men who deliberately created evil genii to serve them in the far past. I know you have been finding it difficult to accept literally what you have been told regarding the actuality of these forms of evil created in Atlantis which were still so powerful hundreds of years later that they could actually be seen and could hold their wretched creator in thrall. I assure you they were only too real. Every powerfully organized thought, good or evil, creates an appropriate form in subtle matter. So it does not need a great effort of imagination to realize what man's cruelty, selfishness, evil desires and actions, has produced down the ages ever since he became capable of thinking positively and charging such thoughts with emotion. He has literally peopled the atmosphere of his world with hosts of evil shapes, which form about him and the earth a great cloud of darkness; and he will continue to increase and energize this by every selfish impulse and evil thought until he realizes what he is doing and reverses the process, breaking up and dissipating this poisonous darkness by pouring in light and love, as clear water will purify a muddy pool. This can only be accomplished by each individual working unceasingly upon his own particular contribution.

"Unfortunately in this age the situation is worse than it has ever been before as man is recovering so much of his lost knowledge and learning how to harness the elements themselves to serve him. Those who deliberately use this knowledge to create destructive forces such as poison gas, death rays, high explosives and the like are also creating, did they but know it, terrific elementals in subtle matter who will follow them vengefully life after life, as those followed you from Atlantis until, to some extent at least they have redeemed them. In fact the parallel, as I have already pointed out, between this age and that of Atlantis is very close.

"The law remains unchanged; so as man becomes increasingly powerful on the mental creative levels, his responsibilities become heavier and the consequences of his actions proportionately greater if he uses his powers wrongly. Even the average man of today is learning through the intensive training he receives in concentration which modern education provides, to think more clearly and precisely; therefore he creates more powerful thought-forms which, whether he is aware of it or not, are projected telepathically far more widely than he could imagine. As a result he can encircle himself with veritable guardians of light or hosts of destructive forces, for thought is magnetic and draws to its creator energies of the same order as those he emanates. These also influence his environment and even his world. You would do well to consider this in relation to what is happening around you today.

"It is for this reason that anyone who is seriously endeavouring to study what is at present known as 'occultism' and is desirous of spreading this knowledge is being especially watched and when possible trained by those on the inner planes whose task it is to try to lead humanity forward along the evolutionary path and to help each individual to break up and disperse this noxious cloud of ancient evil which still blinds man to his true purpose and destiny."

I could understand why people who were making a deliberate attempt to obey the Divine Will and work with the Law instead of against it, might possibly be worth helping, but that did not explain why I had been allowed to contact a teacher in Egypt, for then I had been out for personal gain alone and my motives were purely selfish; nor could I even see why I had been put into such a position of power at all and given such opportunities for the exercise of my very undesirable accomplishments.

"You are taking the average short-sighted view," he admonished me. "Such judgements are usually fallacious because no one—unless he can read not only man's past but even the world Karma of the moment—is able to see the true cause of contemporary events. But we take a wider view. We see things in a better perspective since we can look forward as well as back, and consider the overall plan to be of greater importance than the individual. You must realize, moreover, that there is such a thing as national, racial and even planetary Karma to be taken into consideration. You are too inclined to think of Karma as only applicable to the life of man; but man's life fits into the pattern of greater lives, even as the little cellular lives in your body are part of your own physical state. The consideration of such intricate workings of the One Law may well make your finite mind reel, but at least it can teach you, if it does nothing more, not to be too hasty in your superficial judgements of any occurrences, either those related to the lives of personalities or to more far-reaching events.

"You may now perhaps be able to understand that every instrument must, if possible, be made to serve our ends, even if to the eyes of man it may appear quite unworthy. There is therefore no need for anyone to feel unduly flattered when he is thus chosen by us. There is no favouritism in our methods, we do not use or ignore people because of any personal bias. Our one object is to raise the general level of spirituality, to bring order out of chaos, wisdom out of foolishness, harmony out of discord. Therefore although we prefer those who are willing and able to co-operate with us in this work, from the beginning of time we have always been forced by the scarcity of good material to use whatsoever instruments we could find, even though they may not be particularly competent ones and as likely as not may temporarily ruin our plans through their inefficiency and human weaknesses.

"As for the question of whether or not you merited to be in such a high position in that life, it was not so much due to merit as to your own character and your capacity to seize opportunities. Another might have missed them or failed in action and been defeated. All men have opportunities for power and position at some time; but what they seldom realize is the responsibility entailed and what the Karma of failure will be. If they did they would often hesitate and not be led by vanity into positions for which they are not morally fitted.

"It happened that at the particular period of Egyptian history in which you lived it was essential that the central authority should be at all costs maintained. Egypt was destined to be for centuries to come a focus through which culture, poetry and art—those moulding forces of civilization—could be poured. Therefore men were needed who could rule and by ruling keep the peace; for without security no arts, and eventually no advanced state of true civilization can hope to flourish. There were no men available who were capable of bridging an interlude between two great rulers destined to carry on the work save you who had thrust your way into a position of authority. True, you were a black magician and had all the faults characteristic of a man with such a past, but at least you had strength and resolve. Do not think that a man who has acquired a strong character, even though it has been developed upon the Left Hand Path, has necessarily failed in his evolution. Strength of purpose remains always an asset, for it has only to be given a right direction instead of a wrong one—in other words to be made creative instead of destructive—to become of great value to us.

"So we used you because you were necessary to us; but at the same time, since we could see that you were at a vital point in your evolution, we hoped to be able to hasten the development of one of those individual units which had hitherto been a danger and a handicap to the race. For all evil people by their bad influence upon their surroundings or through allowing themselves to become tools of the Dark Forces—even if unwittingly—act as a brake upon the general advancement. For that reason we will often take more trouble with a strong and wayward man than with the well-intentioned but weak individuals who, unfortunately, as yet still make up the larger proportion of mankind. The Christ made this very clear in his parable of the ninety-and-nine sheep, but as usual few men have troubled to grasp his implication, still less to apply it.

"Do not think, however, that even so you would ever have been allowed that close contact with the Secret Ruler had you not, in your inmost heart, desired help and enlightenment for higher ends and also made a supreme effort to obtain them. For until there is a fundamental urge towards progress on the part of the man himself we are powerless to give him any personal help or encouragement. Individual free will is an essential aspect of the evolution of humanity. We always try to turn man's faults and mistakes to the best advantage for everyone concerned but we never proselytize, for we know only too well that until the desire for regeneration is born and springs up like a flame from within, any outward acceptance of our doctrines would only be ephemeral. Again I return to the teaching of Christ: the house built on sand will never withstand the tempest; so we wait until the man is driven to ask us how he may begin to build it upon the rock."

"Still," I interpolated, "Pharaoh's motives were so unworthy, he only made the effort towards self-betterment out of fear and under the compulsion of choosing the lesser of what appeared to be two evils."

"Do not be in such a hurry to condemn him," he replied with a smile. "Every act and motive must be judged by the circumstances conditioning it. Fear, self-preservation and the like, are some of nature's most successful methods of making primitive or backward men bestir themselves and seek better things. Remember, everything is relative and in those very early stages motives do not matter—desire is enough. So if ever men come to you in fear—of what, matters little—rejoice, as we, the Guardians of the Race, rejoice when we hear the cry of despair uttered by a soul in travail. For fear presupposes sense of lack; and again and again in the lives of every man there come moments when all things fail him and recognizing his lack he recognizes also that he is incapable of remedying it. It is just these moments which so often prove to be turning-points of his evolution. Therefore give all you can to such an one. Do not dare to condemn or to judge him.

"Only we who can read the heart can judge whether a man is ready to receive enlightenment. But be very sure that if the cry is prolonged enough, determined enough, sincere enough, it will be answered. Even as in Egypt when your cry went out, when, in your burning desire you used a Word which might have shattered you to pieces, you were not condemned, you were rather received with joy and your feet set upon the Path."

"But I sense they did not stay on it long," I said bitterly, "what happened to Pharaoh in the end? Did he do his duty and bring peace to Egypt?"

"He did, and thereafter died—insane."

I shuddered. "So he didn't escape, after all?"

"How could he? A man does not change in the twinkling of an eye and become a saint in a day. These sudden conversions one hears of are in reality but the culminating point of long lives of inward struggle and slow growth. None of nature's processes are rapid—judged by man's standard of time. How could such a man as you then were, with bodies attuned to the note of the forces of destruction, atoms poisoned and weakened by centuries of evil thinking, hope to combat for long the results of your own foolishness? Pharaoh learned a great deal through that failure, and that is all that ultimately matters."

"But if he hadn't. . . . That priest used the word annihilation. A terrible word. If all is an aspect of the One Life how could that be possible?"

"The true Self—the Soul—can *never* be annihilated in the sense you use the term since, as you truly realize, nothing that possesses the spark of divinity can ever die. But he was clearly not speaking of the Soul." He sighed. "Whatever one says will almost certainly be open to misinterpretation. But let me put it this way and do not even take this literally for no analogy can express a spiritual truth. Just as in the personality the thread of memory can be broken by illness, old age or other causes, yet the individuality—the true Self—remains unaffected, so can this other thread connecting, by means of a subtler form of memory, life with life, be broken. Or again, just as a polluted stream, impossible to cleanse, can be dammed, yet it still continues to exist although it no longer flows in the old channel. You may find hints here, but no more, for you are touching upon one of the great mysteries, the implications of which are far too deep to express in human terms. But rest assured that this so-called annihilation must happen so rarely, so almost never, that it is hardly worth considering." He paused, "in one sense, and in one sense only—never. I will say no more."

"And what sort of lives followed?" I asked rather apprehensively.

"For the most part they were spent in enforced and grudging service to others, as peasants and as slaves, humble and unspectacular. As you had deliberately undertaken to make the attempt to deal with your past, you had to incorporate a great number of the debased atoms related to it into each of your physical bodies; these made you delicate and unhealthy and prevented you from any intense effort until you had succeeded in transmuting a certain proportion of them.

"But at last you were again strong enough to attempt to combat once more that greatest impediment to your progress—the Demon of Power; in other words, the destructive element which any opportunity for power instantly stimulated within you. You were therefore reborn in an environment which would present you with every opportunity to learn the particular lessons you needed. You shall see and judge for yourself what you made of them."

CHAPTER III

PERSIA

It was in small and disconnected scenes that this life which I am about to narrate was recalled to me. They did not come through me alone, for one part was seen by another of those who participated with me in those first occult experiences in the bungalow. The rest of the life was revealed—not only, I think, because it was probably typical of lives in which once again I was tested by being given a taste of power—but also because my main problem in that incarnation was one with which an increasing number of modern men and women are faced and which has always puzzled and alarmed those who never understand any manifestations of life outside the norm.

The first picture was of myself—a woman—lying upon a divan in a great room. The light was brilliant outside my window; the sea glittered with the transparent blue of jacinth; the sky was white with heat. Someone was weeping by the couch. With a gesture of impatience I turned my head towards the interior of the shadowed chamber and watched two slave-women who, with side-long, terrified glances, were wiping blood from the tessellated pavement. I scorned the girl whose fair head was buried on my knees—yet her I also loved. I stretched out my hand and idly stroked her cheek.

"Why weep, O Ereshem"? I asked "have you never seen a man tortured before?"

"Not thus—O, not thus . . . ." moaned Ereshem, and hid her face in my robe as if seeking to press from her eyes the image of that mutilated body.

"Well," I said sharply, "let this be a lesson to you. And

to you also," I added to the slave-women who had risen and were slinking to the door. "A thousand times I have sworn I will have none but maidens about me." I laughed shortly, "I do not think our Manizha will take a man again!"

When they had gone Ereshem sat up and wiped the tears away with the edge of her veil. "I would I could understand why you hate all men so," she murmured.

"Not men alone. O beautiful jewel of my heart; all life and everyone in it is at times such a weariness to me that it is scarce to be borne. I can be happy only when I am with my father—or with thee." I drew her nearer, caressing her. "Come, little one, let us put the thought of men and their foolishness out of our minds."

But it was not in Ereshem to put the thought of men out of her mind and I knew it well. Therein lay a canker of bitterness, for although she had never loved a man, nothing I could give her satisfied in reality the deepest desires of her nature. I had chosen her to be my favourite and treated her with a mixture of kindness and contempt, passion and cruelty. Now while I continued to caress her my mind beat around her words, angry yet impotent, like a wild beast in a cage.

Well enough I knew why I hated men; it was based upon a bitter longing for their strength and a more bitter scorn of my own inadequacies. From earliest childhood I had loathed this body in which I found myself imprisoned, nor had I ever succeeded in wholly identifying myself with it. The only child of my father I had always been to him a son rather than a daughter, refusing to admit my feminality. Absolutely fearless I rode to lion hunts in man's attire and sought as much as possible to behave like a man. I lavished my fiery love upon women, yet kept always at the back of my mind the bitter knowledge that, whatever I did, I could never be other than the sex I scorned. My body mocked me, so that often I would strike at my breasts with savage hands. Soon I began to loathe all men's bodies because such was not my own. I wrestled and fought with my father's men for sport, yet was suspicious that they allowed me to overcome them because they were afraid of my revenge—and so was the more bitterly ashamed. In these makeshifts of manhood I sought a remedy for this sense of futility, yet something within me acknowledged them as foolish and vain. But to admit myself a woman, to give myself to a man ... The thought revolted me with a contemptuous disgust.

Wearily at last I thrust Ereshem aside and rising began to pace up and down the perfumed, jewelled chamber. Only by domination over the weak and helpless could I prove to myself my own power, yet ever I remained unsatisfied by that proof.

Suddenly the panther chained to the wall yawned loudly. As if goaded by the lazy sound, I seized the whip and like a fury struck the beast again and again, till I had it cowering and whimpering against the wall.

At that moment voices sounded without: "Sanaï! Sanaï! Sanaï Fayiz!" The curtains were drawn aside and my father entered the room.

I lowered the whip and turned about to face him with a gesture in which shame and defiance were mingled.

He was the one person on earth who had the power to soften me; for he alone appeared to understand my dark moods and could read the bitterness of frustration which goaded me to most of the evil which I did. As for me, I loved him as much as my nature permitted. He alone could give me the peace and beauty which I sought but could so seldom find. Seated with him in the rose gardens, reading from some painted, jewelled book, discussing some abstruse point of theology, listening to the voice of instruments, the sweet singing of slave girls, I could forget all my sorrows and frustrations and oblivious at last of sex reach a state which touched on perfect happiness. For he was a wise and gentle man. He had for a few weeks in his youth met the great sage Zarathustra and from that time, instead of furthering his position as a minor official at court, had, in the search after truth, retired into a world of metaphysical adventures in which I was only too eager to join him. We lived retired upon a small estate; and I was content, save when the wild moods of restlessness or ambition seized upon me, then I would weep tears of rage and helplessness in the realization that my wretched body prevented me from accomplishing all the feats of glory I longed passionately to undertake.

Now he stood in the doorway, gazing upon me, stroking his long beard, his eyes full of sorrow.

"What is this I hear, O my daughter? Is it possible that you have had a slave tortured in your presence?"

"He was found with Manizha; I gave him the only fitting punishment."

He dismissed my women and seated himself upon the divan beside me.

"And what right, have you, O Cihrazad, to take this horrible vengeance because a man and woman act in harmony with the divine will and give love to each other? Sometimes it seems to me as if Ahriman and his servitors have taken possession of you. Do not forget that each time you allow them sway over your acts, you weigh the balances against your soul. Man has free will and is his own judge. Would you go down for ever to a burning hell? As for this poor beast," and he pointed to the bleeding panther, "beware lest Geush Urvan, the protector of beasts, punish you for this; some day a beast may tear your body, child." He sighed deeply: "Why do you so fill your life with hatred instead of love?"

I made an impatient movement. "I will be master in my own house: men, women, and beasts shall obey me."

"Whilst you have power they may, but the day will perhaps come when you lose that power—what then?"

I laughed aloud. "I have no fear," I said, "power lies within, I shall never lose it!" I walked up to the panther; the beast made as if to spring at me, but fearlessly I bent over it, drew my hand across its head and spoke deep words. It shivered and crouched at my feet; with a scornful gesture I walked back to the couch.

"You see? I have no whip but it licks my feet"—I struck my breast—"I hold its spirit here!"

I looked down at my father's sad face, and instantly compunction overcame me sweeping my evil mood away. I flung myself beside him, putting my arms about him.

"You have come to me; I am happy. Let us talk here and forget the whole world, foolish men, women and beasts. I care in truth nothing for them. Teach me your wisdom. O my father, thus only can the Jinns be driven from my heart and I be at peace."

He sighed. "Of what avail to pour into your ears the glories of Ahuro Mazdao when you profit nothing by His enlightenment?"

"Perhaps one day I may; only talk to me—it is enough!"

But instead of reading from the poets, or discussing subtle aspects of the Holy Fire, he presently opened his heart to me and revealed that he was troubled because his peace was about to be disturbed. Two famous chieftains had sent a messenger asking for hospitality for themselves and their troops. They were of some importance at Court and could not be refused.

It meant change, excitement, a breath from the outside world; my heart leapt. Then I remembered I was but a woman. Upon the thought came the determination to disguise myself, pose as my father's son and take part in the festivities. Nor could he dissuade me. And so it was arranged.

It was told of Azuri-bin-Zangi and Burandek that they were bound to each other by strong ties of affection as well as of blood; they were wealthy and had a great following; it was very necessary to stand well with them, for their enmity could be dangerous.

So there were feasts in their honour and great hunts were organized, while I, disguised as a boy, joined in the days and nights of rejoicing. One night I gave a banquet in my apartments and so elated was I that I forced Ereshem to wait upon us, caressing her and praising her beauty and her arts in love. It was only later that I remembered that the eyes of Burandek and Ereshem were ever seeking each other and that in those days the girl's moods were strange.

But at the time I did not trouble about her, for my own mind was occupied with others things. A friendship had ripened between Azuri and myself. Together we rode to hunt the lion and the gazelle, each sought to outstrip the other and we returned in peace together, well content. When they made their farewells Azuri gave me a pink pearl strangely shaped, as an amulet to wear in remembrance of him and I gave him a heavy bracelet of wrought silver set with turquoise and rubies.

All the day after their departure I spent alone by the seashore. I swam far out, delighting in the fierce movement of my body through the waves; yet I was restless and bitterly unhappy. I had for a few weeks tasted the life of men—it was this only I desired; even my father's wisdom meant little to me now. That evening in a fever of agitation I called for Ereshem to comfort me, but the girl was nowhere to be found.

Three days later I heard a rumour that a veiled woman had been seen riding with the party of Burandek; then I realized that Ereshem had deserted me for the sake of a man.

A fury of rage seized upon me. I seemed, indeed, as if possessed by all the hosts of Ahriman. Even my father could do nothing. For a week I revelled in an orgy of licence and cruelty so terrible that the fame of it swept through the land. Torn with pangs of jealousy and shame, no woman, beast or man about me but tasted my vengeance, but at last my fiery wrath was replaced by an icy calm, more evil and dangerous.

I made plans, forgetful of everything save my lust for vengeance. I gathered together a band of desperate men and clad in armour, set out after the fugitive.

Of the adventures that befell me I cannot speak, but I must, at that time, have been endowed with almost superhuman power and cunning; perhaps, as my father had said, I was indeed possessed by evil spirits who lent me their aid and drove me on. Suffice it to say that, having traced Burandek to the city where he dwelt and having waited patiently until I heard that he had absented himself for a while, I obtained access to the women's quarters and one night found myself gazing down upon the sleeping form of Ereshem.

I drew my dagger to strike, then paused; for to kill her thus seemed far too easy a punishment; Ereshem must see death approaching by the hands she had caressed and betrayed.

I leant over her, pressing my hand over her mouth. Her eyes opened and, wide with horror, gazed into mine. The dagger flashed, but ere it descended, strong arms seized me; it was wrenched from my grip and I found myself struggling in the enraged grasp of Burandek himself who had returned, unknown to my spies.

The rest of that night, bleeding from my struggle, bound hand and foot, I lay in the little chamber beyond the one in which the lovers rejoiced anew in each other, stirred to fresh ecstasy by the recent escape from death. In agony and shame, in terror of what was to come, I lay there. The following morning, half naked between two mighty eunuchs, I was dragged into another apartment wherein sat Burandek with Azuri-bin-Zangi beside him.

At sight of these two men the cup of my shame was

filled, yet I held my head high. Azuri's anger, however, was terrible, for he felt himself to have been deceived and mocked by the trick I had played upon him. His eyes were like flames and his lips cruel as whips as he arose and approached me. With one hand he tore the pink pearl from my throat and cast it upon the floor. It fell at Burandek's feet; he picked it up.

"It is damaged," he said quietly.

"Worthless, like the woman," replied Azuri.

Burandek looked at me with a certain pity.

"She did what she did for love," he remarked, "she has harmed no one but herself."

Azuri turned away with a scornful movement of his shoulders, but as he did so, his gaze swept over me. The expression in his eyes changed. The hot blood stained my cheek. I was suddenly aware of a danger more subtle than death. I spat out a string of curses at him.

Burandek, watching us, smiled. "What shall I do with her?" he asked, "I do not want her in my house."

"What has that to do with me? Sell her—she should fetch a good price."

Burandek laughed and crossing to where I stood, tore aside my garments.

"She is young, beautiful—and a virgin, my brother," he remarked gently, "will you not take her as a gift from me?"

Azuri stared at me and laughed shortly. "That is true," he said, "she should breed fine sons." He turned to the eunuchs: "Have her veiled and taken to my apartments. If she does not behave reasonably she shall be given as slave to Nahid, my wife; until then—we shall see."

That night Azuri came to the room where I lay bound upon the bed; for twice I had attempted to put an end to my life, so terrible was my despair. Now I spat upon him as I lay there naked and helpless under his eyes and hurled at him every evil curse I knew.

He unbound me. "Arise," he said "and tell me why you hate men and love women, O Cihrazad, who are yourself so fair and desirable a woman?"

Then he stooped suddenly and caught me, kissing me upon the lips; but my nails tore upon his chest and my teeth met in his cheek. Up and down the room we fought, carpets were torn from the walls, furniture upset. Not for nothing had I learned to wrestle with my father's men. My resistance aroused in him a burning flame. But gradually my strength weakened and I who had dominated men and women and beasts knew myself at last as nothing in the hands of a man. Tears of fatigue and shame ran down my cheeks; I was racked by helpless sobs. All the sorrow and ignominy of all the weak things in the world seemed articulate within my weary body as he bore me down at last upon the bed.

· · · · ·

The years that followed are blurred and fragmentary; they consist in the memory of emotions rather than of events, for I always lived in a world of passionate desires.

There was the moment, for instance, when I first realized that I was with child. I felt as if my body had turned traitor to me. To be the plaything of a man I hated was bad enough—but this! I gazed at my body in fascinated disgust, this body I loved, slim, strong, masculine, and felt that there was indeed now nothing left but death. I set my thin lips and swore that I would bear no child to any man. The child was born prematurely—dead.

When Azuri knew what I had done I was confronted with a rage more terrible than I had imagined possible.

"Henceforth," he told me, "you shall be the slave of Nahid—perhaps that will teach you a woman's duties."

Now Nahid and I had hated each other before we met.

I learned later that she had been afraid of being supplanted by me, who was so strange a woman, different from any of those whom her Lord had loved and that through her magical arts she had sought to destroy me. She had studied necromancy long, always having astrologers and magicians by her side to instruct her. Now she was satisfied. She ruled her women with whips and torture, and on me she could vent all her lust for cruelty. She gave me the basest tasks and when I revolted thrashed and starved me until I was too weak to revolt any more. In the end, I think, to save my life, Azuri took me from her and gave me once more apartments of my own.

For there was some curious tie between us, a tie compounded of hate and desire; of repulsion and of fascination. He could neither abandon me nor forget me for any length of time and in the later years a strange friendship grew up between us; for he found that to me he could talk as to another man of things in which the average woman found little interest. I understood, too, his link with Burandek as Nahid, who was fiercely jealous of it, never could.

I seem to have had many children; I know I suffered terribly; my body did not appear to be made for women's burdens. I had no affection for my offspring; only the girls I pitied, thinking how their fair bodies would be used by men, how they would live restricted, prisoners of their own inadequacies.

Moreover I detested the life of the harem with its intrigues, its petty spites and rivalries. Surrounded by women and their cares, by the deep, druglike softness of this life of heavy feminality, my memories of the past soon became the sole means of saving what I felt was my self —my true, unchanging self—from annihilation. So I withdrew into my dreams of those glorious days of freedom and of excitement and with them came also vision of my father and our talks in the garden. Grave, beautiful and full of healing, his words came back to me. Perhaps it was only their wisdom which kept me alive and sane during those long years of misery which I was forced to endure.

No sharp memories arise out of that dark limbo of years. Only one clear flame burns there, the hatred between Nahid and myself which undoubtedly ravaged both our lives.

My loathing was increased by the fact that Nahid remained extraordinarily beautiful, while excessive childbearing had coarsened and enfeebled my fine body and bitterness had left its mark upon my face. For many years Azuri had kept us apart, thus ensuring for himself a certain amount of peace, but at last fate arranged that once more we should be brought face to face and the threads of our lives inextricably bound together.

One day Azuri came to me. He was grave and stern.

"Tonight," he said, "all my women leave for Tallek-el-Bar, my house in the mountains. The tribes of the plains are sweeping upon this city in great swarms; Burandek has already ridden to meet them, I join him at once. If we should be defeated, which Ormazd forbid, we shall fall back upon Tallek-el-Bar and defend it until the last. In the meantime I leave in your hands and in those of Nahid all my possessions, my children, my slaves. I can spare but few men to guard you, and must leave you in the the care of Ashem Vasishtem, wherefrom proceedeth justice and all good. May He protect you. I know full well the hatred you two women have for each other, but at these times enmity must be buried in the grave of necessity; according to your folly or wisdom all may be lost or saved." He took both my hands in his. "O Ciharazad," he said, "there has been between us a bond which I would not have believed could exist between a man and a woman —and it is to this bond that I would hold you now. You could once fight like any man; you were fearless; none could ride better than you, nor cast a lance more straightly

—I speak to you now as that woman you were—nay, as the man you pretended to be. You know full well I love Nahid as my life. I leave that life—I leave her honour in your hands."

I stared at him, amazed and shaken, then turned my head aside. "It is too late; look at me, Azuri! You made me into a woman, I cannot become a man again at your will."

He smiled and touched my face with one finger lightly. "It is to the spirit of the man in you that I make my appeal. I do not trust any of the others—only you. To you I leave my honour—I know that you will not betray it."

Then embracing me, he departed to battle.

For a little while, moved by the common impulse of loneliness and fear, Nahid and I turned to each other with more kindliness. But not in a few days nor by a few words could such hatred as ours, so old, so rooted in rivalry, in blood and darkness, be dissolved. Our distrust was like a serpent ever hissing between us.

Nahid sought comfort and strength in her magical incantations, but I had a deep, unreasoning fear of these and amused myself by strengthening and organizing the defences of the place and practising the use of arms, but even this happiness was muted; for when I would have donned men's garments, I felt I was merely rendering myself ridiculous; I was too stout, my breath was short, I grew faint and my limbs ached intolerably at the slightest exertion; only my spirit was as ardent and as youthful as of old.

The long days of inaction and uncertainty dragged. The mountains closed us in with impenetrable silence. The women wept or chattered; the eunuchs mumbled together and fluttered at the slightest clink of arms; the soldiers drank and diced to pass the idle hours; in her chamber Nahid cast her spells.

Gradually, however, rumours drifted through to us. One day we heard that a great battle had been fought in the plain and that our Lords had conquered. In the midst of our rejoicings came a runner bleeding and exhausted, who declared that they had both been killed and that the enemy were even now approaching Tallek-el-Bar.

I knew how weak the defences were, but remembering my trust, determined to hold the place to the last. All that day Nahid wrought enchantments, striving to discover if what we had heard was indeed truth. Occasionally she would call in one of her women to act as medium for her power, but always they were sent forth with bitter revilings. At last, sacrificing her pride in her necessity she came to me.

"When Azuri left me, he bade you render me any aid I desired," she said, "now, behold I come to ask for that aid. My women have neither the strength nor the courage to assist me. But you and I together may learn the truth for the Spirits will speak; moreover should Azuri and Burandek in verity be slain, then we will recall them even from the Cinvato Peretu itself to give us their strength and council, for surely never were we so in need of it as now."

I would have done it for any but her, for her arts fascinated, even while they frightened me; but here, at last, I saw the chance for which I had been waiting all these bitter years.

I rose, smiling into my rival's face, and with slow and bitter scorn lashed the other woman who now came suppliant to me for aid.

"What matter it," I cried at last, "if Burandek and Azuri be dead? All must die; better be a man and dead in battle than alive, a slave enclosed within high walls and cursed with a woman's destiny. If needs must, I will fight for you, for I have sworn it, but I will not traffic with the Spirits, I will not drag Azuri back to your greedy arms!"

Then while we still contended together, sudden fearful

cries filled the air, shrieks, moans and wailings. We rushed towards the door, but as we reached it the curtains were torn aside and we saw, in the entrance, Azuri his garments rent, blood running from his lips and head. He swayed blindly forward.

"All is lost," he gasped, "our troops are defeated. We fled hither to save you from their vengeance, but they are close behind. Burandek holds the stairs ..." His hand went to his side. "My dagger! Nahid ... use it ... you must not be taken ..."

He slipped to his knees, then fell upon his face.

With a piercing shriek Nahid sank beside him, raising him in her arms. "He is dead ... Azuri ... my heart!" and she fainted beside him on the floor.

But he was not dead. With a fierce effort, as if dragging his reluctant spirit back into its shattered body so as to accomplish the purpose for which he had returned, he raised himself upon his elbow.

"Cihrazad," he whispered.

I drew near, standing above him, staring down upon him.

The noise was increasing below; yells, shouts of victory mingled with high screams of women and of eunuchs.

I knew well what the end would be for any unhappy woman who fell into the hands of these brutal men. I would not be one of them.

"My dagger ..." he gasped.

I stooped and picked it up. A rush of blood came to his lips. He fell back again, but his eyes turned towards the insensible body of Nahid. "Kill her ... swear ..."

I answered nothing, but he read the look in my eyes.

"Swear—Cihrazad. I—beseech you ..."

I looked at him, then bowed my head. "I swear."

He seemed about to speak again, but his voice choked with blood. He was dead.

I stood alone. Without I could hear the rabble upon the

stairs. A child's cry, awful and heart-rending came from the antechamber; it was my child, but I did not move. I was staring at Nahid. I hated her; to leave her her life was the most terrible vengeance I could take for the humiliations, the sufferings she had caused me.

At that moment she stirred and sat up dazedly.

A woman's shriek without; a body falling against the curtain; a mutilated body rolling into the room. Death was nothing—but the cries of the soldiers, drunk with cruelty and lust—and women—always women, the victims and slaves of it. . . .

The curtain was torn down. A gigantic savage form in blood-stained armour, paused there to view the room.

My glance went from Nahid to Azuri, I swung round and the man sprang forward. Like a flash I stooped and plunged my dagger into Nahid's breast, but before I could turn it upon myself he had caught me and wrenched it from my hand.

He held me there, despite my wild struggles, and called to his companions without.

I saw their faces, as they crowded in at the doorway, and seeing them, realized to the full the doom that awaited me. . . .

. . . . .

The woman Cihrazad. . . . Yet how little a woman! Rather the proud spirit of a man, thrust into the restrictions of a female form.

Even the blurred memory of that horrible death was obliterated in my interest in this rational explanation of an age-old problem.

Obviously for life after life I had been polarized as a male before this Persian incarnation. Could Cihrazad be blamed, then, when the spirit within, revolting to find itself imprisoned in an alien and unresponsive form, had sought to take the familiar path again and to ignore the laws of a woman's body, thus twisting her life awry?

How many men and women at the present time were finding themselves in a similar unhappy state and not understanding the inner laws of their nature, were revolting even as I had then done and also seeking blindly by many false paths to resolve the conflict which tore at their whole being.

My mind travelled back along the path of that incarnation with profound interest. The first thing that struck me forcibly was the wild, dark hatred which Nahid and I had felt for each other. She must have been some enemy from my past. Instantly my mind swept back to Atlantis—there was the clue, could I but interpret it. I sat back in my chair, striving to get some connecting link and suddenly the pink pearl came into mind; where had I seen that pearl? Then in a flash I remembered: it belonged to one of our small group of four.

I began to speculate upon the nature of jewels and why it is that they so often appear to be connected with men's lives. What particular virtue can reside in a stone that it appears to have the power to bring back the past or to precipitate events? That my scarab, which had been deliberately magnetized by one who was an adept in magic, should come back to me I understood—but the pearl remained a mystery.

I felt the need of my teacher here but since my efforts to contact his consciousness received at that moment no response, I turned my attention to studying the rest of the life as best I might.

I found it almost painfully easy to get back into that emotional atmosphere. The long period of slavery, the shame and degradation of that trapped and tortured woman made me shudder even now. Indeed I had been made to drink to the brim the bitter cup that in the past I had forced on those dependent upon me for life and well-being. Surely that experience would be graven so deeply upon my undying memory that never again would I show cruelty to the weak.

At last my teacher permitted me to contact him again.

"I left you alone for a little while," he said after greeting me, "as it is far better for you to try to discover for yourself something of the intricate laws underlying Karma although inevitably their deeper significance must still remain a mystery to you. In any case I am revealing now only such lives as have a direct bearing one upon the other, in which effects are working out clearly from previous experiments in living. There were, of course many in which other groups of people were tied to you by the compulsion of cause and effect, lives in which different patterns were worked out with different links and the note you struck through the uses of black magic did not reverberate."

"I suppose those were more pleasant, more happy?"

"Some of them. Every opportunity for happiness as well as progress is given to the evolving man and the circumstances in which he is born correspond to whatsoever side of his nature he is seeking to develop. The whole object of the Law of Reincarnation is that the true self shall eventually learn to create a vehicle of consciousness through which it may mirror forth every aspect of its divinity in perfect equilibrium. It is as if it were seeking to polish a mighty diamond—the true diamond soul—with a thousand facets. To do this it is forced to work in many forms, through many groups of people, to sound its note in many keys, perfecting now one side, now the other. At its best its manifestations in human form can never be more than partial—the restrictions of the body are too great. That is why it is well never to judge another, however low or ignorant he may seem to be; for he may be a great soul working out mistakes in a humble disguise. It is ever difficult to recognize the truth amid illusion."

"I think there was a mutual recognition in Persia," I remarked, "was Nahid not one of my group in Atlantis?"

"Yes. Sudden love and hatred are nearly always the result of some like passion in the past."

"Who was my father? He was the only one I loved truly as Cihrazad."

"He was a link from a happier life. You were born under his roof so that you might be given the opportunity to continue the effort you had made before in the search for wisdom. You loved him because all that was fine in you, all that desired growth, responded to what he had to give as the flower responds to the gardener who tends it; you lost him and all he might still have given you by your own foolishness."

"And what of that pink pearl? You have taught me that there is no such thing as coincidence, yet I cannot see . . ."

"Jewels absorb magnetism just as everything else does," he said, "but they retain it longer, as the mineral kingdom is the most concrete of all and grows so slowly that it appears to have no life whatsoever. Just as your scarab was magnetized in Egypt—except that this was done by an occult process and was therefore the more powerful—so, to a far lesser extent, it is possible for people unconsciously to project some of their own magnetic currents into an object. But in order that this shall have a lasting effect, he who does so must be under a particularly powerful emotional stimulus at the time. If an object so magnetized by hate or love should fall again into the hands of the one with whom it was originally linked, it might, should he be sufficiently sensitive, recall his dormant memories of that event. In any case the contact would be very likely to cause a certain resurgence of Karmic currents from that particular incarnation.

"In fact a jewel returning thus from out of the past may be considered almost a warning signal of karmic debts due to be presented for payment; but naturally in most cases people do not recognize such a signal and would not be able to decipher its message if they did. Life is full of warning lights, of guiding posts for those who are sensitive enough to be aware of them, but for the most part as yet man stumbles from one trouble into another entirely unprepared, then demands indignantly of high heaven why his misfortunes should be allowed, blaming God instead of his own foolish self. I hope," and here I felt once more the glow of his love enveloping me like a pulsing flame, "that in your case this present life will be the last in which you will assail the ears of those who have watched over you with these outcries and fulminations."

I shook my head. To look back thus upon one's past was finally to lose all conceit. "One seems to evolve so slowly—and to forget and fall back again. Cihrazad doesn't seem a marked improvement upon Pharaoh. Just as cruel and passionate and uncontrolled . . . that wretched panther! After all Pharaoh did, I suppose, repent of the evil he had done; he accepted the task laid upon him; he did go forth willingly upon the Path of Return."

"Yes, but as you yourself pointed out, he repented because he was afraid—that is not true repentance. Moreover repentance from whatsoever motive, although absolutely necessary to start with, does not alter the Law by one jot. You may repent, but those currents you have animated by evil do not immediately melt away when you declare that you are sorry. They have to be dealt with and deliberately changed by the man himself. There never were two more pernicious doctrines than those of vicarious atonement and the forgiveness of sins. The Christian Church has built for itself a heavy Karma of retribution by deliberately distorting the words of its Founder and laying stress upon such teachings to gain worldly power.

Man has got to learn to bear the responsibility for his

own mistakes and accept the full consequences; he must do all the work himself. You, as Pharaoh, certainly made an attempt to understand the Law; you cleared the ground before you sufficiently to enable you to go forward; but the true test of this so-called repentance came when you returned to the world, a world full of war, hatred and intrigue, of discords to which the most powerful part of your nature found it almost impossible not to respond. For people, even the strongest, react to the emotional atmosphere about them, especially if it plays upon some weakness in their own character. It was comparatively easy for you to see the advantages of love and wisdom whilst among those who manifested them and to struggle against your Dweller in the peace and solitude of the Temple but such work was only preparatory at best.

"Thus when once more, in this Persian incarnation, an opportunity to exercise power was presented to you, it struck a note to which those entities you had created through the abuse of power instantly responded. For I would impress upon you again most strongly that *the dark forces can only influence and endanger those in whom they can find some affinity to their own nature*. Let the man therefore who thinks he is being attacked by such adversaries search immediately for the flaw in himself which makes such attack possible.

"In Persia these evil entities were reinforced by your inherent vanity and moral weakness which manifested in a feeling of inferiority due to what you imagined to be the indignity of your female form. This hidden conflict made you seek to assert yourself on every possible occasion. Bullies and sadists are always weak people—often obsessed people. You were both. Now I will show you a life which was happier than most, although here again it ended through your own foolishness in apparent disaster."

"And I was a man again, I hope," I exclaimed. "I seem to have crushed enough feminine experiences into that life to last a considerable time. I must have learned something through what I suffered then."

He smiled. "But do you consider that you *did* trouble to learn the lessons of a woman? Did you ever acquiesce in your destiny and endeavour to make the best of it? Were you not to the end unbalanced? Did you ever attempt to understand the mysteries of the feminine side of life and the secret of woman's strength? Did you even learn true sympathy for the causes of feminine fears, pains, difficulties? Did you truly, in deep humility, admit your inadequacy and seek to perfect yourself in woman's form? No; even while absorbing these experiences you did not attempt to understand their significance, but were merely in a perpetual state of revolt. Once again you can see how, without right application, no amount of knowledge is of any use. The aim of evolution, in so far as it concerns man on the physical plane, is the perfectly balanced human being, composed of the male qualities of will and wisdom and the feminine ones of intuition and love; and until these are manifested in equal degree, the soul will seek expression again and again in a form which gives it the opportunity to adjust the balance. Cihrazad never became a true woman, she never made the most of the gifts which were offered her through the medium of her female sex.

"Next time—but you shall see for yourself—and judge. . . ."

CHAPTER IV

GREECE

In Greece I returned to earth once more in a woman's body, but this time I was no longer in revolt against my sex. In the interval I had obviously learned some lessons from my Persian incarnation, and understanding at last how to manipulate the subtle forces that a woman has at her disposal, this time I accepted my destiny and set about attempting to use my feminine potentialities.

But in Persia, even after I had been forced to submit to every possible variant of a woman's life, I had still refused to comply with the laws of nature. I had to the end taken delight in my own sex, choosing lovers from among my fellow slaves. Thus I deliberately perverted that life-stream, which, in its feminine aspect, flowed through my body and in consequence of these excesses, strengthened the purely sensual and material aspect of sex to such an extent that, when I reincarnated in Greece, I was ruled and obsessed by sex currents intensified to an abnormal degree.

Thus, already as a young girl, my life was made a torture by desires which I could neither comprehend nor satisfy.

I was headstrong, moody, with a passionate zest for life and a hunger for experience, for knowledge and for beauty; and because of necessity my outlook was coloured by the normal conventions of the times and place in which I lived, it was inevitable that my mind turned to men, as the only possible means through which I could accomplish my desires.

But there was little chance of any companionship with men for a girl born of Athenian parents. I was brought up in the women's quarters, taught all the arts which would fit me to become a useful wife and mother of children; there was no other possible future for such as myself. But inwardly, I never accepted this uninteresting destiny for, along with this abnormal craving for sex experience, was a strain of very pure idealism and romance. While on the one hand I dreamed of myself ruling men—since in no other way could my lust for power be satisfied—on the other I also dreamed of an ideal and perfect lover who would open all doors to me and would give me that harmony and completeness for which my soul craved.

It is said that everyone before birth is shown in a flash the possibilities of his future life. If so, I must have kept a memory more than usually vivid of what was in store for me, for the thought of a marriage arranged with some sensible and worthy youth I had never seen filled me with revulsion.

Before even I had reached marriageable age I had fallen desperately in love; there were stolen meetings. I imagined that in this man I had found my ideal. Despite the dangers, I persuaded him to elope with me, while my ambitious parents were arranging a suitable match. We fled from Athens to Sybaris, where the laws were more lax and the status of women more advanced. But all too soon I realized that this man did not satisfy me; still following the will-o'-the-wisp of my dreams, I left him for another. My search went on; drawn by this vague urge for perfection and by the urge, not so vague, of my unappeasable flesh, I passed from lover to lover with the inevitable result that fed by the abandonment of all restraint, the until now dormant evil in my nature began to manifest. No longer did I give myself for even the chimera of love. It was not long before I discovered that my body was worth gold, jewel, slaves, all the symbols of power; greed became my ruling passion, greed of the flesh and greed of material things.

I returned to Athens, and there in a few years became one of the leading hetæra of the city. I was ambitious; soon I had collected around me a little circle of the most wealthy, the most intelligent, and the most artistic of the Athenians.

Yet despite my success, in my heart I felt there was something I had missed in life. I was not happy. I tried to forget my dream, but still it haunted me; at last I realized that no possessions, however rare, no knowledge, however strange and erudite, no lover, however passionate, could satisfy this urge which was not of the flesh alone.

One night a feast was given by a wealthy citizen.

The Symposium had begun; most of the guests were already confused by their potations. There were, of course, no women present save a few hetæræ and a number of flautists and dancing girls. The chamber was in disorder, the floor strewn with blossoms and discarded garments. I lay upon the breast of my latest lover, yet I was in no mood for caresses nor for revelry. I had not drunk as much as the others and a strange clarity of vision was upon me. I found myself overcome by distaste at the sight of my fellow revellers. I noticed with scorn that my lover's face was red and blotched, his mouth half open, and the wreath of white roses hung ridiculously over one eye. Presently there arrived a party of fresh guests who had come on from another feast; I was looking at them idly when my gaze was arrested by one of their number whom I had not seen before. He was young and reasonably goodlooking, but beyond that there was nothing to account for my interest.

As I raised myself on my elbow to see him better, he turned and his eyes met mine. We stared at each other for a moment which to me seemed an eternity; neither of us moved. What happened. I do not know, but it was as if a flame of fire passed from his heart into mine. I became as another woman; I saw myself and everything about me with new eyes. I was suddenly aware of a feeling of shame and horror. Hardly knowing what I did, with a swift movement I drew up my robe and freeing myself from my lover's embrace rose to my feet. I saw the stranger speak to one of his companions and thought I heard my name. My one desire was to fly, from what I hardly knew. I picked my way among the recumbent guests, many of whom were already sleeping off their potations and without so much as glancing in his direction, went to the door, calling to a slave to have my litter brought immediately. I waited at the entrance to the house, leaning against a column, faint with agitation, trembling and bewildered.

This must be true love, I thought, the dread, poisoned shaft of Eros. Despite the warmth of the night, I drew my himation over my head and shivered. The sky was dark as velvet overhead with a few faint stars, the air heavy with the scent of flowers; afar off a nightingale was singing. It was a night made for love. . . . O, why were the slaves so long?

I heard a movement behind me and looked about like a hunted thing. What madness was this? How had the sight of one man turned me back into a frightened girl again?

A voice spoke softly.

"Chloris," he said, "I beseech you, wait—speak with me a moment. I am Serretes, a sculptor; all my life I have sought a model for my great work, the divine Aphrodite rising from the waves. I have travelled to Egypt, Persia, among the Isles—I never found her. Now I come to Athens—and my eyes see her at last. I cannot let you go. You are she, the woman I have sought, seen in my dreams. I implore you, pose for me." His voice shook.

I dared not look round. The perfume of the violets with which his head was garlanded made me faint. Overcome by emotion, by this extraordinary feeling of shame and terror, my actions were dictated by mere panic. My litter at that moment arrived. Without a word I entered it and drew the curtain in his face, then, flinging myself on the cushions, I began to weep. I had lost him. I did not know what mad impulse had precipitated my flight. All the way back I sobbed distractedly. When the litter stopped before my house I stumbled out. As I did so a figure materialized from the shadows. It was he.

"I have followed you," he said. "I could not do otherwise. You scorn me, I suppose; it is true I am as yet poor and unknown. You have a great reputation; your lovers are the richest men in the city; I cannot give you slaves, gold, or jewels—but I will do more." His voice rang out and I thrilled to the purpose and the strength of him. "I will do what they cannot—I will make you immortal! In ages to come men will look upon your form and glory in the beauty and the perfection of which you will be the symbol. O divine Chloris, will you not listen? Will you not accept my gifts?"

I turned to him, my face ravaged with tears. The light from above the doorway shone down upon it, but I did not care.

"I do not want your gifts," I said. "I want nothing from you, O Serretes...."

His expression changed, his hands dropped to his sides.

"You reject me, then? Is there no hope?"

I laughed softly, lifting my face to his, opening my arms in a gesture of abandon. "I want nothing from you —I desire only to give you—love. Do I ask too much?"

He drew a quick breath, then flung up his hands to the dark sky. "O Aphrodite, not for nothing did I make vows and sacrifices at thy shrine. O Eros, blessed be thou among the Gods!"

And, catching me in his arms, as a bridegroom carries his bride, so did he bear me across the threshold into my house.

There followed three years of such bliss that I think is rarely given to mortals. I took a villa in the country; there he worked, and there we spent long hours wandering through the groves and over the hills in a companionship so perfect that sometimes I feared we would incur the jealousy of the gods. But all too soon a shadow fell upon our love. Serrete's work began to be acclaimed far and wide and we were forced to return to Athens. There I found myself devoured by jealousy. Only a man as strong and yet as gentle as he could have endured the wild scenes I made. I wanted him for myself alone, was racked with doubts and fears if he were for a few hours out of my sight. I must have made his life a torment, but his patience and his love were proof even against my uncontrolled passions. Moreover, he sought ever to endow me with some of his own stability and with that philosophic outlook which certainly at this time stood him in good stead.

He was a citizen of Crotona and before meeting me had been about to enter the school of Pythagoras and take upon himself the preliminary vows of three years' silence. His mind still turned towards the centre of learning and of wisdom; often he would discuss the possibility of my also travelling to Crotona, which he passionately loved. But I saw in Pythagoras a danger to our close union and although a part of me was also attracted towards the idea, rather than risk having to share my lover even with so cold a mistress as philosophy, I sought to entice him from these dreams and to hold him welded ever more closely to me by the fires of my love.

Then suddenly Fate took a hand in my affairs. War broke out between Crotona and Sybaris. Serretes announced that he must return and help defend the sacred soil of his fatherland.

To me it seemed the end of all my dreams. As a child I had always been obsessed with an unreasoning horror of warfare in any form—the sight even of warriors terrified me still. Now I became convinced that Serretes would be killed. I used all my arts to break his resolution, but his sense of duty towards the city that had given him birth was stronger even than our love. I left him no peace; I upbraided and stormed, I sulked and wept. The exquisite harmony of our life was broken; for the first time we disputed almost endlessly. At last, the day before he had arranged to leave, I made my last throw and threatened that, if he deserted me, I would return to my old life which I had abandoned for his sake.

He only smiled at me and said sadly: "Do I not know it? It is that alone which makes me hesitate—yet even so I must go. Yes, my beloved, I know your necessity, you need men as we need air to breathe. You will always need them to content your tyrannous, lovely body and to satisfy the greed of your insatiable mind. As you had many lovers before I came, so you will have many after. In that we are different. I shall never desire any woman but you."

"Yet you will leave me to them?"

"I must." He came to where I lay upon my couch and took me in his arms. "O Chloris, do not make it so hard for me. Crotona is small, every man must fight if we are to defeat the Sybarites. If I remained here I would never know happiness, even in your arms, for I should feel I had played the traitor to my people in their need. You—are free."

At that I broke down and wept bitterly. "No," I sobbed "I do not want freedom. I did not know love before I met you—I will never love again. I swear I will be faithful."

We were seated in the courtyard. I raised my eyes in despair. It was so beautiful here, but when he went he would take all its beauty with him. I looked at the dazzling sunlight on the pavement; it caught the water from the slender fountain in jewels of colour. Beyond, in the warm shadows, the delicate columns of the Atrium arose in muted whiteness, and here stood his masterpiece, Aphrodite, turning sideways as she arose from the waves, with so exquisite a gesture, so vivid a glance, that life seemed to pulse within her rounded limbs. She was his gift to me—my immortality.

I pointed to the statue. "By Eros I swear that I will remain as chaste and cold as yonder woman until you return."

It was the first time I had acknowledged my defeat. He held me closer, putting his hand over my mouth almost fearfully. "Do not swear, Chloris; I do not want oaths from you, only your assurance that you will greet me again with joy." He drew a heavy ring from his finger. "Wear this for me, it is my pledge to you. Nothing will ever change my love; the memory of your beauty will give me strength; I think it will shield me from death himself."

But like a child I clung to him. "I want to swear," I cried. "I desire to bind myself to you by all the oaths in heaven and earth." I raised my head suddenly. "Serretes, often you have implored me to wed you, but I have refused. Now if you still wish it I will do so, then I will feel unalterably bound. As your wife I must be chaste lest I shame you before all Athens." I wept again. "There is nothing I desire more in the world than to be true to you."

. . . . .

At first, proud of being the wife of Serretes, I kept myself in strict seclusion. I lived for his letters and, having been taught by him the rudiments of his craft, amused myself by endeavouring to copy his work. News came but seldom and at increasingly long intervals. At last all letters ceased. Yet still I hoped. The months dragged on. This unaccustomed existence was little less than torture to me, who had been used all my life to the licentious companionship of the men of Athens. I certainly kept myself faithful, but at what cost! Serretes had spoken truly when he said I was not made for chastity. But I did it out of love for him. Yet when his silence had lasted for months, my determination began to waver. I asked myself what object —if he were indeed dead—would there be for me to continue living in a state of senseless chastity—stagnation of body as of mind; for my body left me no peace, and I felt that my mind could not long stand the strain to which it was at present subjected. Yet I did not dare come out into the world of men again, for I knew my own weakness too well and mistrusted it.

For hours I would pace restlessly up and down, starting at every knock upon the door, hoping it might be a messenger or someone come to visit me. The place was so still. . . . I supposed that very soon I would be forgotten —other women would have usurped my place in the life of the city.

Then, panic-stricken, I would rush to my mirror and spend hours decking myself, working upon my face apprehensively; surely, I thought, grief and anxiety were leaving their mark upon me.

Nearly a year passed. I was becoming thin, nerve-racked. Often I was sharp with my slaves, I, who at least had always counted among my virtues generosity and kindness to all those who served me.

I became frightened at the change in myself; I heard of a new Egyptian physician who was becoming very fashionable and determined to seek his advice.

From the day I went to him, Nectanebes was continually at my house. He fascinated me and at the same time I feared him. Starved of love, longing for flattery, I could never resist listening to his honeyed words; moreover, his knowledge was vast and he gave me glimpses of strange, forbidden lore and a philosophy which, in its way, was as attractive to me as that of Serretes had been, for it promised magic, mystery, power. He laughed at my ideal of fidelity to my lover, and I recalled how Serretes himself had said he did not expect me to be faithful. I was torn between them. Yet for long I refused to succumb to the

Egyptian's pleadings, despite his promises and the skilful way he played upon my vanity, my credulity, and my greed.

One day while we were seated in the courtyard he said: "There is nothing in the world I will not give you, Chloris, even unto eternal youth itself, if you will give yourself to me; together—we might obtain even that secret."

I glanced up in amazement at his words. "Eternal youth? You rave! No man has that power."

He gave a secret smile. "Ah, what do you know of power although you live for it and desire it so ardently?" With a swift movement he seized me by the wrist and drew me to the stone basin.

"Look," he said, pointing down into the still water at my image reflected there, "in that beauty is the whole source of your power, in your white body, in the swiftness, the grace, the hot passion of your youth! Yet these will fade; your eyes will grow dull, your skin will wrinkle and your body become a reproach. You need riches, luxury, admiration for your happiness; without beauty even Serretes, were he alive, would abandon you—do not believe that he would want you bereft of that. But he has already abandoned you for—a city! Other lovers would think more of you than this; even so, they would forget you when you grow old, or look upon you with pity and reproach. What will your fate be?" He thrust this face close to mine. "Shall I prophesy? A poor, raddled harlot, clinging to the rough necks of drunken sailors in the ports —or a begger whining for alms in the gates of Athens? Or death, perhaps—poison for despair?"

His words were like barbed darts, thrusting venom into my veins. I stared, fascinated upon my reflection, and at that moment a breeze, springing it seemed from nowhere, ruffled the water; the image became horribly distorted. Terror seized me. It was true: my beauty was my only weapon, my dearest possession, and I was squandering it, weeping for Serretes who had indeed, as Nectanebes said, betrayed my love for that empty thing he called his honour.

The Egyptian seated himself upon the edge of the basin and drew me down beside him.

"Listen," he said; "in Egypt I had great powers; I studied magic. I am rich beyond your dreams. If you do as I desire you shall have such jewels as no woman in Athens has ever seen; horses from Persia, slaves innumerable—nothing shall be denied you. Furthermore, I believe it to be possible through magical rites to attain eternal youth and beauty, knowledge which will bind men to us for ever. Is it not mad to sacrifice your whole life for an ideal?" His persuasive voice went on and as I listened and saw those glittering visions, the image of Serretes grew fainter. Yet still I was torn this way and that.

"If I do this thing," I said at last, "how do I know that you will give me the secret of youth? By what oath can a man like you be bound?"

He smiled and drew from his girdle a phial of crystal filled with a dull purple liquid. "This is of more worth than any oath in the world, for it is the very elixir of youth that you desire."

"Give it me!" I cried.

But he laughed and held it out of reach. "No, no, there is not enough here. You do not know what strange rites, what mysterious essences go to the distillation of this liquid. One touch each dawn upon the tongue for six months—and it will have done its work. Think, Chloris, eternal youth—beauty—power!"

I sat staring upon it, breathing hard. I told myself that if Serretes was dead, nothing mattered; if he returned I would have obtained such knowledge as might well eclipse all the alleged wonders of the teaching of Pythagoras.

"Where can we obtain—enough?" I whispered.

"At the ceremonies of Hecate. If you will come with me tonight to her temple, you will be shown these mysteries and the future will be yours."

I went, and once having given myself to Nectanebes, fell more and more under the spell of his personality. Athens laughed and mocked, but I did not care. As one part of me had been drawn and responded to Serretes, so did another part find in the Egyptian complete satisfaction. Only one thing, despite all his pleading, I refused to do and that was to return to the Temple of Hecate and take part again in her rites. I had discovered that magic terrified me and I tried to forget all that I had seen there.

Then one day I received a letter from Serretes. In it he told me that he had been wounded and taken prisoner. For months he had been desperately ill. He had been sold as a slave, but had been given his freedom and was returning to Crotona where he implored me to come and join him.

I told Nectanebes and informed him that I was leaving Athens immediately.

He tried to dissuade me, but in vain. I looked at him now coldly; I did not want to remember that he had ever been my lover. Then he began to threaten, and his threats were terrible. I was shaken and alarmed. In order to gain time I promised him I would not leave Athens but would beg Serretes to come to me; but I made secret preparations for my departure and resolutely refused to allow Nectanebes to approach me as a lover.

It was not easy for me to escape. Nectanebes had my house watched and I was almost a prisoner. So the days slipped away; then at last I received another letter from Serretes. There were but a few lines. He wrote that he had received the letter from me saying that I had ceased to love him and returning him the ring he had given me.

"As for me," he wrote, "I will never cease to love you in this life or any other. I have always understood how hard it must be for a woman like yourself to remain faithful, even in thought. But since you are lost to me the world has become empty—even my art is vain. I have entered the school of the Master Pythagoras and by the time this reaches you, shall have taken the vow of silence. In these three years of quietude my thoughts will ever be with you; may the gods keep you and bring you all your desires."

My first thought was for the ring. It was long since I had worn it and I was careless with my jewels. I set all my women searching. It could not be found. I knew then that this was the work of Nectanebes.

When he came I confronted him. He denied nothing. He had sent a letter and the ring. "I wish to take you back to Egypt with me—I can use you there for the great purpose to which my life is dedicated. You will be rich and happy—happier than you could ever be with so poor a lover."

A fierce battle of wills ensued between us, yet try as he might, he could no longer dominate me—the spell was broken and now I desired only that I might never look upon his face again.

At last, defeated, he turned to go, but at the door he paused. "Do you remember the picture I showed you in the fountain? That fate shall be yours, it is my parting gift to the lovely Chloris—I lay my curse upon you."

I flung up my head and laughed. "You are a fool for all your wisdom. Of what avail your curse, when you have given me eternal youth—with this!" and I clutched to my bosom the phial which I carried always with me.

He smiled slowly. "That? It is water stained with the juice of mulberry. Did you think I would waste my magical powers on such woman's trumperies? It was for greater purposes I wanted you."

He passed out without a backward glance. The bronze door slammed. The phial dropped from my hand and was broken in fragments upon the floor.

· · · · ·

There were other pictures in the life of Chloris, but they were but fleeting visions, blurred and uncertain, as if, despite all efforts at fogetting, the acts, by their very associations of horror and degradation, had yet stamped themselves upon the sensitive plate of my eternal memory. I seemed to see a raddled harlot slinking through the narrow, pestiferous streets beyond the quays and experienced her sensations of despair and shame at beauty's slow decay. The Egyptian's prophesy had been undoubtedly fulfilled: "Or death, perhaps—poison for despair...." It may have ended thus, yet in truth this pitiful descent was due, not to the curse—for no curse can be operative unless there is, in the man cursed, some corresponding evil —but rather to her own dreadful inner knowledge that, in failing Serretes, she had failed Life in its ultimate sense— for she had failed herself and thus had killed the very life urge within her. She had been her own curse. Like a canker, her memories had slowly eaten into the heart of her existence, had sapped her energy, had insidiously destroyed all those qualities which hitherto had brought her success. No desire even seemed worth accomplishing; the power to attract and to hold the more intelligent and finer men failed, for she did not care to make any effort to do so. She dropped, like the dead thing she had become out of the ken of living men.

I saw her seated by the still, moon-flecked waters of the Hellespont. Dark rocks rose behind her; the air was warm and scented, but the miraculous loveliness of the summer night could no longer stir her soul. I saw her face illuminated by the wan light and it was terrible, as if ravaged by some fell disease. She was staring with dead eyes at the water below her. Her lips, coarsened by excess, moved in an endless repetition; I heard Serretes's name and my consciousness blending in that moment with hers, I felt this name like a note of despair and agony throbbing through the whole universe.

Her head drooped, her hands beat themselves upon the sharp edges of the rocks. "Could I not have waited—ah, could I not have waited," I heard her say. "Such a little time out of the long, long years. What madness was upon me? What were wealth and beauty compared with—that? What was that but the quintessence of beauty? Only I did not know; I was blind, stupid, ignorant. I served my body as if it were a god. He was my god, and through my body I lost him. For ever. Never again—never again...."

. . . . .

Failure—another failure. But this time a failure of love. Who was Serretes? Could he be Shahballazz come back again into my life, only to be betrayed? What was the result of such a betrayal? Was Chloris right: had I lost again, for centuries perhaps, this being who meant so much to me?

A strange feeling of desolation swept over me at the thought. It was no mere psychological identification with Chloris's consciousness, but a very real and present dread. For well I knew that Chloris's search was in no way unique. In my own life I had often felt this need for some dear companion, some lover or friend who would represent something akin to an expansion, a completion of my own personality; and I was aware that in some form or another such a desire for what is called often a "twin soul" is universal.

What, I wondered, was this basic longing which haunts humanity? Biologists might be content to look no farther than the urge of nature to procreate; that, of course, could easily be its lowest note; but there was, I felt convinced, also an inner meaning far higher.

When I was enabled to contact my teacher again he confirmed this at once. "The search for the twin soul which, with some people, is almost an obsession, and for others is merely a dream," he said, "is indeed more than a biological urge. It has so many aspects and is so fundamentally important that it would be as well if you meditated upon its significance.

"In the life of Chloris, both aspects, the lower and the higher, were clearly mirrored and from a study of her character you can learn much; that is why it has been shown to you in such detail. As ever, it is necessary that the lower aspects of any manifestation should be worked through and understood before those higher and truer aspects can be contacted which, not being of the personality and hence ephemeral, partake of the very nature of the Soul and therefore alone can bring lasting happiness.

"Let those, then, who feel this dominating desire for their twin soul or for an ideal partner, perfect friend, devoted child, or whatever form the vision takes, ask themselves what purpose such an individual is designed to play in their lives. They will probably say that it must be someone who will walk the same road, share in every pleasure and pain, sympathize with their moods, guard them in sickness and health, be faithful unto death. In other words, one who will live only to satisfy their every need. Of course the seeker will also claim to be desirous of serving and loving in his turn; and for many this is undoubtedly true. Even so it would be well for him to consider his motives honestly. He might remind himself that there are plenty of other people in the world whom he ignores, but who desperately need the love and services he is so eager to give to one alone. This might prove to him that this search is, perhaps, mainly activated by desires emanating from the lower aspects of his nature for purely personal fulfilment thus would not be so likely to contain lasting elements of perfect union with another.

"It will obviously not be so difficult for the average individual who is focused almost entirely at the material physical level to find a "twin-soul" or one who is a close affinity; but as man develops and widens and deepens the levels upon which he functions he naturally demands more and more from those who will companion him in life's journey. In consequence he is likely to find his demands increasingly difficult to satisfy and will often experience a great loneliness of spirit. Of course there must be many exceptions for karmic and other reasons, but this can be taken as a general rule. The real answer is that man finds outwardly conditions which reflect what he is in himself. So to find perfection at any or all levels he must at least aspire to and manifest a corresponding condition in himself. Lack of understanding of the fundamental laws governing manifestation are the cause of many of his bitter disappointments in his relationships. More often he demands of life benefits and joys he has not karmically merited because he has not yet developed what might be called the 'receiving apparatus' in his own nature. Therefore even if the opportunity to experience them arises in his life he either does not recognize it or destroys them unwittingly himself.

"The truth is, of course, that the personality can *never* be entirely satisfied, since at best it is only a partial reflection of man's true being. But this is for his ultimate benefit. The dream of perfect bliss with a twin-soul is, in reality, the projection into his consciousness of the love which is the very nature of his Higher Self, a perfect state of unity and harmony. It causes a vague sense of dissatisfaction, of being imperfect, of lack, and so forces him to go on seeking a vaguely apprehended perfection so that eventually he discovers what is worthless and what worthwhile and learns to discriminate between dross and gold.

"The man in whom the higher and lower aspects of self are more perfectly attuned is never so deeply concerned with the search for a twin-soul; he is too occupied in trying to obey the higher will and is seeking deeper and more lasting satisfactions. Also he is usually too busy serving his fellow men."

"But what of such close links as those between Chloris and Serretes?" I asked.

"I said that the man who was closely in touch with his own soul would not have this inappeasable hunger for his affinity on earth," he reminded me. "I did not say no such union was possible. On the contrary, I indicated that it might well bring about such a union; for the two would strengthen each other in work to be done. But to all such questions there are many answers, some too profound to give you now. I can give you only a few hints. You must seek the answers for yourself as you study and learn. I can tell you this: only those who can glimpse something of the whole vast plan in which individual lives play their small part can begin to understand the subtle aspects of the inner relationships existing between individuals.

"On earth men appear to be separate units; but that is an illusion due to the necessity for the individual development of self-consciousness. In actual fact each one is part of a group of souls, each specific group being, if I can so express it, attuned to its own note or wavelength. For remember, upon the inner planes relationships are largely expressed by means of telepathic interplay, we are not hampered as you are by material forms and personality differences which make for separateness. This may be difficult for you to realize, but until you make the attempt you will never begin to grasp the whole complex problem of groups and their work. Again, try to realize that as each small group of cells in your body plays a part in the organization of the whole, so these groups on the inner planes are destined to play specific parts in that final unity which will be represented by the complete body of mankind. For the purpose of gaining the state of perfection essential to each unit, every member of every group incarnates again and again. But since each has a measure of free will, some obviously go forward slowly, some more rapidly. However, the point to be remembered is that until every member has reached a certain stage of development the group, as such, cannot do the work intended for it. You will see, therefore, how grave is the responsibility that rests upon everyone to develop himself as rapidly as possible so as not to interfere with the particular portion of the Plan in which his group is training to play its part. The preliminary steps are, of course, the understanding and control of the personality. Then follows the uniting of the lower to the higher Self, which results in contact with the group. Conscious union between all members of the group both in and out of the body is the next achievement. As each one gains the power to sound the group note more clearly while on the physical plane, so are any others who may be incarnated at the same time attracted to him, thus forming a focus through which those on the inner planes—for seldom or never do all members of one group incarnate at the same time—direct and guide their united energies to the desired ends.

"So does the work proceed in increasing harmony and power, until there comes a time when, by a very subtle method involving the minimum expenditure of force, a group perfects a technique whereby all its members can work freely on the physical as well as the inner planes when they so desire. It would not be wise to reveal more at the moment, but those who are ready for the knowledge will, by meditation, be able to discover it for themselves.

"But you must realize that even conscious union with its own group on all planes is not the final aim of the soul. It is an advance on the purely personal desire for union with some beloved man or woman which is its foreshadowing in the lower self; but it is only a preliminary step to a much greater achievement; for as note combined with note produces a chord, and chords form a harmony, so these groups of souls, once they have developed the power of co-ordination, learn to unite with other groups upon many planes, thus increasing their potency for service and, through this complete and willing participation in the Universal Creative Chord, the outbreathing of God, sound forth ever mightier sound combinations in the divine symphony. When this state is attained these groups of souls, fused in a union which cannot on earth even be conceived, will experience an expansion of consciousness, a realization of Truth and Beauty—a bliss that no two units alone could ever hope to achieve."

He paused. Behind his words I could sense greater meanings towards which my finite mind struggled in vain. Words only helped to veil and confuse them.

"Then you mean," I hazarded, "that the twin soul all men desire is, in reality, God. . . ."

"It is the greatest aspect of the Divine that you can aspire to," he replied. "All things are relative. Yet you see that this dream of a twin soul which haunts humanity has a very real basis and plays a vital rôle in the process of evolution, since it is that urge within the part to find completion in the Whole. The Higher Self on its own plane knows its aim and as it perfects the control over its instrument, the personality, is increasingly able to impress its ideals upon it. You will find that the more sensitive and highly evolved the man, the more acute is usually his sense of dissatisfaction with things as they are and with himself most of all. Thus, aware of his lack, he attempts to remedy it and progress is achieved. So did Pharaoh learn from Shahballazz and Chloris from Serretes."

"But they were not all the same person!" I exclaimed.

"You were all members of one group," he replied.

"Whenever members of the same group meet on the physical plane, being synchronized to the same note, some sort of recognition and mutual interplay is usually inevitable; but unfortunately this is not always the case, for as souls project their reflections deeper into dense matter the discordant and clashing vibrations of the material plane impinging upon them, cause them to lose touch with that note in its pristine purity. This makes recognition increasingly difficult. Sometimes two meet, but pass each other by, neither being evolved enough to recognize the other through the dense disguise of the flesh; sometimes as the upward cycles proceed, it may happen that one more advanced will recognize a brother, but remain himself unapprehended; that is indeed a tragedy, but chiefly for the one who is most sensitive, as it will probably bring him great suffering. But the benefit will be correspondingly great, for such a life is nearly always one of selfless devotion such as Shahballazz gave to you, and this ever brings its own reward."

"But Chloris *did* recognize the note of union, and was not capable of holding it...."

"True; where the recognition is mutual, yet one partner is too weak or too selfish to remain faithful and pay the price for so great a privilege, the results are even more serious. Infidelity in such a case causes a kind of tearing of the strands binding one part of the group to the other, a shattering of delicate rhythmical adjustments. It shakes and destroys the harmony, not alone in the small world of the group, but in affiliated groups also and can have more far-reaching consequences than I could possibly explain to you who know so little as yet of the complexities of group Karma."

"What is the result of such a betrayal of a member of one's group upon the individual?" I asked him.

"Everything depends upon circumstances. If one of a group persists during life after life in sounding forth discords and working on destructive vibrations, he can at last so damage the delicate strands of finer matter joining him to the others that he becomes a positive danger to them. His imperfect manifestations are therefore cut off from the group—as one would amputate a gangrened limb—and any chance of rebuilding an instrument again —at all events, for a great period of time—becomes extremely difficult. That is what nearly happened to you after Atlantis, for you broke your connection with deliberate intent; the Atlanteans had a much deeper knowledge of these mysteries than man has ever again been permitted since he abused it then.

"But such an act as that of Chloris—which is, alas, only too common—results merely in the culprit being cut off from contacting any members of his group for a considerable time, until, in fact, he has learned his lessons more thoroughly. For if there is too great a disparity in evolution between certain members of one group, it is often better for the less evolved that he should not meet the others until he is ready for the responsibilities which are the inevitable concomitants of such a meeting. The severance which is the result of failure is a terrible penalty, since once having experienced the bliss of being united to another member of his group on the physical plane the individual will never be able to forget it in any of his incarnations and will always feel an enhanced sense of loneliness and loss."

"Then why was I permitted to meet Serretes?" I asked. "Why was such an unevolved being as I was then given the chance to do himself and others such harm and to reap the inevitable bad Karma? It seems a little unfair."

He seemed to smile. "A great many things seem unfair to those with a limited vision. But nothing that happen can be unjustified, since everything is there for a specific purpose. Surely by now you have realized this? It must be so since each man is the weaver of the multitudinous threads of his own destiny. Even in your own world is there ever real progress without some risk? But all such questions as you ask require answers at deeper levels. We have been speaking of man being a member of a group; sometimes this group, which, remember, comprises members at various stages of advancement, agrees to give a laggard the opportunity for such a close contact as you had then in order to hasten his development. You may be sure the chances of his possible failure and the long-term results of the experiment are considered and balanced up beforehand. I cannot tell you more than this; but do not forget, no task is ever given, no trial is ever allowed to man greater than he is able to undertake or to bear. His capacities and potentialities are gauged to a hair's breadth. He —in his higher consciousness—is consulted before the birth of the personality as to whether it is desirable to risk the Karma of failure, so everything that comes to him is, in a very real sense his own deliberate choice. Once this fact is more generally understood, men will grasp the truth that they can always be stronger than what they call their "fate". But how few live up to their potentialities—indolence and fear ever hold them back; yet there are in the universe infinite reserves of strength for him who struggles bravely on against apparently overwhelming odds. How often has a man succumbed but a few hours before that precise moment when help would have been sent him. As a matter of fact, in your case the experiment was entirely beneficial. The very sense of loss and dislocation that followed impressed you so deeply that the ideal was never again forgotten. You made a great step forward in your Greek life. You did not die by your own hand as you imagined; you had done that in several previous incarnations and the futility of such an action had remained part of your mental equipment for all time. On the contrary, those years although apparently so horrible and degraded were the most fruitful of all. For, admitting failure, you sought at last to understand *where* you had failed. You no longer made excuses, you no longer blamed everything but yourself. Your inheritance as a Greek—a people who worshipped truth and were possessed of a peculiarly clear and logical mentality—helped you here, as did also the contact you had made with men of advanced intellectual abilities. Free at last of self-deception, you repented; but it was the real repentance. Not based on fear or hope of reward as in Egypt, this was inspired by love and an increased understanding of the Law. You learned, as Cihrazad had never done, that vanity, foolishness and ignorance bring their own curse. You did not alter your way of living—it was too late; but driven down among the dregs of humanity, you developed, with your memories of Serrete's philosophy and devotion to uphold and guide you, understanding, love, and sympathy for your fellow sufferers. Although you knew it not, this experience was a great act of spiritual growth. It was preparing you for what was to be one of the most important of all your lives."

"I thought Egypt was that," I said.

"Egypt was the beginning, but this, in Germany, was the climax. In Egypt you had seen the Dweller—since then you had been combating it blindly. It was not enough. Once again you had to invoke it and fight it face to face. Your lower self had hitherto ruled all your activities and barred your way time and again, but you were never strong enough spiritually to risk an encounter with those Atlantean shapes in full consciousness. Now deliberately you faced and accepted them by taking them into your own body. You sought to destroy their ascendancy, not any longer with the help of a teacher on the physical plane, but as all men must ultimately do, alone, through the spiritual power of the God Within."

CHAPTER V

GERMANY

When my teacher said that in the life he was about to show me, I had taken into myself those mysterious elemental entities which I had created in Atlantis, I could not imagine how such a thing might be, but precipitated back into that past, entering into the mentality of Carl von Schwartzbau, I understood.

At first I saw myself merely as a man in prison. I was aware of darkness, of a terrible feeling of restriction. Then I realized that the prison was my body; it enclosed and tied me—gross, squat, hideously deformed. I was staring into a dim mirror. Behind me sunlight slanted into a gloomy chamber, striking the tapestries upon the walls whereon huge figures seemed to move in a dusty haze. Before me was a great head sunk deep between crooked shoulders, a coarse face covered with warts and blemishes yet lit by eyes so sorrowful, so tragically afraid, that it was as if indeed a trapped soul looked out from behind prison bars.

The eyes narrowed. "An accursed shape. . . ." I spoke the words half aloud. As the man behind me made no reply, with a petulant shrug of my shoulders I moved away from the mirror and crossing to the window embrasure leant my sick head against the cold stone, closing my eyes—the strong light always hurt them.

I felt confused. That dreaded feeling of a gradually lessening contact between body and will was gaining upon me. I was glad Sigismund was in the room; he was the only one who had ever been successful in dealing with these seizures. I pressed my fingers into my eyeballs, trying to shut out the menacing shapes which were beginning to move there. I thrust my head through the narrow window, seeking to breathe. I knew well enough what desperate mental effort it would need to keep control over myself and to drive back those mocking shadows. The struggle became such that it brought a fleck of foam to my mouth while my head began to roll from side to side and my hands beat at the air.

Sigismund, Abbot of Kloster Schwartzbau, who was seated at the table, sprang to his feet making the sign of the Cross.

"Carl! Carl!" he cried sharply.

But I had gained control of myself. I sighed faintly and, staggering across the room, sank into the chair Sigismund pushed forward.

"They were here again," I muttered, for I was convinced that they were devils which attacked me, "but you see I defeated them alone. It used not to be so; once I could do nothing with them—and men say I am wholly given over to the evil one. . . ."

I sank forward and buried my head in my arms. Yet presently I roused myself and with a bitter laugh struck the table with my hand—a shapely hand, belying the appearance of my body even as my eyes belied the bestiality of my features.

"I do believe," I said in a harsh, broken voice, "I am the best hated man in all the world."

Sigismund made a hopeless gesture; he knew too well that no facile sophistry could allay the bitterness of my heart.

"You will not diminish that hatred," he remarked, "if you insist on carrying out your present intention."

I gave a grating laugh and leant back fretfully in my chair.

"Quite so; I am to resign myself to receiving nothing, then, from life? The pleasures of even the poorest of my subjects are to be denied me?" I thrust my head forward with a snarl. "Am I not lord over my people? If I desire this woman, shall I not take what is mine by right?"

"No one has a right over another's body," said the Abbot slowly; "that right is God's alone."

I stared at him. Force was the only law I had been taught, yet such doctrines as his were not entirely alien to my mentality.

"Besides," continued Sigismund, "what pleasure could it give you to take a woman who loathes you and swears she will slay herself rather than suffer your embraces? You know well, being what you are, you would gain nothing therefrom but inward shame. There is, however, a more mundane aspect of the affair you have obviously overlooked. Your people are growing very turbulent; your knights and men-at-arms many of them are secretly in sympathy with Heinrich von Friedfeld; it would not be well at this juncture to give them cause for revolt; methinks they are but awaiting any excuse they can reasonably seize to appeal to him."

I leant forward again, tapping the table nervously with bejewelled fingers.

"Tell me, Sigismund," I said, "why do they so hate me? What have I ever done against them? I have tried to rule them with truth and justice; I feed the people during famines, I defend them from their enemies—yet I can do nothing right." I clenched my fists against my forehead. "Why did I not die in my mother's womb? I breed hate as carrion breeds worms; when my shadow falls upon the ground children scream and run; women would rather die than be touched by me; men plot against my rule and return me evil for good; even dogs shrink from me and horses hate my hand upon the reins. Yet I would love all men and animals if they would but let me. Of what avail is my power and wealth, of what profit music, beauty, art, the knowledge that I am stronger and wiser than my neighbours, when my deformities rob me of the only thing worth having—love?" I covered my face with my hands and moaned aloud. "I am cursed, I am cursed. What have I done to have deserved this fate? I have sought from my youth up to worship God and to promote progress, peace, and justice in my realms, while those about me think only of rapine and carnage. Why has God turned and smitten me alone of our race—I who love the joys of the senses more than any man, and yearn for them continually? Why should I be bound within this prison-house of horror?"

Sigismund shook his head. I knew that these same unanswerable questions had always haunted him. He had been my tutor since childhood and was the only one who understood my true nature and knew the agonies of shame and terror suffered by reason of this deformity and the terrible seizures which the whole countryside firmly believed to be a possession by evil spirits. It had cost him many nights of prayer and fervent searchings before he had been able to reconcile the anomaly that a just God, who was supposed to be a God of love, could create so misshapen a form for a soul which he believed in his love for me to be noble and desirous of good.

While he was still casting about in his mind for some words of comfort and encouragement, I rose to my feet and began limping restlessly up and down the room.

"My poor Sigismund," I burst out after a moment, "do not crack your head trying to reconcile the irreconcilable. We must assume God in heaven knows his own business best, but in the world there is neither justice nor logic. There is no answer to our questionings, nor do I expect any. I am doubly damned in life and death. It may be indeed true what they say, that I am a limb of Satan—if so, does it matter what I do?" I stopped abruptly, shaking my arms above my head. "By the eyes of God, if Satan could rid me of this foul body and render me desirable to that sweet child, I would..." I did not finish, but went back to the window and stood there staring at the fantastic jumble of gables and chimneys of my little town, while my fingers drummed a tatto upon the sill.

But Sigismund was by my side in an instant, one hand upon my shoulder. "Carl, you are mad! Take back your words or I will take them upon myself." As I made no reply he lowered his voice and continued in a tone of horror: "Is it true, then, what rumour whispers, that you are consorting with the Dark Powers?"

I threw up my head. "Ho, it lacks but that to garnish my reputation! They are premature, the good folk. I have not done so as yet." I frowned, biting upon my lip. "The Dark Powers? What precisely does that mean? You who are supposed to know so much about God should also be able to give me information about his enemy, the devil" I laughed scornfully. "But methinks you do not know as much of either as you pretend, else you could explain to me why God mocks me with this crooked back and yet would apparently be angry should I seek to set it straight."

"It is his will, Carl, as I have told you a hundred times; who are we to imagine we can ever understand his mysteries? He loves us, therefore all must ultimately be for your benefit, of that I am well assured. As for this traffic with the evil one, what would it profit you in the end? Would you risk damnation for what at best could be but a temporary advantage? We live but once on earth and by that life prepare our souls for Heaven or Hell."

"Thank God we live but once," I cried; "to live again is my idea of Hell—well, it seems I cannot escape damnation, dead or alive."

"You should go on another pilgrimage; there are still wonder-working shrines...."

"And leave my lands unguarded? Though, by my faith, the people would be more glad if Adalbert ruled them than I."

Sigismund frowned thoughtfully. "Who is setting afoot these rumours about you? Who has already told the people that you covet Elsa?"

"How should I know? They all hate me."

"This Father Niedhart, he seems to me a man very apt for power. He has a great love for Adalbert and the boy is a veritable slave to him. It might suit him very well if you were slain and Adalbert ruled instead of you."

"Absurd!" I cried. "Why, next to you he is the best friend I have. It was he . . ." I broke off.

"He who first led you to Elsa's house in the wood when you were hunting."

"Well, what of that?"

"Nothing, save that it fired in you this mad desire to possess her and filled you with renewed horror at your bodily deformity because she shrank from your advances."

"You have always hated that man."

"Hated him, no; feared him, yes. He is a turbulent, ambitious priest. I am well persuaded that he joined the Church because he saw in it his only chance of worldly advancement."

"Do not most men do that?"

"Some, I admit; but often the beauty of the truth weans them from their foolishness; not so, I fear, with him. I am convinced, Carl, he is your enemy. I beseech you, walk warily; your enemies are too strong and it would be disastrous if you fell. Adalbert is a charming boy, but he is not fit to govern himself, much less this fief; so if you love your people . . ."

"Love!" I mocked. "What is this love? I can see nothing about me but hate—hate—hate. Yet I want love—I want peace—I want all those gifts that are said to be of God—but all things are denied me! God is my enemy!"

Sigismund raised his arms. "Beware, Carl, this is blasphemy."

"Blasphemy?" I laughed. "Then I wish he would strike me dead for it!" and with a violent gesture I strode from the room.

Like a furious beast I stumbled away through the castle. The men-at-arms fell back before me, whispering. They feared me, my dreadful shape, my strange, mysterious seizures, my aloofness, even those impulses of an almost womanly pity and tenderness which stirred me always at the most inauspicious moments, separated me from all my kind.

I came at last to the little garden under the ramparts. Here was peace. The grey walls above me were entwined with creepers. The grass was velvet-soft, powdered with daisies; flowers bloomed in every crevice of stone, and a cloud of birds, attracted by the sure knowledge of crumbs and dainties which I daily brought them, fluttered down, settling fearlessly upon my shoulders and hands. These, I thought bitterly, were the only creatures that did not notice my deformity; yet these only loved me for what I had to give.

Below me, clinging to the castle rock as if for defence against the world, hung the town, red and grey, twisted streets running upwards, blossoming trees like flurries of snow, blue wood-smoke biting upon the scented mountain air. Beyond these again cut the line of the ramparts, then the river, a silver thread, then the black, wooded hills. All this was mine, the towns, scattered hamlets and farms, mine to govern and to guard; a precious heritage.

But I had no joy of it—although, if what Sigismund said was true, a man filled with the love of God might find joy in service alone. Joy? My mind slipped back to the figure of the peasant girl, Elsa: innocent, lovely as light, her two fair plaits to her knees, her eyes blue as mountain periwinkles, her laughter like a bird's singing. I desired her. I clenched my hands and groaned. I had always held aloof from women, occupying myself with statecraft and with war. I had been wise. Now I was stricken with a worse wound because I was well aware of the hopelessness and the utter absurdity of my dreams.

I was disturbed by a man's step. The birds flew up into the shelter of the creepers; I turned and saw the figure of Niedhart, the priest, approaching me.

I did not know at that moment whether I welcomed him or not. But the thought came to me that this was probably the only man who could bring about my desires.

The priest smiled. He had a curiously expressionless face, like a mask drawn over something vital and fierce which yet pierced it through. He would have been an insignificant man save for this veiled aspect of power which all those who met him instantly felt. He had had a terrible childhood and in one of my sentimental moments I had taken him into my household, had helped him enter the priesthood and made him tutor to my young brother, Adalbert.

Now, remembering the conversation with Sigismund, I studied the face beside me. I had always liked to imagine Niedhart grateful and my friend; but I knew instinctively that it was not so. Sigismund had been right. This man was set upon power. If he could obtain it with me still lord of the city, well; if not he would have no scruples in plotting my downfall. Here was another good reason, I told myself, for me to enter into whatever plans he might be maturing. At all costs I must keep the upper hand. I was glad to find so excellent an excuse for what I had already determined to do.

I turned to him abruptly. "Why do you hate me and plot against me?" I asked. "If you put Adalbert in my place he would not be able to hold von Friedfeld at bay for a week. I have a gift for war, whatever else I lack—even though I hate it. I could have all these petty princelings at my feet if I chose—and you know it. I have brought peace and safety where they have not been known for hundreds of years. It is only in a state which is secure that wisdom and the arts can flourish—that is my aim. Why do you combat it?"

For a moment he looked disconcerted, then gave his blank smile. "I do not combat it—I applaud it—moreover I seek to help you gain that—and all your desires. Why do you say I hate you? I am your best friend."

"Nay, I have no friends—except Sigismund and perchance the birds."

"You are too modest, my lord. We who know the greatness of your heart love you well. It is only your deformity that still stands between you and the respect and devotion of those who see in it a scourge of God and the mark of the devil. And this," he continued, since I made no reply, "is not so difficult to remedy as you persist in believing."

I laughed. "I have been to every miraculous shrine in the country; Holy Church, it seems, is helpless to aid me save by giving me counsels of patience and virtue—which lead nowhere."

"I have told you," said the priest, glancing round and lowering his voice, "that there are other Powers...."

"Yes—of the devil."

"Not necessarily. There are powers of earth, air, fire and water. Holy Church can use them if she will, she can bind them for her purposes." He stooped nearer, "I can bind them...."

I stared at him. We had had many such conversations before, but he had never spoken quite so openly; and even though there were dangerous rumours about that I was interested in black magic, such rumours were very common in the age in which I lived and actually I had so far done nothing more than try to understand some strange books that Niedhart had lent me. They held a deep fascination for me, as did indeed any fresh knowledge or any new thing. I was not sure whether or not I believed the priest's words, but if there were a chance, however incredible and remote, would I not be a fool to refuse it?

I looked with deep yearning upon the town and the valley where the spring fields told of harvests to come. These people were my children; I loved them, even if they did run from me and curse my name in superstitious fear. I had a swift vision of myself straight and comely as other men with some lovely woman for wife and heirs of my body to perpetuate my line. I would be loved and obeyed; I would be able then to bring about reforms which, because they seemed strange and unaccustomed, but chiefly because it was I who sought to inaugurate them, were now impossible. It by some miracle I were made into a normal man, these people would believe me blessed of God and would be ready to trust and obey me.

"So if I do use forbidden powers," I reasoned to myself, "it will be for a good purpose; surely then God will understand and forgive me."

The priest had not stirred. He too was staring at the distant scene, but I knew his inner vision was embracing the whole world. Whereas I wanted power to help the people and to heal them, he had long since admitted to me that the height of his ambition was even the Chair of St. Peter itself. Well, let him have it! I did not desire world dominion, there seemed to be more than enough to deal with close at hand.

Our meditations were broken by the barking of dogs and the tinkling of mule bells. I rose and leaned over the wall. Below I could see that they had lowered the drawbridge. A procession was moving slowly across it.

"My good cousin the Abbot leaves us," I remarked.

"I fear," said the priest, "he is displeased with me; although I know of nothing I have done amiss, he severely reprimanded me an hour ago."

"He would not do that without cause," I answered dryly. "He is as just as he is wise. Without his care," I added, "I do not think I would be alive—I do not know whether to thank or be angry with him for the gift."

Niedhart came up behind me and laid his hand on my humped shoulder. "You have not yet begun to live," he murmured, "you do not know what living means!" He waved his hand vaguely as if indicating a world of light, colour, joy, and love. "Yet life awaits your commands. It would be but a small experiment, yet I dare to hope you would return from it—yourself, your true self, at last. Why do you hesitate? There is a full moon just a week from now. It would not be safe to perform the necessary ceremonies in the town, but I have found a ruined chapel on the Western edge of the forest, going down towards Rahlstedt."

"That is where—she—dwells," I exclaimed almost involuntarily.

"About a league away." He hesitated: "I will have to persuade her to come—we will need her."

I swung round. "Never! I shall not permit it!"

"Do you not want to win her love? For that it is essential; your destinies will be linked by these rites." He smiled. "Remember, she will see you grow beautiful; for one instant she may even have a vision of your soul. So even if the experiment should not succeed and your body remain as before, she will never forget what she has seen and her heart will always be yours; she will know the man beneath the mask."

I gave a deep sigh. For an instant my whole body was suffused with ecstasy—pain was forgotten. To be loved—desired. . . .

Niedhart must have been aware of the change in me.

"Will you not come?" he asked persuasively, "there is no need for you to have anything more to do with these experiments should this one not be successful."

I began moving restlessly up and down. I found a hundred reasons why I should attempt this trial, and so few in its disfavour: only the stern decrees of the Church against sorcery and the threat of the awful doom which would befall us should we be discovered. For a long time I did not reply; at last I turned.

"This once I will join you," I said, "then I shall be able to judge what truth there is in these claims you make. But you must swear to me that Elsa will come to no harm and run no risk at all."

"I swear it. She will not even know for what purpose she is required. You understand it is essential for this particular ceremony to have a young, innocent virgin to act as a medium through whom the Powers may work. I believe her to have the requisite mediumistic qualities. I have been reading much lately of these things in some very ancient books I was fortunate enough to discover. Three men are also necessary and Adalbert will join us. Ah, do not fear! Would I risk him whom I love above my own life? But even so is not any risk worth the prize? You do not yet know what I purpose to do if this experiment be successful." He sprang to his feet, his head thrown back. "I will become a great leader of mankind—I will change the world! Not alone will I provide them with spiritual truths until now hidden from our knowledge, but I shall have at my command the very elixir of life itself and with it all power, all riches." He laughed aloud in exaltation. "You need not fear for any of us, my lord—we will, I assure you, be well protected."

"Protected?" I muttered, and stared at the priest doubtfully but did not care to question further.

In the days which followed, I suffered agonies of fear and indecision. I hardly slept; and when I did my dreams were haunted with hideous scenes and visions in which I seemed to be participating in magical ceremonies so obscene and horrible that I wondered if they could be warnings or if indeed I were already deserted of God and my soul given a foretaste of Hell. Ever since I could remember I had felt as if surrounded by evil beings who, suddenly leaping upon me, would rend my body in paroxysms of rage or vengeance. But now they seemed to have drawn even closer, hemming me in on every side. Yet the consideration that soon my back might be straightened and Elsa be made to love me influenced me even more than my fears.

I visited her one day while out hunting, hoping against hope that she might not repulse me; but the sight of my hideous face and misshapen body sent her cowering against the wall and she refused with equal loathing the gifts I had brought. I departed more set than ever upon my purpose.

The day before the full moon I went to make confession in the Chapel of the Monastery; yet even while I prayed I felt those evil presences behind me, turning all I did into mockery and sacrilege.

Sigismund seemed very far removed from me when later he showed me portions of a book of meditations he was engaged in writing and some lovely illuminated manuscripts upon which several of the monks were working. He walked serenely by my side. I envied him. He asked no more than to be Abbot of his little community, to teach and serve them; he was happy in this life. But I—where might I find happiness? As we walked together in the garden where the novices were bedding out herbs and hoeing the moist, sweet-smelling earth, a mood of hopeless yearning for peace and beauty descended upon me. I said farewell to this man I so loved with a greater emotion than I had ever felt before. It was, indeed, like a final parting.

"God knows," I thought, as I held Sigismund's hand under the grey walls where the apple blossom hung and starlings cried in their small voices to one another, "if we shall ever meet again; but if we do I shall not be the Carl you now know—something must change after this night."

I had not yet spoken to my younger brother about the attempt we were to make. I had always held myself aloof from Adalbert, well aware with what repulsion he looked upon my deformed body—for he had the intolerant scorn of his age for all physical weakness. I did not blame him nor anyone else for such an attitude of mind; my own horror of ugliness was so great that I could well understand a like sentiment in others; that did not, however, allay my bitterness nor help to bridge the estrangement there had always been between us.

But this day, meeting the young man coming from the mews, his favourite falcon on his wrist, I felt it necessary to break through the barrier of cold politeness with which we both protected ourselves.

"Adalbert," I said, "has Father Niedhart told you the true purpose of our attempt tonight?"

My brother dropped his eyes as if to hide some embarrassment. I stared enviously at his tall young body gallantly clad in a parti-coloured cotehardie of blue and gold, white hose which showed off to perfection his shapely legs, and long-toed shoes of scarlet leather; at his handsome face, clear skin and auburn hair. How simple life must be, I thought, to such a one!

"I understood that we were to make an attempt to— cure you, Carl," he said, "at least the good Father said that was our main purpose."

"So it is; yet—" I hesitated, "I had rather you should not risk yourself for me. For there is a risk. Perhaps Father Niedhart has not fully explained it to you. He is going to summon forbidden powers and if our ceremony were discovered we should all of us be burned for sorcery."

The youth's face twitched slightly at the word, but he threw up his head boldly enough.

"I do not fear. He can protect us." His eyes flashed. "It will be a wondrous thing should you gain a straight back.

Besides," he smiled brilliantly, "Father Niedhart asked me to come also because it would help him and might make me great and powerful, which is his dearest wish." He flushed and added ardently, "I would do anything in the world for him."

I had been deeply moved by my brother's first words, but at these my face darkened. I was disturbed by this friendship and by the restless ambition Niedhart was fostering in the boy's mind.

"Then I cannot dissuade you," I said coldly, "for I well perceive your mind is set."

The night of the full moon Niedhart and I rode together to the meeting place. Adalbert had preceded us in order to fetch Elsa and take her to the Chapel.

It was sunset when we started out. The sky was aflame as if there burned a mighty conflagration beyond the black, close-set pines. A deep excitement akin to this flame stirred within me; I felt as if there were Powers upon my right hand and my left.

Soon we were riding in darkness, but presently the upper branches began to glow with a faint luminosity and soon the moon was shooting fingers of light through the cavern-like gloom in which we rode; I thought them like the petals of silver flowers. When we came into the open glades the moon rode with us up the starless sky.

I would have been glad to ride in silence, but Niedhart talked of his plans. He had managed to gain Elsa's promise of co-operation only after he had convinced her that what we were about to do was for the good of the townspeople and in the name of Holy Church. "It flatters her vanity," he said dryly, "to consider herself chosen of heaven for a high destiny. It makes her feel superior to all the poor girls who were not good enough to be thus honoured. There is nothing you cannot do, Count Carl, if you know how to play upon vanity. It is the devil's touchstone."

At that moment I hated him.

"I bribed her too," he said, and laughed. "Promised her a fine dowry—I think I can count upon you to keep that promise for me. It was absolutely necessary to be assured of her silence, one word might ruin us. There, so far as I can see, lies our only danger. But I think she'll be wise. Her mother is a suspicious old woman, she's got a nose like a hunting dog for a mystery; but we must take some risks—'tis unavoidable."

Almost, then, I had turned back; but I bethought me that they would undoubtedly go through with the ceremony now and at least I could defend the girl from harm. All my distrust of Niedhart had been stirred into life by his words.

At length we reached the chapel. It was a ruin. Blocks of masonry littered the ground. A few of the side chapels and the sacristy were still in moderate repair, gaping like mysterious caverns, but there was no roof and the east window was an empty space wherein a sapling had thrust its dark and swaying head. Upon the ground, where the altar once had been, was a curious stone, far older than the cult which had erected these walls unwittingly around it; the stone seemed indeed to have conquered it and cast the walls down.

As we entered we perceived Adalbert by this stone. Beside him in the moonlight which, to my eyes, appeared to encircle her in a glittering aureole, stood Elsa.

I had never imagined her so beautiful; her hair, unbound, fell to her knees over a white shift; her feet were bare; her hands clasped over her breast. Her eyes were wide, fearful, yet full of dreams.

She started when she saw me emerge from the shadows. She had not been told that I was to be there; instantly she was on the alert.

But Niedhart soothed her fears. "The Count desired also to participate in this service to his people," he told her, "he and his brother are here to pray the Holy Mother for success."

She bowed her head in acquiescence.

Through the broken windows trees were visible; they shook as if the passing feet of unseen spirits had brushed their crests.

In the silence we all four stood now about the ancient stone.

Niedhart turned again to the girl. "You must have great faith, Elsa, and do instantly as you are bidden. No harm can possibly come to you."

He placed her against the east wall and bade us stand upon either side.

Then, advancing towards her, he began speaking a strange medley of babbling words, making passes before her eyes, intoning great vowels with a tight-lipped humming.

Adalbert and I spoke no word. A mist seemed to be enclosing us, shutting us off from the outer world.

Adalbert had no eyes save for Niedhart; I, however, was aware of some strange conflict taking place within me. I was sharply vigilant. Instinctively I felt that I must keep perfect control over my mind and body, if only for the sake of Elsa; for I realized now that the priest had lied: we were all in terrible jeopardy. Yet even so my curiosity was still greater than my fear. For protection I tried to fix my thoughts upon the Christ; but I found I could think of nothing save the woman.

Elsa stood rigid, the moonlight upon her face. The priest touched her, she did not move. Her eyes stared blankly.

"Come!" he said.

She advanced then, like an automaton. We followed.

"Unclothe her!" he commanded.

When her shift fell to the ground, I could have cried aloud at her beauty; my lust leapt up within me, burning every other thought from my mind. I knew there was nothing I would not do to gain this woman for myself.

We laid her upon the stone; and now the priest drew around us and her the mystic circle. In a brazier at her foot red coals sent a fragrant perfume into the windless air.

From a bag he drew horrible and mysterious objects: a skull, some bones tied together by a strange fibre, a loathsome substance, the nature of which I could only guess, and other nameless things.

The skull he placed upon her breast, the substance he smeared upon her forehead; the remaining objects he placed upon the palms of her hands, upon her feet and upon her mouth. From a jar of curious shape he took some unguent which he rubbed over parts of her body, the odour of it was sickly, yet indescribably foul, and knowing something of witchcraft I could imagine of what it was composed and shuddered with horror.

The horror gained upon me as the obscene rites began. I had the curious illusion of being two people: one part of me an aloof being, clean, wide-eyed, a guardian with a sharp sword, standing there watchfully; the other, a foul fiend, the misshapen creature of my body, licking his lips with eager lust, waiting to partake of the unclean thing. The inner conflict increased. I felt that somehow a final and terrible choice was about to be forced upon me. With which of these twain would I identify myself at the last?

The moon had sailed behind a clump of high trees; only upon the stone and the white body there a long beam of radiance fell; all else was steeped in profound darkness.

Suddenly, as the figure of the priest swayed in an ecstasy of supplication, the circle upon the ground began to glow with a faint luminosity. Sharp-tongued flames trembled from it; a cold wind rushed through the building; the brazier flared up in a livid flame of green and at the same moment an unearthly whispering arose about us emanating, it seemed, from the trees, the earth, the stones.

Niedhart, standing at the girl's head, raised his arms sending forth with fuller strength that incomprehensible rush of moaning syllables.

His arms fell, spread out; he beckoned us to follow him and began pacing round the stone from West to East.

His voice rang out over our heads: "Sathanus, Sathanus, Sathanus!" He broke into Latin: "I conjure thee, I conjure thee! By Earth, by Air, by Fire, by Water, by the Symbols which are here prepared, come hither! Descend! Arise! Speak!"

The sharp tongues of white fire burned higher; these and the glistening surface of the girl's body which glowed now as if with an inner phosphorescence, were the only visible things in a void of darkness.

A tremor ran through her; slowly her lips parted. A stuttering, hissing sound struggled through her clenched teeth, then abruptly ceased.

Niedhart bent over her, as if driving power into her body.

"Sathanus, Lord," he cried, "speak and obey us who command thee by these acts and words! Cure this thy servant of his crooked back; give unto him the heart of this woman. And unto me and this youth give Power and Glory and Strength and Dominion, and the secrets of the Elements which thou dost rule!"

Once again the girl's lips opened. Agonizing sounds came from them, as of a voice striving to speak. Then slowly, stiffly she rose to a sitting posture. A change came over her, creeping into her livid features and behind her blank, staring eyes, invading them with an alien life.

Her expression became hideous, her lips drew back in a fiendish grimace, foam flecked her mouth.

At last, booming from the throat, the voice came:

"Greeting, my servants, I am here; I—the Eye, the Ear, the Voice. What is your will of me?"

I felt my senses slipping from me, overwhelmed by

a flood of darkness rising from the founts of my own being.

That voice—what was it? The voice of one of those fiends we had summoned to our aid, the same perhaps who had so long tormented me, seizing upon my own body, racking it, possessing it, even as they now possessed the body of the girl I loved? In my imagination I saw them all about us, black devils with horns and tails and fire-breathing nostrils. These would cure me! I shuddered and groaned. Cold drops ran from my face.

Again I heard the voice. "Come hither, Carl, Graf von Schwartzbau, give utterance to thy desires. Fear nothing."

I felt my feet being drawn close and yet closer to Elsa's body.

Now I stood looking down upon her, upon that ghastly, distorted countenance, dewed with a pale, shining sweat, sealed with the symbols of the Powers who waited to serve me. I looked, and slowly my terror was drowned by a great tide of understanding which seemed to sweep up from within my own mind. These waiting powers were a very part of myself. Through acknowledging them, accepting and obeying, I would become master of them. All my desires could be gratified: I could become strong and tall, I could have this girl to love and cherish me. The Being we had invoked could give me all I had ever dreamed.

Exultation filled me. I lifted my arms in ecstasy and in a ringing voice cried aloud:

"I desire freedom from this miserable bondage of my misshapen body; I desire that this woman shall love me; I desire that I may be enabled to bring peace and joy to my people, so that I may be beloved by them. I desire, O you, whosoe'er you be, devil or god, that you give me above all things the secret of happiness."

For a moment I stood there, uplifted by the glory of

my own demands. About me was absolute silence; the whole world held its breath and waited.

The chapel was filled with invisible yet powerful shapes; they pressed upon me, whispering with their soundless voices. My lust, my ambition, my desire for all the gifts of life which had been denied me were like burning chains about my limbs drawing me nearer and nearer the final consummation, drawing me down towards the girl upon the altar. Now my face was touching hers, my hands were upon her breast. At that moment, as if a veil had been withdrawn, her countenance regained all its wonted fair serenity, and like a sharp sword a flash of wild desire leapt from her body into mine. Closer I stooped, the awful weight of my crooked back pressing me lower; every limb ached now with intolerable pain. . . . To be free! . . .

Free . . . free . . . what were those shapes moving about us? Her eyes looked into mine—strange eyes; they flickered, calling me. . . . They were not her eyes! Bewildered, dazed, with a supreme effort I tore my own away from that magnetic gaze and glared round, seeking I knew not what in this turmoil of burning darkness which was slowly engulfing me. I perceived the form of Niedhart, arms upraised, his face a quiet mask of triumph; I saw the face of my brother, gazing at Elsa's body with an expression so maddened and bestial, that a pang of horror stabbed me to the heart; for in that instant I knew—I, that one who still watched aloof—that in my own face the same light shone.

I looked at her again, so white, so still, with those empty, lascivious eyes. Elsa! And suddenly I was shaken with loathing to think of this fair being I had known profaned by that Thing which now possessed her. As with a breath my desire was blown out. I was no longer two but one; no more identified with the deformed body, slave to demons, I forgot myself and thought only of her, of how

I might yet save her; of my young brother who, wide-eyed, swaying a little, was still gazing as one bereft of sense, waiting with dreadful eagerness for that to which, I knew, all that had gone before was but a prelude.

My arm shot out. Adalbert reeled back outside the circle. The priest shrieked aloud. What happened then, I hardly knew; something rent me from head to foot, disembowelling me, tearing at my brain, flaying my whole body. A roaring filled my ears. I became blind with blood; the whole world was falling upon me. But with a supreme effort from Elsa's breast and hands and feet I swept the symbols; tearing off my cloak I flung it over her, covering her white body as a cloud covers the whiteness of the moon.

The earth rocked under my feet, clamorous voices deafened me. Kneeling beside her, with both arms uplifted upon the thick, fetid air I made the sign of the Cross—the only gesture for protection that I knew—and called in a choking whisper upon the name of Christ.

An appalling darkness fell upon me, yet I saw as through a red veil of blood, Niedhart with foaming mouth battling as if with an unseen adversary, and Adalbert rolling upon the ground with shrill, persistent screams; I saw Elsa breathing in long spasms, her eyes closed at last, her head turning from side to side. I dropped across her body, covering her with my arms. Her eyes opened and I saw terror and loathing come into them—but I was glad, for those eyes were once more her own.

I raised my face, staring into the darkness, and sobbed again and again in my extremity of helplessness: "O Christ, O Christ, have pity!"

Presently I was aware of a cool breeze laden with the scent of pines upon my brow; the voice of whispering trees filled the chapel like a benediction. I raised myself slowly and looked round. My brother and the priest had gone. I noticed that the cloak had slipped aside and I replaced it, drawing it up to her chin and covering her bright hair as if protecting her against every evil; but now there was no more need, for the chapel was empty. Elsa still seemed dazed, occasionally giving a faint moan, and I began to consider how I should get her safely to her home. I wished the others had not deserted me.

While I stood pondering, I became aware of a new sound mingling with the voice of the wind in the forest. It rose and fell, a broken, discordant chant, filled somehow with menace. Stronger it grew, sweeping forward like an approaching storm from the direction of the town. Now I could distinguish loud cries, clamorous shouts—it was the voice of a raging crowd.

In a flash I had seized Elsa and dragged her from the altar to her feet. Despite her bewildered struggles I fled with her from the chapel towards the thickest part of the undergrowth.

Now the uproar was upon us, filling the night. As we reached the bushes, the first men of the crowd broke into the clearing.

A wild cry arose, for as she ran the cloak had fallen from her, and her naked body was clearly visible in the darkness.

"The witch!" they screamed, "the witch! Death to the witch!"

I pushed her behind me and drew my dagger. "Run!" I cried. She fled away. Stumbling among the briars and the bracken, I rushed forward to head them off, but I did not realize that in the confused shadows of the undergrowth I was practically invisible.

A few men set upon me, but even as I fought, I knew with dreadful certainty that Elsa was doomed, for the crowd had broken, and men and women were running through the forest in her wake, still crying: "The witch— the witch! Death to the witch!"

I fought with reckless despair. One man fell; while I engaged another, the third ran after the crowd calling for assistance. I stabbed at my adversary's heart, and the man, falling upon me, bore me to the ground and together we rolled into a ditch. I struck my head upon the stump of a tree and for a few moments lost consciousness.

I was aroused by cries all about me. I struggled but was unable to release myself from the sprawling body of the dead man in that restricted place.

From where I lay, through the bracken I could see the glade above me filled with dark, agitated shapes lit by the smoky glare of torches. The crowd swayed and parted and in the midst of them I saw the white shape of Elsa, drooping between two men. A woman rushed at her, tearing her face with her nails; another followed, for a moment she disappeared, borne down beneath the weight of their venom; then the men dragged her up again: "Leave her," they shouted, "see if she sink or swim! The witch, the witch, to the water with the witch!"

Then I heard her voice raised in agony: "Save me! O, save me! It is not true! Have mercy. O have mercy!"

I struggled frantically to free myself, but nearly fainted again with the agony shooting down my leg; I could not move, nor in the uproar could my hoarse cries be heard.

They were dragging her away. I saw a woman pull her head backwards by her long glittering hair; I saw her white face streaked with blood, tipped upward to the sky as if imploring it still for mercy. About her, like fiends themselves, the crowd danced and tossed, ridden by a passion of lust and of destruction as if the evil spirits we had invoked had entered into them. They passed out of my sight. Once, above their clamour, I heard a shrill, despairing scream, then slowly, like the dying of a storm their voices faded into silence.

It was nearly dawn before I succeeded in freeing myself. I stood in the half light uncertainly, wondering whither I could go. I was weak from the blow on the head, my foot was sprained, and there was an agonizing pain in my ribs.

Return to Schwartzbau I dared not; for I believed I had been recognized by the man who had escaped me, and I knew only too well that I would fare no better at the hands of my enraged people than Elsa had done.

My only remaining hope was to reach the monastery and claim sanctuary there, at least from that dreadful death.

But even while I stood hesitating, I heard in the distance the sound of cries mingling with the deep baying of dogs. They were already out in search of me.

I learned that day the helpless terror of all hunted beasts. Down the still forest aisles, through brakes, by untrodden ways of glade and stream they hunted me. Faint with weariness, racked by pain, tortured by fear—not for myself alone but for my brother whose fate I could not guess; haunted by that picture of Elsa borne away by the crowd to a horrible and unmerited death, I stumbled on, desiring the oblivion of death, yet ever fleeing it. I grew gradually weaker. Once, hidden in a ditch, I watched the hunters pass. It was but a league or so to the place of refuge, but ever, it seemed, the way was barred to me.

That night I slept among mossy rocks; but towards morning suddenly out of the bushes a great hound sprang, like a nightmare shape, its eyes green fire, its jaws agape. I recognized one of my own hunting dogs and desperately called it by name; but like all the other animals it had always shunned me, and now my scent was not that of a loved master, but merely of the mantle I had dropped and which had been given it. I was borne backwards fighting for my life. Its teeth slit open my cheek; I struck at it blindly with my hunting knife again and again; I hardly knew how I fought free of it.

I staggered on, half fainting. My whole body was torn

and bleeding; I held my hand to my injured face and moaned as I went; my eye was a raging furnace of pain. I could not see clearly; bushes struck at me, brambles. wound themselves about my feet; trees barred my path "All nature is against me," I thought stupidly, "I have loved the forests, I have loved the beasts, now they have become my enemies." I felt indeed that I was forsaken of God and that the end must be near.

That day was a blur of such memories; but towards evening, looking upward through that mist of blood in which all objects hazily swam, I perceived the buildings of the monastery quite close across a space of grass. I lay within the shelter of the bushes, gazing at those calm, grey walls. Would the monks admit me, accused of sorcery? Would I reach the sanctuary of the Altar in time —and even there would I be safe?

As I watched, a postern opened and a monk came out and walked down the slope, shading his eyes from the sinking sun. In a moment I had slipped into the building.

I gained the chapel. Sigismund was kneeling by the Altar, a few monks gathered about him, deep in prayer. With my hands outstretched I stumbled forward and fell upon my knees at the Altar foot, crying aloud: "Sanctuary! Sanctuary!"

For a long while I lay in a cell hovering between life and death. Sigismund and a few brothers sworn to silence nursed me. Only when I had recovered sufficiently did I learn what had happened. Adalbert had escaped by hiding in a hollow tree and reached the castle safely by a secret way. Niedhart, however, had been captured.

"He was handed over to the secular authorities," said Sigismund, "and has been burned at the stake for sorcery. They tortured him first to discover the names of his accomplices: he showed great fortitude, he never revealed them. I talked to him much, exhorting him to repentance; myself I held the crucifix before his eyes at the

GERMANY

last, thrusting it even into the fire. I pray that his soul was purified indeed in those dreadful flames and that he has been saved from the wrath of God and the pains of the eternally damned."

I groaned. "He was no worse than I; where then shall I find hope? As the dog tore out my eye, so will the devils tear my soul from my body and carry it to perdition."

Sigismund smiled then. "They have already done so if the townspeople are to be believed. Since you disappeared it has been rumoured that the devil was seen in person flying with you over the river. But it is as well, perhaps. They can prove nothing definite against you; you were not actually recognized, but you are strongly suspected. and I doubt if you would be safe even here if they knew you were alive. Adalbert they love and will obey, but he is only a boy. There are rumours that Heinrich von Friedfeld, hearing of the disturbances is already gathering his men on our frontiers."

"And I can do nothing—all my life's work will be undone." I lay for a little while in silence. "Elsa," I muttered at length, "my lust for her was the cause of everything."

Sigismund crossed himself. "And she was innocent—a most foolish child; why she even dropped some hint of her intentions to her mother who came to me after Elsa had gone. I enjoined the most strict silence upon the woman, but alas, she too must have talked indiscreetly. Poor soul, she paid for it; yet as you say, your mad lust was the true cause ... Ah, my son, what a sin you have upon your soul!"

I turned my head upon my pillow and wept. "I meant no ill to anyone," I said brokenly, "least of all to her. Yet all I do is as accursed; so many have done worse things and for more evil motives, yet have escaped. But I escape nothing. I were better dead than alive."

Sigismund shook his head. "That is not true; for although we live but once and our bodies perish, remember the soul is immortal and may be saved from damnation through the sweet pity of our Lord. He may yet give you the opportunity to do penance for your sin so that you go not down alive into hell."

I shuddered and answered nothing, listening to the voices of chanting monks rising from the chapel.

Presently I opened my eyes. "You speak truth. I am now determined what I must do. I have heard there is a monastery of Carthusians hidden in the mountains where the rule is more severe than any in Europe; there I shall bury my vile body with my sin. Perchance by penances and scourgings and a life devoted to the mortifying of the flesh, I may learn to destroy this evil which possesses me and so may at last win to pardon."

A few weeks later in the early dawn I stood at the monastery gate ready for my journey. Sigismund and I wept as we embraced. We knew we should never meet again. As I turned away I looked for the last time across the valley to where the little town I loved, encircled by the glittering river, orchards and meadows, climbed to the apex of the castle in which I had been born. It had been God's trust to me—and I felt I had betrayed it. I did not dare look again at Sigismund standing there surrounded by his monks, but bowing my head resolutely set my face towards the mountains.

· · · · ·

What had happened to Carl, I wondered, shut up behind those grim walls with the Trappist monks—he who so desired to work in the world and to turn his dreams of progress and happiness into a reality for his people? I could not believe that he had found there either peace or happiness. But at least now I understood the distaste I had always felt in my present life for the Middle Ages and monasticism; also my almost agonizing pity for anyone ugly or deformed. This was the result of something approaching a state of inner remembrance. As I meditated upon this it became clear to me that many of the likes and dislikes, the fears, emotions and characteristics peculiar to individuals which the psychologists are so busy labelling at the present time, might conceivably not spring from causes generated in this life, but be the reflections of past events precipitated by karmic currents upon the mirror of the mind.

Was not Carl's idealism due to the fact that some faint light emanating from his past had been able to influence his outlook, making him so spiritually alien to the violent and brutal men of his age? Did not the fascination that magic held for him mean that intuitively he knew that at one time through magic he had indeed had power to work what might be called miracles? Yet there was still here much that puzzled me. I could understand how, having once chosen to face the creations of my past, it was inevitable that the desires generated then should be resurrected and that consequently my body should reflect this conflict and be open to madness or obsession; but why I should have been given so hideously deformed a shell—why such restrictions should have been laid upon me as to make it almost impossible for me to manifest in the world the qualities which at last appeared to be developing in my consciousness, this I could not explain.

The death of Elsa—a child innocent of any crime—also raised seemingly unanswerable questions. She was indeed an example of that apparent inconsistency of Fate which so often seems to punish the innocent and allows the guilty to escape. There was also the strange enmity that the animals felt for Carl. It is usually said that animals can sense the good in what may appear to be the very basest of men, yet Carl was not base or cruel, and he loved them—here was another enigma. But I knew that some definite cause must be as much responsible for this as for Carl's crooked back.

So, desiring enlightenment, I retired to a quiet place and sought, by stilling my mind and attempting to align myself on a higher vibration, to contact my Teacher. For as time went on I was beginning to find that less and less was he descending, as it were, to my level, and only by an increasingly powerful effort on my part could he be reached for guidance and information. Sometimes when for all my efforts I did not receive a response, I felt that he himself was withdrawn in deep meditations on far planes of thought which I could not hope as yet to reach. But this time I was immediately answered.

"Can you not see," he said, "that the life you led in Greece brought as an inevitable consequence a diseased and deformed body? It is curious how difficult man finds it to apply occult truths to the everyday facts of life! As I have told you, by your thoughts and deeds in one life you build the vehicle which will incorporate your spirit in the next. If you impoverish the constitution of your bodies, you will return with similarly impoverished—or almost moribund—atoms and will have to nurture and develop them afresh. Thus an enfeebled mind is often the result of mental laziness or of intelligence wrongly used, and those who weaken their bodies through excess and perversion may reincarnate deformed, epileptic, with some disease, or some fault in the brain, weakness of will, and inherent tendency to their former vices through which any malignant force from their past can more easily manifest. Vanity also reacts upon the physical vehicle; for the man who lives for his body alone will return a slave to it; a glutton for example, might inherit from his past a faulty digestive system, which applies also to one who has deliberately starved himself through foolish asceticism. Thus people are born into families from whom they can inherit the specific weaknesses they have themselves created by past errors.

"You began such a physically destructive process in

Persia and continued it, although on different lines, in Greece. These two lives made your bodies so deficient in the pure, vital forces necessary to build a strong constitution that poor Carl was the result."

"But didn't I come back between Greece and the Middle Ages?" I asked, "it seems a long interval."

"There is no fixed interval, it is a matter of the soul's needs. But in your case several attempts were made to build a body strong enough to deal, without too much risk, with those destructive forces which still stood in your path; but you were too handicapped by that impoverishment of your atoms of which I have spoken. You incarnated as a Roman, but the body was too weak to serve your ends, so you quickly abandoned it. You made the attempt again several times but each was a failure; you either died stillborn or did not survive for any length of time. At last you sought the East and came through parents who, having studied Hatha Yoga were enabled to render you more assistance than any Western parents could have done. You later studied this form of yoga yourself and, although unfortunately the evil forces within were too strong for you and you failed in that life to accomplish your purpose, you did learn enough to enable you to incarnate as Carl, who, despite all his weakness, was yet strong enough to face and grapple with these forces at last.

"So now perhaps you see more clearly the necessity to seek behind appearances for the answer to all these questions which so trouble the more thoughtful. If you meditate carefully upon this particular life you will find that many problems will be resolved. This is why it has been shown you in such detail. Take such a case as Elsa's which I know has been causing you much concern. She appeared innocent enough, as indeed in her personality she was. But in many incarnations she had used magical means to attain her ends. What is more, in one of them she had initiated so-called religious persecutions thus being the cause of death to many. She needed to experience the terror of death at the hands of a mob. Vanity largely impelled her to the act which was the direct cause of this particular disaster; but had she not had this evil past she would have escaped the horror of such an end, even as Adalbert did who found a place of refuge and you, who had further lessons to learn and were trapped in a ditch until your way was comparatively clear."

"But the animals—why did that dog injure me—or was that just chance? Yet they all hated me. . . ."

"Look back; had you not injured the animal kingdom in Atlantis? You exploited them too in other lives you have not been shown as you could hardly stand the strain and there is no real cause why you should remember them. But I need only tell you that you were cruel and brutal—you killed for sadistic lust or out of sheer indifference. The animal kingdom also has a 'soul', though of another nature to that of man, and impressions of cruelty made upon it remain. Because of what you had done to it, there would be discord and destruction between you and that Kingdom until you, being man and therefore pledged to serve and help in the evolution of your younger brethren, succeeded in adjusting the karmic unbalance.

"Whatever Kingdom of nature you injure, pervert or exploit you will at some time have to reconcile to yourself through love and service. Until you do there will be enmity between you; its members will be inimical—not deliberately but because you have placed yourself in opposition to them and therefore your vibrations strike a discord with theirs.

"The death of Niedhart was the direct result of the perversion by him of the element of fire in the past.

"Thus you see that the idea prevalent in the Middle Ages of the purification of the sinner by fire or water had in it an element of truth: for a certain residue of the ancient wisdom had percolated through from the past into that age, but naturally in a totally distorted form. The medieval Church in its ignorance of the law of Karma arrogated to itself the right to impose an entirely erroneous purification upon those it chose to regard as sinners. In consequence those who were instrumental in causing the death of men and women in this way brought upon themselves the same condemnation, as He whom they professed to worship had predicted when He said: 'By what judgement ye mete it shall be meted to you again.'

"Some of these inquisitors and other churchmen were definitely allied with the forces of the Left Hand Path and were merely indulging their sadistic and perverted appetites in torturing their victims; but many also were upright men who were blinded by ignorance and confused by the mental atmosphere of the age in which they lived.

"Numbers of these latter are reincarnating now, for instance those scientists who are risking their lives experimenting, for the benefit of their fellow-men, with subtle forms of energy which will eventually be used to cure most of the ills of humanity. These men, compelled by an inner urge are, although they know it not, endeavouring to pay back some of their ancient debts by learning to work with the elements as healing agents instead of destructive ones. Many of them are called upon to make the uttermost sacrifice and sustain injuries in the process so that ultimately their bodies are destroyed by the same element they once used upon others. This is a form of purification.

"But of course there are many other people, not yet sufficiently evolved to make such an effort to work constructively with these forms of energy, who expiate the past by contacting the destructive might of fire, air, water or earth. At this period in which you now live an intense effort is being made by advancing souls to undertake these readjustments with the elemental kingdoms, as a few moment's consideration of present conditions will prove to you. Thus does the Law fulfil itself in all things, perfectly and without the possibility of evasion. Nothing is fortuitous; if man could but see into the past he would understand the cause for even the most glaring apparent miscarriages of justice."

"But what seems to me the worst injustice of all," I said, "is that man is allowed to stumble on in the dark, not remembering. If he recalled the past and the mistakes he had made, he would never repeat them, as we all do. Who would be cruel, violent and insatiably ambitious if he could remember the Karma such acts had brought on him before? With conscious memory of the past man would surely make an instant advance in virtue and wisdom."

He smiled then. "He might—for a while; but it would be from fear alone, thus such progress would last only for as long as the emotional urge to repeat the mistake was not too overwhelming. Then he would conveniently forget, or would imagine that this time he would somehow evade the consequences. No, no; progress does not come through fear of the Law, as I have already tried to show you, only through change of heart. While a man is still slave to his emotions he will commit any foolishness—for he is driven by something stronger than reason. Consider a moment: have you never, in this life, made the same mistake twice? Have you taken every lesson experience has brought you to heart and applied it? I do not think so.

"It is no more necessary that you should be burdened by the remembrance of all the events by which you gained the qualities which make you what you are, than that you should keep in your consciousness every detailed hour of your school life and all the childish episodes in which you were taught the commonplace decencies of life. It would do you no good to live perpetually in such a lumber-house. But actually, as you know well, nothing is forgotten. Man's unconscious mind is that lumber-house of rejected memories while his super-conscious holds, as it were, the inventory of it all and the key to the right utilization of everything there, however small and unregarded. For acts are, after all, but causes; it is the *result* of these causes, the man as he *is*, that matters.

"Moreover, as you yourself felt after contacting your Atlantean life, if the average man could recall all the mistakes, tragedies, losses, and crimes of his past he would, as like as not, spend all his present brooding upon them and would soon become unfitted to deal with the problems he was brought into the world again to solve. Remember also, a man—more particularly one who is unevolved—takes colour from the age in which he lives and the actual facts of the past would not help him much to deal with facts in the present. There have, indeed, been people who, having brought over the faculty of contacting their past incarnations, without the balance and discrimination necessary to counteract the dangerous effect this clear knowledge can have upon the mind, have wasted the whole of a valuable life in dwelling upon past splendours, thus compensating themselves for present deficiencies instead of seeking to remedy them.

"To return to Carl. His life as such was almost more than he could endure; it would have overwhelmed him—probably sent him mad—to recall the past, for at that time there would have been no one capable of explaining the meaning of those memories to him. Yet the past was there—in him. That was enough.

"You have already remarked upon the fact that impressions from the past were beginning to affect Carl's personality with increasing frequency and strength. That was due to the fact that your Higher Self—the true God within who *knows*—was becoming able to impress its personalities with its own undying memory. That memory is what men call conscience. But its voice cannot be heard through the turmoil of the senses, until its instrument—the body—is sufficiently refined and controlled. Thus in some men the voice is unheard, in others it is a clarion call which the personality dare not disobey.

"As man evolves, the closer becomes this *rapport* between the personality and the Higher Self, and consequently the more clearly can experiences from the past be related to similar occurrences in the present; for sensations reoccur upon identical vibrations, thereby stimulating memory. Thus when past and present become very closely associated, inevitably this acts as a magnet, drawing causes out of latency, so to speak; which automatically bring debts up from that particular past for settlement. Here is another good reason why men should not be permitted to recall their past lives at will; it is too dangerous, for it may precipitate Karma upon them for which they are not ready and with which it may not be desirable that they should as yet attempt to deal.

"In Carl's case this closer contact between the higher and the lower selves inevitably stimulated those powerful forces of black magic still untransmuted within him, for any intense effort in one direction always arouses a compensating opposition—that is the Law of Equilibrium. Action will cause reaction at all levels. Man, upon the physical plane will only cease to suffer from these repercussions when the mystery of how to balance the pairs of opposites is better understood. This conflict was portrayed in Carl through the alternating obsessions and strivings towards good and progress. Through the magnetic currents of his past he met again one with whom he had worked in Atlantis—one who had also struggled along the Path of Return, but had not yet quite reached the same stage as himself. Yet it is significant that this time even while Carl invoked again the forces of evil, he finally rejected them, inspired by the voice within.

Thus the victory was his, but for that invocation he had to pay in much mental anguish and by losing some of the ground he had already won."

"What happened in the monastery?" I asked, "what was his end?"

"He lived a life of great austerity and penance, doing battle with those entities which had obsessed him hitherto and which had naturally been strengthened through his lapse into black magic. It was a most undesirable waste of life, for had he only been patient and not sought to hasten events by taking short cuts through forbidden ways, he would have gained eventually the love and fealty of his people. Opportunities were awaiting him in the near future. Through his natural gifts in strategy acquired in Egypt, he could have finally defeated Heinrich von Friedfeld, earned the admiration of his soldiers and increased the happiness and security of the population.

"Moreover, shortly after his flight, the plague broke out, followed by famine. Through his foresight and a certain knowledge of healing acquired in a life which you have not contacted, Carl would have been able to bring great benefits to his people. As it was he merely built around himself a fresh set of difficulties for his next life and acquired a mental equipment compact of erroneous concepts, of fears and of hysterical regrets. In those long years among the Trappists, brooding morbidly over his sins, he so influenced his subtle bodies that in his next incarnation he returned obsessed by that abnormal sense of guilt so characteristic of the churchmen of the day, accentuated in his case by an exaggerated fear of sex, since it was through lust for a woman he had fallen.

"Consequently your lower nature was unbalanced and torn by conflict. You incarnated therefore in a country and at a time best calculated to resolve that dualism by giving you experiences which could assist you to achieve a more rational outlook."

CHAPTER VI

ITALY

"You were born," my teacher continued, "in Florence at the time of the Renaissance. Your desire to contact again and thus to renew in yourself the best qualities of the ancient Greeks after your sojourn in the Dark Ages precipitated into your make-up forces in harmony with that age of enlightenment; you were therefore incarnated in a period in which much of the Greek wisdom was being rediscovered and men were seeking, however inadequately, to adjust their outlook in conformity with those half-forgotten traditions and ideals.

"Being, as I have said, weakened by reason of the conflicting influences brought over from your monastic experience, you were of a moody, vacillating temperament, with no definite sense of direction and much given to extremes. Half of you—that related to the reincarnated Greek—was passionate and sensuous, worshipping beauty in every form, yearning after all the pagan wonders with which Italy was being flooded. For dormant memories were stirred in you by every fresh discovery, and this being so it was inevitable that art, sculpture and the teachings of the philosophers should affect you profoundly, since they were symbols—albeit unrecognized ones—of the perfection you had lost there. Thus these shapes of beauty and these words of wisdom stirred in you the desire for some vague but transcendental ideal of which you felt anything related to this past was somehow the partial reflection.

"This was one side of your nature; but as so often happens to those who have been monks or priests in past incarnations, there was another side which, desiccated by the sterile imprint of monastic training, was terrified of worldly things, regarded beauty and sexual desire as snares of the evil one and was perpetually haunted by the terror of purgatorial fires.

"There are many such in the world today. Torn by passion one moment and by repentance the next, they are destined to be the victims of their temperament and bring sorrow and perplexity into the lives of those who love them by their violent and strange reactions towards normal sexual relationships which they yet ardently desire. Fanatical and violent, sensitive and idealistic, they do not understand their own unhappy natures, nor do they realize that only by attempting to see things as they are, by neither idealizing nor degrading them, by a close analysis of motive and control of impulse can they ever hope to resolve these discords which shatter the harmony of their being.

"Much depends with such people upon the kind of influences that are paramount in their lives.

"You, for instance, were the illegitimate son of a petty noble and a peasant woman—an arrangement nicely calculated to give you a certain steadying and simplifying element from the gentle and pious girl who adored you, combined with an excellent education and facilities for mental development which you received from the upbringing in your father's house—a situation which was in those days quite usual.

"For a man ever gets the parents he deserves—or needs. Sometimes parents and children are enemies from the past, drawn together in order to discipline each other and to endeavour to adjust their differences and their old enmities through mutual service. Such a situation implies, of course, a very unhappy home, since friction, bitterness, jealousy and revolt are its inevitable concomitants. If the true reason for such conflicts of personalities could be understood, much unhappiness would be avoided, for all concerned would realize that until sympathy, love and understanding had transmuted the destructive elements in their natures, such conditions would be theirs for life after life. Home life is the chief testing ground of many souls, and one of the most difficult; for there is, of necessity, such an intimate relationship between all the elements—chiefly those of the physical bodies and those which go to make up the personalities—that friction is more difficult to avoid than in most other relationships formed, at least in the first place, through some kind of attraction.

"In your case, of course, Maddalena was a strong link of love from the past and her influence was most important. Until the end of her life it was to her you turned in difficulty, in sorrow, in triumph and in failure. She was indeed to you a very symbol of stability—what you most needed. She was as nature herself—the deep peace of the earth, the shade of trees, the song of water, the breath of flowers. She had the calm, the unalterable steadfastness, the serenity of a Demeter—or of the Mother of God. She satisfied both the pagan and the Christian sides of your nature. She had no preconceived ideas about life but accepted it as it came to her, complete. Neither clever nor subtle, she had yet that deep wisdom which is only born of great love. There was peace in your home, for your father always loved your mother, holding her in esteem and consulting her about your upbringing and your future. At your birth, as was customary, your horoscope had been cast and when it was seen that your House of Marriage was severely afflicted and your nature such as to make any family life and all relationships with women so difficult as to be almost impossible, your father decided that the Church would give you the best chance of advancement in life. At first you too desired this, as from a child you were afraid of life, although eager for it; but after a short trial it was obvious that you had no vocation, for although in those days the Church was rather a political than a religious institution, suddenly, for no apparent reason, you revolted from the idea and your father being some remote connection of the Medicis you were placed in the household of Lorenzo.

"He was the next to stamp his image upon the plastic clay of your youth. You worshipped him. You were dazzled by the glitter, the munificence, the learning at his court. For a little while all monkish scruples were swept away in the stream of art and beauty down which you were carried in rapturous abandon; yet you still had hours of self-questioning and violent reactions from the licentious life around you. These, however, did not last long in the spate of laughter, love, music, dancing, which tossed you like a small golden leaf, caught in the dazzling foam.

"It was at the palace of Lorenzo the Magnificent that you met and married a young and beautiful girl. With the utter lack of discrimination so typical of those at your stage of development, you chose one most unsuited to understand or to help you: charming, frivolous, with not much intelligence, inclined herself to be neurotic and unbalanced—small wonder your marriage was doomed from the beginning to disaster.

"You were passionately in love, but a few months after marriage you already began once more to experience those dangerous reactions to which such ex-monks are so often prone.

"Something within you rejected the licentious life of which you were yet a part, and Beatrice often appeared to be a symbol. An ideal, which you could not yourself distinguish, haunted you. You did not know what you wanted—you only knew that nothing satisfied you; therefore, vaguely connecting these feelings with sin, you supposed that you were somehow guilty and scourged yourself accordingly. Thus the conflict between the two opposing elements in your nature instead of being resolved through love of your wife, were but increased; for being violent in all things, this passion and asceticism combined caused you to project your fears upon her and gave birth to a fierce jealousy. Although depriving Beatrice of your love and even of your presence for weeks at a time while you indulged in orgies of repentance for what you imagined to be your sins, you yet expected her to remain faithful and to retain for you her original feelings of love and respect.

"She, however, bored and not a little frightened by your, to her, almost insane moods, had met during one of your absences a young man with whom she fell wildly in love. He—unlike yourself—was perfectly normal and far better calculated to make her happy than you, being also a closer link from her past. The loose standard of morality of the age made it quite reasonable that she should take a lover; a code was arranged between them, and whenever you went away he would come to visit her.

"But by chance a message from him fell into your hands. You were seized by a very madness of jealous rage. All the latent evil in your nature was roused; old forces of hatred, pride and cruelty surged up from the past again to attack you. It is through man's emotions that the powers of destruction can most easily control him; thus through your fatal lack of balance you became an easy prey to obsession and were rendered indeed for a while, what men still call insane.

"You showed no sign of your knowledge to your wife; but with cold cruelty you began to subject her to a type of mental torture well calculated to unnerve her. You played with her as a cat with a bird; announced your departure only to return suddenly, made love to her while you knew she had been hoping for her paramour. And all the while you planned what you would do to him—and all the while you suffered as a man in hell.

"You waited; you laid a trap for them. Then, when you

knew they were together, you entered her room by a secret door, dragged him from her bed, and thrusting a dagger into his hand, bade him fight for his life.

"It was an unequal combat from the first. He was young, unskilled in arms. You played with him, mocking him and the woman who loved him and who was forced to be a helpless spectator of his approaching doom. When at last he was at your mercy you struck—not to kill but only to maim. He fell bleeding at her feet and she, instead of fainting or weeping began wildly to laugh. She had lost her reason.

"At that dreadful sound your own madness suddenly left you. Terror took its place. You bade your servants take the wounded man away and leave him outside the city walls, while, overcome by remorse and panic at the realization of the catastrophe your own act had precipitated upon her whom you now found you still loved, unable to plan or to think, you fled for counsel to your mother's house.

"She had been very ill for some time and was on the point of death, yet thinking of nothing save your own disaster you did not spare her. It was only later that you realized your selfish outburst had probably hastened her end.

"But her words were to remain with you always. Illuminated by her love and perhaps by the approach of death which so often clarifies the mind, she gave you the fruit of all the simple wisdom life had taught her. She would not allow you even to remain with her, but bade you go back to take charge of Beatrice. Sternly she showed you where your duty lay. The young man must be found, brought back, tended and healed. Here she believed was your one chance of salvation. Neither your arguments nor your protestations moved her from this decision.

"At first you refused. 'He is my enemy, I hate him,' you cried. 'Why should I do anything for a man who has only got his deserts, who has stolen my honour, ruined my life. It is through him, not me, that Beatrice is mad. . . .'

"But gradually her words, playing upon your plastic mind, aroused once more in you that other side of your nature which passion and hate had overshadowed. Before you left she had succeeded in making you realize that perhaps you were as much to blame for the tragedy as they; and despite your reluctance, she made you swear a most solemn oath that you would never henceforward abandon either of these two whose lives you had ruined and for whom, therefore, you must consider yourself responsible.

"You did not see your mother again, but her spirit remained by your side in those first dark weeks while the young man struggled for life and Beatrice walked like a crying ghost from room to room. Your first idea had been to provide her with guardians and servants and every luxury, send the young man to some farm, paying him an annuity and escape yourself, either by retiring into a monastery to do penance for your sin—for by this time you were in the throes of violent remorse—or by going abroad where there would be nothing to remind you of the tragedy. But the memory of your mother's counsel made you very soon reject these plans.

"Faced with these problems and many other difficulties your reckless act had precipitated upon you, you were impelled to turn from your previous indulgence in self-pity and take yourself firmly in hand. There was no one now to help you with wise counsel. The varied advice of friends, all light-hearted and frivolous young men, was useless to you. You stood absolutely alone. And in those months once more—only in a different guise—you faced the dark places of your own nature with nothing to guide you but the wavering light of your own soul.

"Slowly, during long hours of self-questioning and tortured broodings, the seed of your mother's wisdom began to take root in your mind, fed by the dark, hidden streams of the bitter experiences and lessons which were your legacy from the remote past.

"She had said: 'Somehow I never feel that penitence is quite enough, my son. Should we not try to bind up the wounds we have made? Should we not seek to mend that which we have broken?' The words struck some string in your heart which vibrated as if to a familiar note. You could not forget them, nor could you escape their implication. It would not be a light thing to break such a vow as you had made to her. Still you hated Neroccio—still you shrank from the wild words and gestures of Beatrice; but now the balance was upon the side of remorse and shame. You knew you had sinned; no escape was indeed possible. Despairingly, seeing no gleam of light ahead, you came to the decision that the welfare of your wife must in future be your personal care. Could poor pathetic Beatrice really be left to strangers? And this Neroccio? He was a wandering student and appeared to have neither friends nor relations. It was certain he would never be capable of taking up life again for, although he was gradually gaining in strength, he had been so severely injured that the physician said he could not possibly live longer than a year or so at most. To him, then, who by your hand you had deprived of everything, you must give all you could until his life should end.

"There were struggles still, moods of black anger and wild revolt, but gradually you gained a certain calm—yet at the cost of some of your sensitiveness. You formed around your hurt, your inward fear, your ever-present feeling of guilt, a protective shell without which you could hardly, indeed, have struggled through those dark years; for, as if life itself were determined to test you and see how deep and enduring were these resolves you had made, very soon you realized that Beatrice was with child, whether yours or Neroccio's, you could not know. At first the shock was such that you felt you could not keep her lover near you, as you had planned. You had always desired, above all things, to have a child; this was indeed the most ironical gesture that Fate could have conceived.

"You were saved, perhaps more than anything, by the gradual realization that the situation was not without some elements of humour; true, your laughter was bitter, but even so it was a surer sign of your progress than you could know; for to be able to laugh at himself and whatsoever befalls him implies that the man has begun to acquire a sense of proportion.

"You told Neroccio nothing—afraid lest he might not view the situation in the same light as you were beginning to do and would, therefore, be overwhelmed and perhaps weakened by the burden of a fresh complication. For his attitude towards you constituted a problem which needed all your tact, patience, and care to resolve.

The difficulties of that household during those months I have no need to enlarge upon. You can imagine them for yourself. Sometimes you felt incapable of continuing along the stony road you had chosen, but grimly you persisted, knowing you had no choice. For the first time you co-operated with the great Law even while revolting still against it.

"When the child came you had it brought into the ante-room next to that in which Neroccio sat among your books, still sullen, suspicious, yet already beginning to melt beneath the kindness and the care which you had forced yourself to lavish upon him who was your rival in this life and had, indeed, been your enemy in many another."

· · · · ·

I saw that scene clearly. Once more I found myself identified with an alien personality which was yet somehow closely allied to me.

ITALY

It was growing dusk in the long room; through the wide-open windows, under which the young man lay stretched upon a couch, two cypress trees raised their black pointed fingers against a luminous sky of primrose wherein the moon floated like a pale bubble blown over the distant hills.

I paused, wondering how best I could approach the subject; the baby decided the question: it let out a thin wail.

Neroccio started. "What was that?" he asked.

"A gift from God to—us both, Neroccio," I said ironically and, crossing the room, leant against the window, smiling down on him. "Life has of late placed me into such fantastic situations that, by my faith, I begin to find it almost diverting."

"So do not I," muttered the young man.

"I know—it is too hard for you; at your age I would not have done so either, yet as we grow older . . . But I digress." I touched him lightly on the shoulder. "We have hated each other—and with reason—I have sometimes hoped that the worst of that hatred has been assuaged; but, believe me, you have never hated me as I have hated myself. Yet of late that, too, has grown less. Hatred, I think, never did any good to anyone. Chance threw us together in this strange way, now—having, I must suppose, a sense of irony—she has chosen to bind us by one more thread." I grew serious then. "And since," I continued, "we are so indissolubly linked, let us seek to look upon things through each other's eyes—to perceive some saving fantasy in it—thus we may, perhaps, find it more bearable."

I called the nurse's name. She entered, carrying in her arms the new-born child. Advancing to Neroccio's side, she held the baby out and drew back its veil.

Neroccio stooped over it and his gaze went to my attentive face, which yet showed traces of an ironical smile.

"What . . . what . . . ?" he stammered, and pointed to it with a hand that trembled.

"It was born of Beatrice yesterday."

"But . . ." Neroccio stared at me, apparently bereft of speech.

I shook my head. "I do not know whether it be yours or mine."

The young man clasped his hands about his head and gazed at the child with an expression of horror.

"I can see no cause for mirth in this," he whispered at length.

"Well," I replied, "I am discovering in the last few months that the only way to keep sane in life at all is to find cause for mirth in everything. Yet I think you must admit this situation is somewhat diverting." As his face did not change, I grew serious. "Do not be so stricken. One good thing has come out of this: Beatrice is divinely happy. You shall see her soon; hardly could I get the child away. There is a new and saner light in her eyes—that dreadful terror is gone. I believe this may be her salvation."

Neroccio started; his hands dropped; slowly his gaze wandered round the library; there was consternation in his eyes.

"Then I—will have to go," he said slowly.

"That will not be necessary, for I think she will never clearly remember the past. We did well to keep you apart; she has never even spoken of you and thinks I am her father. Of course, if she becomes sane . . ." I shrugged my shoulders. "But I think and hope all those past unhappy events are wiped from her mind and will remain so, and that she will find renewed life and happiness in her son."

"Can that be possible?" marvelled Neroccio.

"Why, yes, all things end in forgetfulness, even those for which we have ruined half our lives."

I gazed down at the puckered face of the babe and thence to the brooding one of Neroccio.

"Truly I begin to wonder," I said at length, "if anything on earth is worth the pother that we make about it."

. . . . .

I quoted those last words which came to me aloud. "A rather cynical and negative conclusion to a life," I remarked.

"Certainly," my teacher replied, "but at least it showed a better appreciation of relative values than before. Did I not say that the most difficult thing man has to learn is to acquire discrimination? It was not possible in that life for you to discover which were the objects of true worth—the things to strive for at all costs and which those that should be relinquished if true happiness was to result. Cynicism is usually the result of disillusionment and therefore but a halting place of the evolving man on his way up the mountain of truth; he must in time be disillusioned of cynicism also, since such an attitude of mind is purely destructive. In your next life you applied the knowledge you had gained through the experiences of this—but not immediately, for you had by no means controlled your emotional nature nor had you destroyed the remnants of those ancient forces which once entirely possessed you.

"That life is the one preceding this. It is close to you; your links with it are strong. Although comparatively uneventful, it marked a tremendously important epoch in your evolution, for in it you began to recover the occult knowledge which once was yours, thus paving the way for your developments now. As a child you remembered some of that life—think back and seek through those memories to contact it again."

CHAPTER VII

ENGLAND

The memories to which my teacher referred were a remarkable series of dreams I had had in my childhood in which I was always a man dressed in garments of the eighteenth century. A whole string of episodes had thus come to me; but what has chiefly interested me about them since is that neither the experiences nor the emotions could possibly have emanated from a child's unconscious mind, for they were essentially those of a mature man. Yet they also influenced my waking hours, for I used to live a whole secret life of my own in those days, always imagining myself to be this man, creating about me a world of historical fantasy.

Still, occasionally, I have such dreams, and a psychic once saw me change before his eyes while we were talking into a man of that time, and told me that there was a resemblance between his face and mine. Another psychic again saw, while this book was being written, a man in the dress of somewhere about the same period leaning over the back of my chair, and got from him that he had been a friend of mine during a past life.

I was not, therefore, surprised when the words of my teacher confirmed the fact that I had lived in England in that age.

I asked him how it was that I still seemed so closely identified with this eighteenth-century gentleman and whether it was desirable.

He explained that it was partly because this last life was comparatively close and I was now engaged in working some of the debts contracted then and trying to develop qualities I still conspicuously lacked; also partly because the old personality shell in which the dead live for shorter or longer periods in the world next to the physical had not yet entirely disintegrated. He gave me at the same time some information regarding such "astral shells" as they are called, which, he said, can remain for long periods upon the lower planes particularly if their ex-owners have been materialists and strongly orientated to the physical world. Occasionally also they can be used and to some extent re-animated by those sufficiently advanced in occult knowledge to do so.

Unfortunately it is not only the true owners who can use them after they have been completely abandoned and in process of disintegration, for they can be animated by wandering spirits who are earth-bound or, worse still, by malicious and evil entities. These may end by obsessing the medium or even the sitter who invokes them. This is the reason for some of the mistakes made by clairvoyants and spiritualistic mediums who have not been properly trained and who take the apparition for the person of whom it is only a simulacrum.

He also warned me of other dangers of deception to be encountered by those who venture into what is veritably a world of illusion; but this is not the place to enlarge upon them.

Those dreams I had had and the sense of contact with an earlier age made it easier, therefore, for me to piece together some, at least, of the main events in the story of the man I have called Charles from the outline I was given by my teacher.

On the surface it does not appear to have been a particularly interesting or dramatic one, save in so far as the events in the lives of one's ancestors, through their very strangeness and different setting, often seem endowed with a colourfulness and a glamour usually lacking in one's contemporary existence. Actually it was much the same as that of the average man anywhere, compact of the usual pleasures, pains, frustrations and bereavements common to humanity.

Again I made many of the same mistakes as previously, but my attitude towards them, being coloured by those old experiences which I was at length learning to turn to account, was changed.

To begin with, I made another rash marriage; carried away once more by romantic ideals and a mixture of vanity and passion which I mistook for love. The girl, pretty, pathetic Elizabeth, had a tragic home; we eloped and were married at Gretna, followed by the curses of her father, a fanatical, unbalanced creature who never forgave her for marrying one he considered to be a godless libertine, damned to eternal fires.

I was at that time nothing of the sort. Having evidently been generous in a past life and learned to administer my wealth wisely, I inherited a reasonable income which enabled me to live in accordance with those rather extravagant and dissolute standards demanded of young men of my social standing; for I was by way of being unoriginal, following closely the conventions of my day. Nothing in fact would have roused me from the idle rut in which my life's wheels were set save some sharp blows from Fate. These were not to be denied me. Charles was to be the clay which my Higher Self was ultimately to refine sufficiently to create a vessel through which the inner light might begin to percolate. This process could only be carried out by suffering.

The first blow was the death of the son whom I adored, the second the infidelity of my wife. I will write of these more in detail, since each played so important a part in that process of spiritual education for which I had been born. For whereas in my previous lives the most shattering blows had had, for the most part, but little effect save to make me more rebellious and bitter or to send me flying somewhere for refuge, now each event had a vital influence in my development.

I was riding down a country road. It was spring. I raised my head and drew a long breath of the sweet air. Across the pale-blue March sky white clouds rode behind the patterned boughs of oak. The lichened trunks were chequered with cold sunlight, the hazels were misty purple with opening buds; dell and copse were aflower with primroses and anemones and vocal with the song of thrush and finch, blackbird and robin. The road, a cart-track more or less, heavy with black loam half flooded by recent rains, wound down through these woods then upward to the rise which shouldered the open sky.

Four ways met upon the top of the hill, two deviating through more woods, the fourth like a ribbon running between open fields towards the Kentish Weald. I loved this country, knew as an intimate friend each tree, each hedgerow. It had always been my habit when coming home from Town to pause on this hill-top, breathing in the air, basking in a pleasant sense of ownership. But now I found myself indifferent to it all; looked on fields and woods almost with distaste, while in my pocket my hand clenched and unclenched itself round that letter from Elizabeth which had brought me back from London.

I fumed now to think that she should even have spoilt my delight in nature. What right had she or anyone to affect me so, to take all the colour out of life for me?

I jerked angrily at the reins and the horse turned of itself towards the left.

I sat upright, heeding nothing. My mind was still a little numb. I could not quite believe it true that she had really left me, eloped with some stranger whose name I did not even know—she, this docile, lovely creature whom I had snatched from a cruel life—a life of brutality and degradation, to whom I had given, not alone an honoured name and every material benefit, but my love. For I had loved her—I told myself this fiercely. I had been repeating it ever since I left London, until by this time I had come to believe that I had loved her as few women in the world ever had been loved and that consequently I had been injured beyond belief; how dared she treat this rare gift as nothing and shame me wantonly under the mocking eyes of all my world?

I writhed at the thought of how they must have laughed at my cuckoldry. Now that I knew the truth, several of my friends had told me of the gossip which had long gone on behind my back. I ground my teeth together; well, they would not have food for mockery much longer. I had taken all the proper steps whereby alone my honour might be vindicated. There could be but one end.

My horse stopped suddenly and began to crop the grass. I glanced round and found that the animal, acting on an old-established habit, had brought me to the lychgate of the church. Almost automatically I dismounted and, throwing the rein over the hitching-post, walked through the churchyard until I reached a corner where a young cypress reared its slender shape like a dark candle over a little grave almost hidden now beneath a mound of spring flowers.

Here I paused and stood staring blindly down at that place where the remains of the being I had loved beyond thought or expression lay forever hid. Even after five years the loss was as fresh, as terrible, as on that day of my son's death. Here Elizabeth was forgotten; all the angers and shames of the past week were wiped out by these other memories which crowded in upon me every time I stood by this small patch of earth.

I had worshipped the lad with a love akin to idolatry. From the moment the child was placed in my arms I had felt that at last my own life's purpose was accomplished and perfected. I would not be parted from him; grew jealous even of his contact with his nurses and his mother. I forsook my friends, my normal pursuits, shut myself up in my country house and spent my time playing with the child or planning out his career which was to be the most marvellous in the world. All my own frustrated dreams, hopes, ambitions were transferred to my son; in him I began my own life afresh. I even neglected Elizabeth in this wild, absorbing passion and, by the irony of chance, it was indirectly through Elizabeth that the accident befell which robbed me of the boy.

Elizabeth's father had never forgiven her marriage. He had sought without ceasing in the early days of our union to force her to return to her home, and occasionally even in later years he would suddenly thrust himself upon us, breathing threatenings and slaughter, until, losing patience, I gave orders that he was not to be allowed upon my estates.

But on this fatal day, the boy's sixth birthday, while Elizabeth was riding with him mounted upon his new pony, suddenly out of the bushes Nathaniel had materialized, dressed in a scarecrow cloak he always affected, waving his arms and warning his daughter against the fires of hell. The pony shied at the apparition, throwing the boy. He was picked up dead of a broken neck.

To me it was as if my own life had ended. At first I had seriously contemplated suicide, but partly out of pity for my wife, partly by reason of some inner revulsion from the idea which I could not myself explain, I had refrained.

Instead I had enclosed my grief within a hard shell of indifference and had striven to forget, plunging into wild dissipations of every kind. There were senseless orgies in town, women, gaming, drink. When this did not serve, I would disappear for weeks, taking long, wild rides through the country-side; indulging in mad acts of bravado when I courted death battling with the elements, storm and sea and the icy embrace of snow-covered wastes, or sought out the haunts of highwaymen and footpads; yet I returned unscathed and the more disillusioned, with the memories of that small, gallant figure, those eager, laughing brown eyes, that subtle, vivid mind, as unstained, as clear, as poignant as they had ever been.

No, not even with the passing of years had these changed or grown dim. You couldn't kill out a thing like this. As I stood there in the bleak March wind, the depth of my loneliness was suddenly revealed to me. At least until now there had been Elizabeth always awaiting my pleasure: charming to look upon, although growing a little plump; good-tempered, kind; futile, perhaps, wearisome often, but at least someone who loved me, who could minister to all my bodily needs and whom I could love when a kindlier mood was on me.

But now she, too, had gone. Life had deprived me of my last chance of that quiet, more stable kind of happiness, which, despite all my wildness, I had always really desired. Everything was ended.

Overcome by an impulse stronger even than my pride, I knelt down and pressed my face on the cold soil beneath the primroses. Their fresh, damp scent enveloped me; a lassitude descended on me; I never wanted to move again, but to lie here, to sink into the earth beside all that was left to me of life. An idle wish, for there was nothing left —anywhere. The boy was cold in the earth—finished utterly; Elizabeth was in another man's arms, mocking me, perhaps, or more likely having already forgotten me.

I rose heavily and, climbing back into the saddle, turned my horse's head in the direction of Windstalls.

Bah, what did it all matter? Life was a game of hazard that you were forced to play whether you willed it or no; yes, and this God that men prayed to and revered was nothing but a trickster who loaded the dice against you at every turn. Perhaps it was as well the boy had died. He too might have had high dreams and ideals which would none of them have been fulfilled. He, too, might have lived to discover the fruits of life turning bitter in his mouth. He, too, might have married into a family that was a curse upon him.

"Well, she'll pay for it all now," I muttered savagely. "I've done with this weak pity—an eye for an eye is my motto for the future."

I thought that the man who came forward from the stables to take my horse when I arrived at Windstalls looked at me slyly; no doubt the servants were laughing at me too. My eyes narrowed; I had half a mind to dismiss the lot of them.

"Is all well?" I asked sharply as I stooped to calm the excited antics of a pack of dogs that had rushed from all sides at the sound of my voice.

The man shook his head and jerked his thumb towards a cottage which could just be seen through the trees on the other side of the ornamental water.

"She's been at it again," he remarked cryptically. "We took food and left it outside, but we daresn't go in; she was screaming, shouting of devils and suchlike—we thought best to leave her alone."

I relieved my pent-up feelings in a bitter tirade of abuse at the man's cowardice.

"She may be dead, you miserable pack of curs; is it thus you attend to your duties? I'll go and see to her myself, and do you fetch some fresh food and bring it along presently."

It was nearly a quarter of a mile to the cottage where Elizabeth's mother lived. She was not fit to be kept nearer, for her habits were unclean and, when drunk sometimes two men were needed to control her.

Entering the stuffy lower room I was, as usual, so struck with revulsion and with pity at the squalid condition to which she had been reduced that for a moment I forgot my own misfortunes.

I called her name and a hoarse voice answered and bade me wait.

I did not sit down. The stale smell of spirits and of things unutterably foul sickened me; my fastidiousness recoiled from any contact here.

Poor Adela, I thought, what an end was this! She had been a beauty, a young heiress, courted and spoilt before Nathaniel Chalmers met her; now she was bereft of everything—money, beauty, reputation, even of her wits.

I could never enter here without recalling that tragedy. Nathaniel, a man of most rigid virtue, had swept like a burning flame into this girl's life, denouncing her petty vanities, her frivolous ways, even her wealth, as of the devil. Why she had loved him, what she found in this hysterical fanatic, no one had understood; but she had abandoned everything for him, following him out into the bleak world in which he moved, going with him from village to village, while he exhorted people to repent and flee from the wrath of God.

I had never heard what first made Adela fall a victim to the terrible lust for drink; I only knew that Nathaniel set himself the task of casting out this devil which he believed had gained power over his beloved wife; for to Nathaniel the world was peopled with the predatory hosts of the evil one. So great was his anxiety to save her that there was no cruelty, no austerity to which he did not subject her in order to attain his goal. And she, in her love, had been pitifully eager to submit to everything, although his penances and scourgings only weakened her body and destroyed her will.

But she grew rapidly worse. At last Nathaniel imagined she had been unfaithful and cast her out in an extremity of jealous rage. For several years she had wandered about the country, sinking lower and lower, whoring, thieving,

lying, selling herself body and soul to any creature, however debased, who would procure her the drink she madly craved. Thus at last, half dead, she arrived at Windstalls and had straightway thrown herself upon my charity.
The boards in the room above creaked with an ominous sound. I heard a heavy body descending the narrow stairs. So large had she grown of late that she could scarce pass the doorway. She stood now on the threshold, staring at me stupidly, her grey hair straggling down her flabby, mottled face, her shaking hand holding a soiled wrapper together over her hooped petticoats. She had obviously not yet fully recovered from her recent drinking bout.
Despite my repulsion I was in some queer way attached to this woman. She had, I thought, a humanity and a tolerance not to be found so easily in the world. Her forthright speech and bawdy wit were refreshing after the simpering affectations of the ladies of fashion who, though bawdy too, were yet bawdy with a difference. Her vagabond and tragic life seemed to have taught her some queer sense of proportion to which these others could never attain—they who were, after all, for the most part but glorified ladies-of-the-town and in the long run just as wearisome.
There had always been a kind of sympathy, too, between us; so that now, standing there facing each other, we communed without words.
"So you know . . ." she mumbled presently. "Well, 'tis you drove her to it, when all's said."
I drew a quick breath. "Me? You crazy fool! If anyone did I dare swear it was yourself; you knew all about it, you haven't forgotten how to play the procuress, I'll warrant."
She gave a hoarse chuckle and laboriously lowered herself into a chair.
"D'you think Elizabeth could keep anything to herself for long? Of course she told me; and the scenes she made!

Wept, she did—said she must give him up—do what was right. . . . Ha, ha! There's a streak of my poor Nat in Elizabeth. She prated of marriage vows—and your ruined life—as if she, silly little fool, was the only one you'd ever been to bed with! But I . . ." her voice dropped, into her bleary eyes crept a sly look, "I knew. I knew what'd happen if she didn't have her way—she's the kind that dies slowly, goes into a decline—or worse. For, mark you, she's properly in love—a little mad with it. Of course you've not noticed, but it's been in her eyes, in her gait this long while. Or perhaps you thought it was your charms?" She laughed again. "She never was in love with you like that, save at the very first. Since then she's been grateful, affectionate—like a dog is. Did I say it was your fault? Well, so it was. You—you frightened her. The first night, Charles! Ah, you may wince. Haven't you ever realized she's not made for your kind of passion—nor mine, either; you and I are something alike, my pretty Charles—although you'd not care to own the likeness. Ho, you've got hot blood enough, but not she—not my Elizabeth?"

She leant forward across the table, looking up at me with her bleared eyes; her voice had taken on a monotonous quality; I knew these moods in her, when she appeared almost like some old sybil. They always fascinated me into silence.

"You're right, I did help her," she said, "because I want her to be happy. She can be; she's simple. Neither you nor I are made for happiness. We want too much—" Her head sagged.

"I know," she continued, "I know. We're all of us looking for something; that's what life is. You too under your cold, proud air, you're just like the rest. It's love we want, I suppose, or perhaps just something that's bigger than ourselves that we can serve—aye, and worship; something to bring us happiness. Some of us know what it is we want. I found it—in Nat—but I wasn't big enough perhaps—or he wasn't—I don't know any more. Now Elizabeth's found it in Basil, and you—" her voice grew fierce —"you'd rob her of it just because you lost yours when your boy was killed...."

At the mention of my son by those drooling lips my control broke down and my bitterness against this woman and her brood who had wrought me nothing but ill all my days, flashed out. At the malignant glance I gave her even she, besotted, already falling into a sort of maudlin coma, shrank back, galvanized by my passion into a renewed awareness of me and my purpose. Yes, she had indeed been right, I could hate as fiercely as I could love and beneath the veneer of cool and cynical indifference with which I had schooled myself to cloak my feelings I could suffer intolerably.

"Elizabeth," I said, and my voice was level and ice-cold, "will learn her mistake and return to her duty as an obedient wife—that is, if afterwards I choose to allow her to return."

Adela raised herself heavily. "Afterwards? What are you going to do, Charles? What devilry are you planning?" Her voice rose again as I remained silent. "Charles, Charles, you'll never drag her back against her will? You'll never do Basil an injury?"

"I have made all my arrangements," I replied. "This Basil—as you call him—will be taught his lesson. That is all."

She clutched at my sleeve. "You'll not kill him, Charles?"

"Why not? Has he not shamed me before all the world?"

Holding me still by the sleeve she dragged herself up towards me; although I tried to shake her off, I found myself, by her inert mass, being slowly forced to stoop nearer so that her foul breath fanned my cheek.

"Rum," I thought idly, "I wonder how she got it? I told the men..." Then her voice brought me back.

"You've got to let them go. You don't know what you'll do to her—you don't understand—but you've got to—you've got to learn. Don't look at me with those cold eyes. Oh, you're all alike, you men, hard, self-righteous, thinking of your own pleasures. You'll do to her what my Nat did to me—but she's weaker than I was, you'll kill her—kill her soul. What right have you to ruin two lives —and for what? Your honour! Ha, ha, a nice thing for you to talk of, you with your fine ladies and your trollops —you who only took Elizabeth on a romantic caprice, thinking yourself a noble, gallant fellow. Honour! Hypocrites, all of you, who deck out your lusts and your selfish vanities with fine names, whilst we—we..."

She suddenly let me go and sank forward muttering and weeping on the table. For a moment I glared at her, too disgusted and furious even for speech, then swung round and strode out of the place.

All the way back to the house my rage boiled within me; the few servants who met me drew hurriedly aside, frightened no doubt by my set white face, tight lips and blazing eyes.

Round and round in my head went Adela's words. The devil of it was there was truth in them, a truth which something within me recognized and acclaimed despite my superficial furious protests.

I strove to ignore it. Elizabeth—it was all her fault, from the beginning. Had she not seduced me when I was but a foolish boy? I saw her again as I had seen her first, so lovely, so appealing and romantic, crouched weeping in a meadow with a weal from her father's cane across her plump, white shoulder. Well, perhaps Adela—curse her for a witch—hadn't been far wrong there, I may have been as much in love with my own fancied chivalry as with her. But I had been young—I'd loved her since, hadn't I?

Elizabeth—Adela—Nathaniel—between them all they had robbed me of my peace—curse the lot of them! Hadn't they murdered my son? But this was the end. Now I knew them for the enemies they were I'd be rid of them all: Adela could go back to the gutters where she belonged—and Elizabeth might follow her; as for Nathaniel, if ever the chance came my way I'd keep the vow I had made over the boy's dead body and make him pay a hundredfold for all the evil he had brought me.

Still plunged in these bitter thoughts I found myself in my wife's room; I had not meant ever again to enter it, but now, amid her familiar dresses, her perfumes, all the small intimate, delightful things that spoke of her, I paused.

The tallboy was open as she must have left it in her flight. There were empty spaces and a disorder which spoke of feverish packings. I fingered for a moment a sprigged muslin she was wont to wear o' mornings; most of her shoes were still there, tiny and somehow pathetic now, abandoned of their owner. A hat, all coloured bows and flowers—I could see her laughing face beneath it. Yes, I knew, as I stood in this room with the fragrance of her presence still about me, that I had, indeed, loved her in my fashion whatever Adela might say.

I could not bear to linger here but passed on to my own apartments. The first thing my eyes lighted on were my rapiers lying upon a chest. I took one up; as my hand closed round the hilt a thrill of exultation went through me. I bent it, testing the steel. In this art I was indeed a master; I had made a name for myself as an adversary to be avoided, and this fool—this raw country lad from some outlandish Northern part—had dared defy me! I began to make swift passes as if at an unseen opponent. I remembered Adela's cry: "You'll not kill him?" Kill him? I had only thought of wounding him severely—but —why not? Suddenly, from deep within the unknown recesses of my being, a flood of hatred swept up, a hatred of such virulence that blood suffused my eyes and my body trembled. I gripped the hilt wildly. "Kill him?" I cried, "I'll do more than kill him, I'll maim him for life, torture him! I'll teach him to steal my wife!"

I stopped, appalled at the tones of my own voice. The rapier fell from my hand, but I did not pick it up, only stared at it with shrinking and with horror.

What had come over me? Was I going mad? I, who always prided myself upon my perfect self-control, to cry aloud for blood—to think of maiming. . . . Shuddering, I sank upon the bed, covering my face with my hands, struggling to regain command of myself.

Presently when I could think more calmly I tried to understand what had happened; how came I to consider even for one moment so hateful and degraded a notion? That madness, that passion, whence came they—strangely familiar yet withal so alien? Presently I laughed bitterly. "Come, Charles," I said, "have done with this self-deception. Adela may be a drunken sot, but she's more often nearer the truth than most." I'd fooled myself long enough, but now, faced with the fact of my own behaviour at that moment, there was no more avoiding it. Had I not, all my life, been aware of something within myself like to a chained beast which must be carefully held in leash? From childhood I had been terrified of any display of emotion, either in myself or in others, and had always held myself in check, disciplining myself in secret, so that even to my intimates I had ever appeared cold, aloof, indifferent. I had known, even then, that any slackening of the control and that chained thing might break loose. Only once it had got the better of me, its master; that was when the boy had died and I had no longer cared what happened to my body or my mind. But even that had not lasted long; shame had driven me back to the old paths; the conventions of my time—the rigid code of the society of which I was a part, combined with that fear which dwelt ever within me—a strange fear like a threat of destruction—had saved me. But this lapse was worse than anything I could have imagined possible, so barbarous that I could, even now, scarce believe it of myself.

I got up presently and flinging open the window took a deep breath of fresh air.

"God," I muttered, "am I in truth as base as this?"

The next morning a messenger rode in to say that the meeting was arranged and that Basil Tremayne had chosen pistols. I was glad, as somehow I did not feel like touching those rapiers again.

The next few days I spent going about the estate among my horses and dogs, setting everything in order. The duel and what subsequent eventualities might develop therefrom I resolutely put out of my mind. I had been more shaken than I cared to admit even to myself, by that curious happening in my room which seemed, somehow, fraught with some profound inner significance I did not pretend to understand nor seek to explain.

Then, one night while I was sitting by the fire with my dogs round me, drinking my after-dinner wine and wondering whether it might not be better to send for the old fool of a parson for a game of cards rather than spend another evening alone, the door opened and Elizabeth came fluttering across the room towards me.

I stared at her, aware, at sight of that pretty creature, so fair, so plump, so made for ease and laughter, of a queer feeling of sickness and of loss.

But I let none of this be seen, only made her a bow more elaborate than the occasion warranted.

"Welcome home, Madam," I said, "so you've repented, I suppose? You've come back perhaps to tell me you've seen the error of your ways? 'Tis a little late, I must confess."

But instead of wilting at my sneers as was her custom,

she flung up her head and faced me with more spirit than I ever guessed could dwell within her placid body.

"I'm never coming back. I've found my happiness at last. I've only returned tonight to beg and implore you, Charles, to release Basil from this horrible obligation you've thrust upon him."

"Ho, so your fine Basil is afraid of giving me satisfaction like a gentleman, and has sent you to be his messenger! A gallant lover you've found yourself, my dear."

"'Tis a lie. He'd never forgive me did he know. But I—" Her voice faltered, "I cannot endure the thought of this encounter. I cannot live through the agony of it. I shall go mad. . . . I cannot face waiting to know what you have done to him."

"Faith, what pretty sentiments! They do you credit. And for me, your husband, you'll have no anxiety, I take it?"

She looked at me. "You?" she whispered, "you . . ." then burst into tears and turned away.

I took my opportunity then and whipped her with the bitter irony I knew well she could never counter, for her slow wits ever lagged behind. It was not a pleasant hour we spent together. Mutual recriminations are rarely dignified and I was always particular about my dignity. She had no dignity at all, but she revealed other qualities which, until then, I had never suspected in her. For Elizabeth, placid, gentle Elizabeth was alive at last—even her beauty became a vivid thing and the more desirable; while the sharper became her speech, the more I found myself liking and admiring her for her spirit.

I goaded and played with her, it was cruel sport enough yet not all cruel since the result was the birth in her of something new and fine. At last she rose from the chair into which she had sunk exhausted. She faced me, flushed, defiant amid her tears.

"You never loved me," she cried, "never, for all your

pratings. I have been your doll, your toy, the spoilt child of your idle hours—yes, and your housekeeper, the mother of your son, but never more than that. That is not love! Ah, I have known how in your heart you have oft despised me. Never to me, but to other women have you told your deeper thoughts. I may have been a fool, but you never troubled to make me wiser; you did not need me thus. But I—I have desired always to be everything to the man I loved, and Basil . . ." her voice broke on the name, trembled into soft harmonies so that the word took on an unwonted beauty, "Basil," she continued, "loves me for my mind—not only for my body; he asks my advice, we think alike—we are indeed as one. I cannot lose him, for I shall lose all . . . all. . . ." Then breaking down suddenly she fell upon her knees imploring me to spare her lover's life.

I dismissed her at length with harsh words, but listened to her sobbing grow fainter with a feeling of irritated compunction.

I found myself wondering how she had come; whether her coach was waiting to take her back to Basil, or whether she would stay the night with her mother. I did not like to think of her in that sty, but it was impossible now to recall her and ask her to sleep at Windstalls. Besides I had an uncomfortable feeling that she might turn on me and refuse with scorn.

I laughed; it was certainly a novel sensation to find myself afraid of Elizabeth.

I did not attempt to go to bed that night but instead sat over the fire, sipping my wine at intervals and holding the spaniel pup, Caesar, on my knee. It was somehow comforting to feel that soft, warm body, full of blind devotion pressed against me. "Horses and dogs," I thought wearily, "they're the only creatures a man can safely trust, when all's said."

But the problem of Elizabeth was not to be as easily

disposed of as her presence had been. I was not a man given to introspective musings, believing in action rather than in thought and despising people who did little but read and dream. But from thought tonight there was no escape. Adela's words came back to me, reinforced by all that Elizabeth herself had said. As the hours wore on I began to see the pattern of our lives in a better perspective. Adela, with her devilish clear-sightedness, had been right again. I had loved my son too much for sanity and through this wild absorption I had lost Elizabeth. She had admitted that it was while I had been away for months seeking forgetfulness that she had first met Basil Tremayne. As I thought of this I began to pity her. She must have suffered much in those five years—pangs of conscience as well as of love. Gradually as my imagination got to work, my pity increased. Could I add to her torment the hellish tortures of further deprivation? What, moreover, would I gain by plunging her into fresh sorrow through destroying her lover? And even if I got her back, what would it profit me to drag an empty shell by force into my arms?

Backwards and forwards swayed the tide of my thoughts and resolutions. Often enough vanity got the upper hand; my hurt pride could not brook this situation and cried out for vengeance. All the conventions in which I had been reared assured me that my attitude was right, yet again that something within me forced me to look deeper although I would fain have turned my eyes aside and deafened my ears to a conviction more profound than any of the rules and usages of my kind. But at last when, utterly weary, I dozed for a little while, I thought the boy stood beside my knee, smiling at me with his wide, brown eyes and pleading with me to spare his mother—to set her free and make her happy. I awoke with a start, crying aloud the boy's name, clutching wildly at the space where he had surely been.

Perhaps it was this dream that finally decided me; perhaps my decision had in truth long since been made, and this but put the seal upon it; yet even so I found myself confronted with a problem which it would need all my ingenuity to solve.

Withdraw from the duel I could not; I had not sufficient courage to face the sneers, the scorn, the complete social eclipse that such an unprecedented action would bring down upon me; but I was nevertheless determined that the young man should not be injured, and what was more important still that Elizabeth herself should be spared from all the terrors of uncertainty.

But at last when the cold, dead light of dawn crept into the room, touching the litter of glasses, the ashes of the fire with revealing fingers, I reached my decision. There was but one way out; I knew what I must do.

Next morning I prepared to ride to Town to see my lawyers and make all arrangements; but first I went once more the round of my estates. I loved this place dearly; now that I was leaving it, probably for ever, I realized what it had meant to me. I hoped Elizabeth would care for it as I had done.

At the end of the long drive I turned in my saddle to give one lingering look at the house with its mellow brick walls, the graceful Elizabethan chimneys, the dark background of fine trees. A squall of rain spattered against my face. The sky was massed with enormous clouds. How black were the pines and the cedars! Upon the little artificial lake two swans floated. Everything was veiled, soft and heavy with rain. It was a lovely place, set in its hollow of lawns and gardens, white pigeons circling upon the roofs, peacocks upon the terraces, hounds and horses in the stables. But now it, too, seemed insubstantial, as if a shadow had been cast over its reality; deep melancholy exuded from the very earth.

As my gaze wandered towards Adela's cottage I saw

her walking up towards the house. She wore a dark mantle and hood, and her hoops swung out from her short, ungainly figure, giving her, I thought, the appearance of an elderly, obese duck.

"Well, she'll be able to drink herself to death in comfort now," I thought as I turned my back on it all and guided my horse out of the park gates.

I stopped at the churchyard and stood for a moment beside my son's grave. My mood was a very different one to when I had come here but a few days ago; so different that I seemed to myself unreal, as if I were living through a dream.

"Did you want me to do this?" I asked that which lay beneath the primroses, "did you really come to me last night? But you couldn't, you are dead—dead as I'll soon be. There's nothing after, of that I'm well persuaded; those are but parson's tales to frighten babes. But even if I should be wrong, it doesn't much matter. Either you'll be with me again—which is my idea of heaven, or there'll be nothing at all; in any case this is the door out of what's been hell for me these five years since you left me alone."

It was not such an easy task to frame my letter to Elizabeth. I did not want her to realize what I was doing, yet wished to calm her mind so that she should not suffer those hours of agonized expectation. In the end it was rather a clumsy affair, but the promise not to injure Basil was clear enough.

So in the early morning in a secluded field just beyond Vauxhall Gardens, I faced Basil with a pistol in my hand and a strange, light feeling about the head, combined with an emptiness of the stomach which I put down to a very natural shrinking from annihilation. Yet withal there was a gaiety about me which had been with me ever since I had come to my momentous decision. For I was as a man who had stepped out from chill clouds into clear sunlight. I was aware that, for the first time, I was in reality afraid of nothing any more, not even of myself. My friends noticed the change in me and commented to each other upon it.

The sun was pale as silver behind the bare boughs; there was rime upon the grass; a thrush was singing, its notes like crystal drops upon the keen, sweet air.

I looked at Basil. "So young," I thought, "but his clothes are dreadful." I looked up at the sky and smiled little. "I only hope," I said to myself, "my poor Elizabeth won't grow to find him tedious."

At that moment Sir Harry Bellairs gave the signal.

. . . . .

The lime trees outside my window made a green, scented shade, murmurous with bees. One branch had been cut away so that I might, through this space, look upon my world: a corner of terrace, herbaceous borders vivid with flowers; the lake, a dark, polished jewel with swans nesting on their reflections like encrusted pearls; and beyond, the rolling parkland where I might never ride again.

The sun etched delicate patterns of leaves upon my coverlet; Caesar, the spaniel, lay curled at my feet.

Propped up on my pillows I stared into the sunlight.

How bored I was; how intolerable was life! I should have died that morning of the duel, should have been permitted to make the heroic and romantic end I had planned for myself.

But the Fates who seem to be ironical rather than romantic in their disposings of men's affairs, had decided that, instead of killing me, Basil's shot should merely wound me so severely that for many weeks I hung between life and death, and recovered only to succumb later to the retarded effects of the injury.

I should have died after that duel, but instead, as if the

absurdity of being forced to live were not enough, when I did regain consciousness, the first thing I saw was Elizabeth's white face bending over me.

During those early days while I was too weak to bother much about anything, I merely supposed that she had returned for a little while out of a kindly regard; but she did not go away as I expected, and only later, when I was strong enough, did I learn the wicked havoc those same ironically-minded Fates had made of my intended sacrifice.

For, what with my friends' account of my behaviour in the duel and what I had written in my letter to her, Elizabeth had soon come at the truth of the matter, whereupon, torn by pangs of conscience and by what seemed to me hysterical regrets, she and Basil had decided to part for ever, Elizabeth returning to my side where she considered her duty lay, and Basil embarking for the Colonies there presumably to work himself into forgetfulness.

So none of us would be happy after all. For it soon became clear to me that Elizabeth, by her return, had indeed ruined everything. She had vowed to serve me, and serve me she did, but with such ardent zeal and so little humour that life became a burden to us both.

Had she stayed with her Basil, I would have remembered her always as that small, courageous being who had whipped me with her tongue and disclosed to me my own inadequacies; as the years passed by undoubtedly I would have lost the original Elizabeth in a poetic mist of sentiment and transmogrified her into a being regretted and adored. But as it was, soon—far too soon—the real Elizabeth was filling the house again with her trivial talk and her tinkling laughter. Had she been struggling with a broken heart I might have loved her still out of pity, but I found it most hard to forgive this easy forgetfulness—even of a rival. For it revealed her to me at last for what she truly was: too shallow even for tragedy to darken her ways for long. Basil had been well quit of her I thought bitterly; by burying himself in those far-off Colonies he had retained the dignity of his little tragedy; but for me Elizabeth was rapidly turning all our sufferings into farce.

It was the Regent's own physician who, some time after the duel, had told me that he believed the old wound to have developed into a cancer.

For a long while I utterly refused to believe him.

All medicos, I declared, were fumbling fools, hopelessly ignorant, guessing blindly and bleeding you for everything. It was nothing—just something that had not rightly healed—it would heal soon enough—as for cancer, it was amusing no doubt for them to give names to that of which they could know so little but I was not to be deceived by their pomposities.

To prove to myself that I was well, save for this stupid pain which seemed to be returning when it was supposed long ago to be pronounced cured, I deliberately took up the old life again, was seen at White's and Boodle's playing for preposterous stakes; forced myself to go to the races, to routs, to join in every extravagant gaiety, meanwhile fighting with silent yet grim determination this enemy which seemed to have taken possession of the citadel of my body. I had always been proud of my superb health and endurance, and I was not going to give in so easily. For a few desperate months I had kept it at bay until one night I fainted of pain at the opera and had to be taken home by my friends in a jolting coach which I thought would finish me.

I was beaten and knew it. Since that day, already two long years ago, I had been slowly growing worse, and now I spent all of my time in bed with little hope of ever rising again.

I lay propped up by pillows, a dark frown upon my brow. For an hour or more no one had come near me. It was unprecedented. I pulled the bell-rope and waited, biting my lip. Where was Elizabeth? Never during my illness had she deserted me for so long without any explanation.

A butterfly fluttered to a tassel of lime-blossom which had blown upon my coverlet. I watched it idly; it was gone again, out into the sunlight. I closed my eyes and groaned; then became aware that still no one had answered the bell. I jerked at the rope with such force that it fell like a snake upon my pillow and I cursed it and the maids and my wife and the whole world with much precision.

I had become accustomed to relying upon Elizabeth's constant ministrations, to the sight of her placid form sewing beside me, to using her as whipping-boy whenever an evil humour rode me, which was often, for inaction and helplessness had not improved my temper. Now this inexplicable neglect struck me as an outrage. Was it not enough for a man to be sick and helpless, dependent upon the whimsies of a pack of women, torn by the evil pangs of a cancer, without being deserted thus for hours by the people of his household?

I was working myself into a rage, when a servant-maid appeared.

"Where is your mistress, girl?" I snapped.

The girl looked frightened. "She—she is indisposed, sir. She fainted in the hall. She recovered for a space and bade none of us tell you, then she swooned again. We have put her to bed."

"Indisposed?" I sneered, "why, she's as well as you! 'Tis no doubt but a fit of the vapours...."

"I fear she is indeed ill," muttered the girl. "Mrs. Langly hath sent for the physician."

"Egad, she's getting beyond herself. Am I not master in this house any more, that she should send for him without consulting my pleasure?"

Someone called from below, the girl turned nervously to the door.

"Oh, get you gone, then," I growled, "and bid your mistress come to me when she thinks fit to recover."

I sank back on the pillows exhausted, pressing my hand to where the pain tore at me as with talons of steel, daily increasing, invading the helpless structure of my body with that agony which nothing, no medicine, no drugs, no bleeding could allay.

An hour passed. It was beyond the time for my meal.

I lay listening to the noises of the house, hurried footsteps, muffled voices; once a dog barked below and the spaniel upon my bed answered it. I felt as if I were already dead, a ghost, cut off from the world of moving, active beings. The bell being broken, I banged upon the floor with my stick, but still no one came.

Elizabeth ill? I felt aggrieved. Stupid woman not to take better care of herself. But she was like that, so irritating for all her good intentions. An increasing restlessness invaded me. My impatience and curiosity became intolerable. I could no longer bear inaction, and, although I knew I would pay dearly for my imprudence, at last I got out of bed.

I struggled into my dressing-gown, glanced at myself in the mirror almost instinctively—for I was still vain of my person—flicked at my neckcloth, put my hair straight, and set out to my wife's room.

I reached it at last, although the distance seemed to have increased since last I had walked that way.

No one heard me; no one saw me enter.

They were all grouped around her bed: a number of whispering servants, the physician and his assistant with a basin and blood-soaked cloths, Mrs. Langly, the head maid, and a dog sitting anxiously behind them.

The dog saw me first; it leapt up and rushed upon me; as I pushed it from me the physician stepped back,

"I fear—" he began, then saw me.

He advanced with fluttering hands, "My dear sir, this is a terrible, a most distressing misfortune, 'pon my soul, it is! But who told you? You should not be here—I had no idea . . ."

But I did not heed him. I was looking over his shoulder at my wife's face motionless among the pillows.

·   ·   ·   ·   ·

The house seemed very silent now that Elizabeth's vapid chatter was for ever stilled. I was amazed to find, as day dragged after day, how indispensable she had made herself and how greatly I missed her. Although she had irritated me at times beyond endurance, she had yet succeeded in bringing a kind of muted happiness into my troubled life. Indeed I had never appreciated her truly great qualities so much—her thoughtfulness, her patience, her kindly nature—as now, when I was deprived of them.

I was desperately lonely, for I had few friends about Windstalls, and when my illness struck me down I had retired proudly into myself. I had always had such a horror of sickness that I believed all those old fair-weather friends of mine in London would be infinitely wearied by me, if indeed they had not already forgotten my very existence, as I, in like case, would probably have forgotten theirs.

But to lie there alone, with no occupation, with nothing at all save the prospect of a lingering death perhaps still far ahead: empty days, weeks, years—nothing more appalling could have been presented to a man such as I was.

I had ever been essentially a man of action; men and women—chiefly women, had been my lesson books, but now, deprived suddenly of all that heretofore had made my existence bearable—for Elizabeth's friends had kept her informed of all the latest gossip of the Town, and that had always been the breath of life to me—I was forced to seek distraction of some other kind.

In the library were old books full of strange lore which my grandfather, a learned man, had left to become a legacy of wisdom and comfort to this unborn grandson in his time of need. These I began to read out of sheer desperation. At first my unaccustomed brain soon tired, but gradually my interest was aroused. It began to dawn upon me that, until now, I had walked through life like a man blind and deaf to the real world about me; I found I knew little or nothing of those greater movements of thought and of scientific discovery which flowed on, indifferent to the average man and his little adventurings. Angered at this discovery of my own deficiencies I determined there and then to remedy my lack which I found so unbecoming in a man such as I, until now, had considered myself to be.

Like a fever the urge towards discovery, the lust for understanding grew upon me, as if the doors behind which my true self had been enclosed had suddenly been thrown open. Soon my bed was piled with volumes old and new. I waded through Hume and Locke, struggled with the medieval Mystics and discarded them, then swung back to Aristotle and Plato. Bacon fascinated me; Browne did not tell me of medicine what I had hoped. Here was a fine confusion, but I did not care. I was determined to discover Truth, and felt that somewhere in this welter of contradictions it must be hid. But I returned always to Plato, and sometimes as I lay there, pictures of that ideal Academy, of those men talking wisely and peaceably together flashed before my eyes and I found myself wishing with a kind of sick regret I had lived then and had participated in that fellowship.

Although I was hardly aware of it at first, my whole life was being changed by these books I had found.

While Elizabeth still lived, I had awakened each day

with a feeling of horror at the long, dragging hours ahead; but now even the sleepless nights lost some of their terrors, and I watched the daylight grow, eagerly wondering how much time the pain would allow me to finish this thesis or work out this or that train of thought.

It was indeed as if all the immense energy which heretofore I had frittered away in the common usages of life, in emotion and desire, having no longer any focus in my enfeebled frame, was being gradually freed through the pain and disintegration of my flesh, to turn towards more intangible yet more enduring things.

I began to write as well. I got the idea that all this knowledge, these many-sided speculations should, if there were any fundamental truth in them at all, be capable of being sifted and correlated in such fashion that at length the ultimate verities—if such in fact existed—would emerge. I became engrossed in this task to such a degree that the thought of my end, which once I had courted and often prayed for, became intolerable. My existence was, indeed, a race with death. For hours, sometimes for days at a stretch, death had the laugh of me; then I became helpless with agony, a mere lump of tortured flesh incapable of thought. Yet the intervals of relief were the more valuable.

Once I said to the spaniel who usually kept me company when he had nothing better to do elsewhere:

"Do you realize, Caesar, what this Basil actually did for me? If it hadn't been for him, I'd have gone on to the end not knowing that the universe held anything more important than Charles Carrington and his little tragedy. If I knew his whereabouts I'd write and thank him. Gad—and I wanted to die! If I'd done that I'd have died half finished—all bottom and no top so to speak—a damned unpleasant sight, I, who dislike unbalanced things. Now I suppose I risk becoming all top and a rest of me that won't bear much thinking of—which is just as bad. But no, perhaps I'll see the way whereby all parts can be unified. I can't yet quite believe one goes on after death, though the evidence of the united belief of better men than I seems to point to the possibility, but I do like to think that anyway I won't be too crude a product when life's finished with me."

Then one day some time after Elizabeth's death, when the trees were turning golden and great winds swept about the house with melancholy sighing, I was disturbed from my books by the distant sound of shouting voices, the roar of what seemed to be an angry crowd: it was a sound which, for some reason unknown, always sent a chill of terror down my spine.

I frowned, turning towards the window.

"What can that be?" I muttered nervously. I pulled the bell rope and waited. Then since no one answered, turned to my books again and was soon so plunged in speculation that I hardly noticed when the door opened and one of my servants entered the room.

The man came forward and I looked up.

"Well," I asked, "what's all the pother in the garden? Have we started to emulate the French? Am I likely to be strung up on a lantern?"

"It's the villagers," he replied, "they're out after a man, and he's taken refuge here. They're raging mad—they'll kill him like as not if they get him. He's hiding in the kitchen. Mrs. Langley let him. He says you know him, sir, and craves your protection. His name is Nathaniel Chalmers. . . ."

I dropped my book then with an oath and stared at the man.

"Nathaniel Chalmers . . . ?"

I drew a long breath and leant forward. "You tell me they're after him—they'll kill him? And he's come here?" I gave a low laugh, "after all these years—and they say there's no God who answers prayer!"

I sat for a moment still, my head bent. Vividly before my eyes I saw again that tiny, limp body lying on a hurdle between two men, tears streaming down their faces, and Elizabeth half fainting on the path at my feet. But I had not wept. Instead I prayed to whatever power listens to the curses of men: "Give me a chance to revenge myself; put his life in my hands that I may take blood for blood."

That had been many years ago; now my prayer was answered.

I looked up. "They'll kill him, you suppose?"

"Tear him to pieces, I should say. It wouldn't take much to finish him, I'm thinking; he's nought but a scarecrow as it is."

"But what's he done?"

"Preaching at 'em, but it's not the kind they like. Talking of liberty; they say he's been in France. Your people don't want that kind of liberty here."

"Why should they? I've never stinted them."

I closed my eyes and leant back. "Tear him to pieces?" I whispered. To be torn—yes, I knew what that was like; but by a crowd . . . hands clutching, the writhing flesh, the agonized screams. I seemed to know them too, those screams, but how I could not tell; it was horribly familiar, that blood-cry of a maddened mob. It turned me cold.

Well, this indeed was vengeance enough to please any man. Vengeance—but for what? Queer, I could not recapture that old mood. What had Nathaniel done—what could anybody ever do—bad enough to merit any pain, much less such pain as this? Why, even to run with a crowd at your heels was terrible enough. . . .

And suddenly great pity welled up within me, drowning all my anger—all my hate.

"He must indeed be half dead, poor devil," I found myself saying. "Call out my grooms and bid them whip those curs back to their kennels. Tell 'em if they even so much as touch a hair of any human being's head I'll turn 'em out from their holdings and their cottages neck and crop. Thank God I'm their landlord and can do it! Give him a meal and a good bed—and tell him I'll be glad to see him when's he's rested."

Nathaniel. . . . How I had hated him! I had lived with hate. And now suddenly it was dead—finished. And I knew that I was glad. He must be old, I thought—and ill. Perhaps he's come hoping to see Adela—he loved her, but he was a little daft—not his fault, that. He doesn't know they're both dead—poor devil, too late, of course, one always is. Well, he'll be company. He was no fool, I remember, for all his madness. My eyes fell on the book propped up before me: Marcus Aurelius. . . . Religion had been an obsession with him; odd that it had almost become one now with me. But a very different kind. I grinned to myself, "I'll tell him I believe we live again in the flesh. In any case it's as sensible a reason as most for all the stupidities of fate. How he'll rant! But if he doesn't rant too loud, it may be amusing. There's Adela's cottage, he might like to live there—if he'll consent to stay with me at all; he was proud, I remember—still he may have changed, we all soften down a little, I believe, though most of us are too vain to admit it. I don't doubt I'll be able to persuade him to take the chance of a bit of peace and comfort in the end . . ."

.   .   .   .   .

How close in some ways, I was to this Charles still, how close—yet also how strangely remote. There was a gulf between his mentality and mine; yet when I thought of the child I had been in this present life I seemed to perceive there a Charles reproduced in miniature. Those weaknesses with which he had passed over were still all too apparent, but much of what in him had been but potentialities, in me manifested at once, this time, as definite characteristics. At any rate it had not required another long incarnation of suffering and mistakes to lead me to the realization of what my goal was to be and what I was determined to learn this time.

Cancer! It had needed that to turn Charles from an aimless, embittered idler to a seeker after wisdom. Cancer. ... Suddenly a picture of that scene in the Cave Temple of Egypt flashed into my thoughts and I recalled the terrible, crab-like creature I had seen there. I had realized even then that one day I should have to absorb it into myself, but had not known that when that day came, it would turn out to be a blessing for me and not a curse. Truly had my teacher once said: "There is no evil save that which a man creates through his own lack of understanding" while a greater than he had enunciated the same truth when he declared that all things work together for good to them that love God. Well, I hadn't consciously loved God, but perhaps the search for truth and wisdom was a form of that love.

I recalled then that once, when my teacher was giving me information on the karmic cause of certain diseases and the relationship between diseases and cycles of time, which I have not the space to write of here, he explained the reason for the prevalence of cancer in our day, pointing out the close connection between this particular disease and the use of certain forms of black magic in the past. He also told me that, until the poisonous substance which it generated had been absorbed and transmuted through man's body, certain steps in development cannot be attempted. This work, he had said, is now being rapidly undertaken. Some more advanced souls deliberately volunteer as an act of devotion to take such matter into their own physical bodies for transmutation, thus sacrificing the personality to the general good. Only when this general process of transmutation has reached an advanced stage will a genuine cure for cancer be discovered.

But so far as I was concerned there had been no such noble motive. The poisoned substance was my own and until I had brought it up to the surface into physical matter and had to some extent at least dispersed and purified it, it would continue in whatever body I built, to constitute a handicap and a potential source of weakness and danger.

Yet as I looked back I saw that even this attempt, personal as it seemed, had not only been of benefit to myself, for through the results of that suffering I had undoubtedly gained enough wisdom to understand the unhappy Nathaniel, to forgive and probably to help him.

My teacher confirmed this. "You even gave him a taste for philosophy and thus rid him of many prejudices which would have hampered him again in his next life, had he not dealt with them before passing over. A great achievement."

"Does one go on in the new life from precisely the place where one left the old?" I asked in some surprise.

"Yes, there are no gaps—no jumps in evolution beyond the space of time which must inevitably elapse before the new physical vehicle is of an age at which such capacities as have been acquired in the past can manifest. Were this more generally understood, the aged would take a very different view of their last days and not waste so much time going back into the past when they should be synthesizing their experiences and projecting themselves towards the future. Both you and Nathaniel did this, and profited considerably by those last years when you were forced by circumstances to turn inward upon yourselves."

"Was he not an enemy from my past?" I asked.

"Yes, so was Adela, but in a lesser degree. They had both been associated with you in Atlantean magic and were endeavouring also to do battle with the elementals they had invoked then and which were obsessing them both, driving Adela to drunkenness and to crime and

Nathaniel to such an unbalanced condition that he was practically insane. You had to pay off your old debts to them at some time and your Higher Self seized this opportunity and impressed you to serve them both as you did."

"But why," I asked, "should an Atlantean elemental drive a man to a state of religious mania? It seems a little incongruous."

"Nathaniel was genuinely trying to battle with evil, but often when there has been excess in one life, the personality—still branded with the stigmata of its past—will swing to the opposite extreme in an effort to readjust the balance, just as you did in Italy. Such men make the most passionate reformers. Violent socialists, for example, are often people who have ruthlessly crushed the working classes in an earlier life and now—not having yet acquired discrimination in the interval—while determined to help the poor, are prepared to crush, just as ruthlessly, everyone else! Religious fanatics may also be reacting from a series of licentious and immoral lives and in consequence feel impelled to try and deter others from falling into errors similar to their own. But unfortunately this is not always so; fanaticism can be the result of vanity and ignorance which are at the root of so much evil, cruelty, and violence; and since such fanatics do more harm to their religion even than its adversaries, the Dark Forces use them through their weaknesses to this end. That great Adept through Whom the Christ manifested His wisdom, found present hope for all save such zealous hypocrites; He knew that the man who so violently condemns errors in others is usually not far removed from similar weaknesses; by scourging them, he is but whipping himself away from something to which he is still secretly drawn. It may be that in his next life such a man will fall a victim to these very vices and will, thereafter, develop understanding, pity and love by becoming himself an outcast and walking hand in hand with sinners. Therefore it is well never to condemn people, since you cannot know what difficult Karma they may have courageously determined to work out, nor what are the forces arrayed against them in the deeps of their own nature where the eye of the ordinary man cannot penetrate.

"So small a part is perceptible on the physical plane of what a man is and of what he is striving to become, therefore ever greater understanding is needed to guide these wayward children. The modern psychotherapists realize this and are seeking to open to mankind the door of freedom through the power of the great occult formula *Man —know thyself.* But more is needed still; in the future, when the educationalists and healers have been able to develop the higher clairvoyance and can perceive the true condition of their brothers in affliction, a great change will come over all the methods now used both with regard to the treatment of the sick, that of the insane and those with criminal tendencies. But it is essential for this development that the Law of Karma and reincarnation should be more generally accepted and studied than it is today. When it is taught, as it will one day be, from earliest childhood and taken into consideration in every circumstance of life, men will not continue to suffer blindly and revolt against the apparent cruel compulsion of living in a universe governed either by blind fate or a capricious god.

"Look at your own past life and the cruel death of your son. How many parents have cursed God at such a bereavement even as you did then. No two causes can be quite similar, but behind them all is the Law. He was one of your group. This time you loved him enough, but it was the wrong kind of love, selfish, possessive, so unbalanced as to be almost criminal. You would never have allowed the boy to live a life of his own, never have given him the opportunity for individual development that he needed, for from the start it was obvious to Those who watched you in this test, that, like so many parents you were determined to live again through your child. Since, therefore, he had not deserved to suffer from such loving tyranny, such jealousy; since you, moreover, were still so unfitted for the joys and responsibilities of such a contact, he was taken; mercifully for him—and for you."

"That is the third time I have failed my Group in love," I said.

"Yes, it is one of the hardest tests, it demands the utmost that a man has. But the test must be passed; this problem in love will return until you do solve it. For no one is allowed to shirk his problems. Looking back even upon these few lives you have been shown, you must realize how the same problem is presented to the man again and again. To escape from bondage by breaking your shackles is no escape; it is merely transferring the bondage to another time when it may have become by the accretion of other incidents, more complicated and difficult; for such bondage, being the result of man's free will, is part of the immutable Law of his own being. No man can escape from himself, as you discovered in Egypt—no, not if he flees to the uttermost part of the earth—for that self is a part of the one Life. Therefore the sooner he realizes this and faces up to his Karma the better for him. In your eighteenth century life you faced many problems of the past and solved them; you forgave your erring wife, spared her lover, and had pity on your enemies, Adela and Nathaniel—that was a real advance.

This time you have returned determined to clear off as many as possible of those other more urgent debts contracted in the past through neglect, cruelty or ignorance, —some of which you have at last recognized. Until this work is accomplished you cannot progress in the way you desire.

Your relationship with Elizabeth had been left imperfect, so you have been born in the same family as she, and she it is, in a new form, whom you have always felt a deep compulsion to serve and to protect. You both failed each other then, but although you forgave her, you were the worst offender, for her fall was largely due to your neglect; therefore it is you, this time, who have been called upon to make the greater sacrifice.

"Although sometimes in moments of rebellion you have believed that this service stood in the way of greater occult development, of wider experiences and the freedom you have always craved, fortunately for you, love holds you now as duty alone might not have done, turning duty into a willing sacrifice. For what you have always imagined to be a barrier is in reality the very key to the door you desire to unlock. Had you not striven to perfect this relationship and sought to create harmony where before there had been tension, you would never in this life have been permitted the contacts with us that have been yours. For it is nearly always the commonplace and often despised incidents and problems of ordinary life which are used by the teachers on the Inner Planes to test would-be aspirants to the Path of Wisdom. The man who cannot deal wisely with small things is not yet fitted to undertake the far more strenuous efforts which will surely be demanded of him then. Sometimes, indeed, difficulties are deliberately put in his way so as to test the strength of his aspiration and to see whether he is so resolved to achieve his goal that nothing will shake his determination nor cause his footsteps to falter.

"You may thus recall how, for years, you practised your exercises in meditation without any obvious result; how difficult it was for you to obtain any information on occultism so that you were forced to seek it from within, and how, in your daily life, you had to struggle along without assistance and often without friends. This was all part of your training and a preparation for what has happened since, although you did not recognize it as such at the time. The trouble is man is so bewildered by the vortex of physical plane activity in which he is immersed that he is inclined to set up an entirely false scale of values.

"He is, indeed, as one who weaves a tapestry upon a tremendous loom; so close to it is he working, so engrossed is he in sending the shuttle back and forth over his tiny patch, that he cannot perceive the beauty and magnitude of the complete pattern. Yet it is essential that he should do so. One of the difficulties under which you all labour is that you are bound by erroneous conceptions of time and space; yet even the discoveries of your scientists should have made clear to you that time and space cease to exist for him who can enlarge his vision, step away from the confusing detail and view the whole. At present, being only in possession of that partial vision which the limitations of man's development impose upon him, he still sees lives, personalities, and events as separate broken fragments, having little or no relation to each other. But there is no break in continuity, no lesion anywhere. There is but *one* life, *one* consciousness, *one* supreme manifestation. To realize this, not academically, but in such a fashion that it colours his entire viewpoint, permeates all his activities, inspires every thought, dictates every action, is his ultimate aim. Until he has done this he will continue to be limited by the supreme illusion of Separateness, and remain bound upon the Wheel of Re-birth."

EPILOGUE

I SAT alone at the foot of the rough wooden cross marking the summit of a mountain in Central Europe. Around me was a desolation of scattered rock interspersed with short turf redolent with thyme and starred with brilliant Alpine flowers. Below stretched the narrow valley I had left that morning winding into the distance, its white torrent visible like a thread uniting the various villages which could be distinguished by a darkish blur or by the flash of sunlight on panes of glass or the steeples of a church. On and on the valley went until it lost itself at last in the blue mists of distance where lay the great town, representing to these people of the solitudes that outer world barred from them by a chain of rocky heights which could faintly be seen steeped in sunlight, a fantastic barrier, fairy-like and unreal.

Before me so close that one felt it would be easy to leap across the valley to those snow-piled flanks, dazzlingly white against the pure blue of the summer sky, stretched four magnificent glaciers, so cold, withdrawn and calm that they seemed to reduce all man's ant-like activities to their true proportions.

I was exhausted by a long and somewhat arduous climb in the great heat and lay still, allowing my thoughts to drift idly. That I was here for some purpose I did not doubt; but by now I knew from experience that it would reveal itself at the right moment and not before; so long as my senses were alert and my mind like a well-trained dog ready to come to heel at the slightest sign, nothing more at the moment was expected of me. The preliminary physical effort had been made, now I had only to await events.

But I had a great sense of expectancy. In some ways I was reminded of the atmosphere at the bungalow by the sea before those strange revelations which had marked such an epoch in my life and in those of my friends. Now as then I had been drawn away from the world into the solitudes; now as then I was aware of the presence of more powerful nature forces than usually surrounded me. But fire and air ruled this upper world; there one had felt more a part of the earth and the voice of the sea had been the dominant note in one's days and nights. Here was the mountain-top from which one could view one's little world in a truer perspective; there the range of visibility had been more circumscribed. Analogously here it was the realm of mind, there that of the emotions.

My thoughts travelled back to those weeks when our group had re-created for a moment that lost world when water ruled. How much had happened to us since then! Having evoked the past, we had all in our different ways been called upon to deal with it, not in conjunction but separately, since in Atlantis we had chosen the path of separation and only now were just beginning to realize the power which lay in unity—that other word for love.

Almost immediately we had been forced by the exigencies of our different types of work to go our several ways. Naturally we met whenever opportunity offered, for, however full of discord and hate our distant past had been, our relationship had radically changed, and the consciousness of the past was now helping to cement us in growing bonds of comradeship and affection.

But those meetings for a time became increasingly difficult. Each had obviously to work off his own Karma and undergo various tests and training in accordance with his particular line of development. On the other hand our Karma had been remarkably similar. There had been for all of us periods of enforced loneliness, many frustrations, financial loss, payment through service of debts to various personal links and also a good deal of illness and mental stress.

Since we had all been starting on a new cycle at that period these were the inevitable preliminaries to any further progress.

Whilst I had been engaged in writing my book and was receiving undreamed-of help and intensive training, I had become so accustomed to contacting those forces which were being drawn to my assistance that it had never occurred to me that any other conditions could supervene. But there came a time when I was warned that there lay ahead a period when it would be necessary for me to work off much Karma alone and utilize the powers I had acquired without such assistance before any further step could be taken. Slowly, almost imperceptibly then the forces began to withdraw, until I found myself, not alone —knowing what I did, that could be impossible—but certainly bereft of conscious communion with my teachers and therefore thrown once more upon my own resources. "We have hitherto made the effort to descend into your atmosphere and contact you," my teacher had said, "now it will be for you to learn how to rise mentally to our plane and contact us."

But what seemed to me at that time most incomprehensible was that my book remained unfinished. Do what I might, I could not succeed in completing the work which I had begun with such zest and such assurance.

The interim, as I have said, was filled with struggle, disappointments and difficulties. The waiting time had indeed seemed long and sometimes I feared never again to experience that unique sense of union with which no human companionship could ever compare. What I did not realize at the time was that, as everything in existence is governed by the law of cycles, so are the inner tides of man's development; even as the wave rises to its crest, breaks into far-flung spray and is followed by an apparent withdrawal into the depths, so does man progress, working forward to some intense effort or some important experience arising from a past cause and then, that wave of energy temporarily dissipated, retiring into what may appear to him to be a period of rest or even inertia. This is in reality a moment of pause allowing for the accumulation of fresh force. It follows the rhythm of universal life, that of night and day, of life and death, of eternal becoming.

These years were a time of experimentation in which I had to learn how to synthesize and apply the knowledge I had received in practical living. To accept willingly and gratefully such a gift as this teaching is one thing and comparatively easy; but to apply it with discrimination, to adjust it to modern conditions, even to sift the wheat from the chaff which is bound to accumulate in this field where weeds from the personal prejudices and unconscious resistances inevitably mingle with the good grain, is quite another matter.

The beginner, inexperienced and easily confused by the new conditions with which he is bound to be faced during this period of readjustment, must tread very warily if he does not wish to find himself in trouble. This is more especially the case when the teaching itself comes largely through psychic channels rather than from books or even a teacher on the physical plane. Discrimination and a critical and detached attitude is always essential. For all teachers, even the best intentioned on the lower levels are fallible and even teachings coming from far higher sources can be distorted and perverted by those who receive them as happened with the teachings of Jesus.

At the beginning of this period in my life false messages would occasionally be received, the veracity or otherwise of which I could only discover for myself.

What must never be forgotten is that it is through the subconscious mind that one can most easily be influenced until one has learned to tune oneself in more perfectly to the vibrations emanating from the superconscious mind—that is to say from the soul, and has learned to discriminate between the two. Herein lie many dangers, since the subconscious mind contains in effect the sum total of most of those undesirable elements left over from the man's previous physical plane experiences, not to mention those he has himself consigned to these regions of his being during his present life, which have not yet been assimilated and transmuted through the influence of his higher consciousness.

When he is determined to make the attempt to climb what might be called the spiritual mountain, and is beginning actively to co-operate with the divine law instead of struggling against it, his efforts often tend to galvanize the residue of the past and bring it up to be dealt with. This phase is essential because until this is transmuted to some extent at least, it would not be safe for the aspirant to greater wisdom—and therefore to greater power—to advance very far.

It is said that in certain cases these forces from the past can actually be seen by clairvoyants in the form of a "dweller" as was shown to me in Egypt. But the term can also be symbolical and stand for unresolved complexes and the dark turmoils controlling the aspirant from the unconscious. We all have such "dwellers" as every psychiatrist knows; powers in the hidden places of our being which influence us far more often than we know. It follows that any attempt to speed up our evolution inevitably produces reaction from these more primitive levels which have not yet been integrated into our personality and are in resistance to our efforts to allow the soul to control us.

This attempt at integration in preparation for a next step forward is taking place more widely today, largely owing to the work of the pioneers in psychology who are endeavouring to explore this underworld and bring its denizens up into the light where they can be revealed for what they are; for only then can they be controlled and rightly directed. When this is accomplished they will no longer be destructive and dangerous but rather valuable allies to the evolving man. Until he does learn to know and understand himself he cannot hope to change himself; and until he changes his whole polarization it will not be safe for him to rely upon any extrasensory or "occult" powers he may develop since they will inevitably be coloured and distorted by this subterranean self which he neither knows how to check nor control.

In view of this danger communication by automatic writing in my own development ceased as soon as possible, as it is one of the methods more open to interference by the dark forces than any other, a certain attitude of negativity being almost a *sine qua non*. This is an invitation to these ancient powers to make an effort to gain a footing in the pupil's subconscious which, once attained, would be a perpetual menace to his progress.

For as soon as a man makes a genuine effort to fit himself for the service of the spiritual leaders of the human race he inevitably attracts the attention of their antagonists whose whole object is to prevent the development of the higher qualities in man.

As the law of action and reaction operates in every realm, it follows that when positive force is poured down, forming a vortex of energy about the pupil to facilitate communication from higher levels, a vacuum invariably follows when that energy is exhausted. Unless he is aware of this and knows what measures to take to protect himself, these negative—or what are called evil—powers can manifest and communicate in the vacuum thus formed. They can even give themselves the appearance of the teacher to those who can see but cannot verify their vision by sensing the vibration which accompanies it. For the specific rate of vibration indicates the *character* of the entity and cannot be simulated.

As every man has a teacher upon the Right Hand Path, so, through his errors in the past, he has nearly always at some time linked himself to some influence upon the dark side which, naturally, will make every effort to divert him from achieving success and will attempt to shake his confidence and lure him away to other lines of development. For this reason it is dangerous for would-be pupils to invoke a teacher. The usual result of such invocations—based for the most part on ignorance and vanity—is that a "teacher" will appear but he may be an enemy in disguise full of flatteries and promises, and woe betide the man who is foolish enough to listen and follow such a one!

Therefore the ability to discriminate between subtle rates of vibration is the first thing a pupil has to learn. But before he can do this with a certain amount of confidence, it is necessary for him to evolve a type of equipment which can act as a kind of sounding-board and be capable of registering these different emanations which are, as it were, the wave-lengths of Those who desire to contact him. This recognition of a teacher's vibration is one of the greatest of all safeguards in occult work, but it can only be established when a certain proficiency has also been attained in the control of the mind and the power to direct it and hold it at will. It may be a long time before one can be absolutely sure of such contacts, although that inner certainty which is undeniable increases with practice.

Every phase of a man's development has thus to be tested, tried and judged in the light of experience. Ordinary common sense, emotional balance, and above all a very receptive attitude towards what is loosely termed his "conscience", are excellent guides through this morass of difficulties he is called upon to traverse during any rapid development of inner sensitivity. Nothing that goes against the man's own inner knowledge of right and wrong should ever be accepted. No matter from what high source the instructions purport to come; nothing that could remotely harm another, that would cause sorrow or fear to those who are not ready to understand such experiences, should be accepted and acted upon without the most serious consideration of the possible results. To seek to develop one's own powers to the detriment of others, leads to a very different goal. The true student considers always the feelings and capacities of those about him; this applies in small things as in great. But here again discrimination is a most essential factor; to gauge exactly where the importance of his own development ceases and its harmful reaction on others may begin, is one of the most difficult lessons to learn. This can only be done by experimenting, by failing many times, paying the price of failure and recommencing. But if he is animated by genuine love, if his intuition is awakened and he seeks enlightenment through communion with that god which dwells in the heart of every man, he will be less likely to err.

He must never forget that his aim is to work for humanity—not for himself, regardless of humanity; and that while he is in a physical body this work is obviously intended to be on the physical plane among his fellow-men, a fact, which although apparently so obvious is very often overlooked. Any attitude which tends to minimize unduly the importance of the physical plane, so that all its manifestations become unreal and seemingly valueless, can safely be taken as inspired from a doubtful source. No knowledge of inner planes, no contact with past lives, no wanderings into spheres of light, no powers, voices, visions, are of the least use to him unless they make of him a greater force for good in the world, unless they help him to deal wisely with the innumerable little problems which arise in his own life and which will be brought to him increasingly by others in distress; unless they teach him indifference to the blows of Karma, and above all to transcend misfortune and turn every experience into progress and power. It may take him many incarnations before he begins to mirror forth a gleam of the splendour of the Light Within, before his training begins to take practical effect in wider spheres, but the results should be instantaneous in the small circle of his life on earth. If he cannot be a good citizen it is useless to call himself a good occultist; spiritual advancement and bad citizenship are incompatible.

The irrefutable truth of these observations which my teacher had impressed upon me before I was left, so to speak, to my own devices, I had occasion to prove again and again.

My endeavours to develop those necessary capacities of body and mind were the cause of many difficulties and a great deal of ill-health. But no man can hope to progress very far by developing one part of himself at the expense of any other, and while he has an unreliable physical-plane instrument, he will find himself handicapped at every turn; groups of maladjusted and feeble elements in a body are always a source of potential danger, should any exceptional strain be put upon it—and this, in occultism, is always likely to occur; therefore as a preliminary to the work it was essential for me to endeavour to remedy such deficiencies.

My teacher had once said: "Remember, any effort causes resistance, and resistance in man's body registers as pain. A large proportion of pains and sorrows come about by people resisting the Law of Karma and resenting the necessities that it imposes upon them; the cultivation of a balanced mind and a reasonable outlook would do much to mitigate this. When a man has succeeded in eliminating from his vehicles all discordant elements, so that every atom of all his bodies is vibrating in harmony with the Divine Will, no activities on the physical or any other level will have any more the power to cause within him friction or disturbance. This is the secret of that perfect health, that inner peace and superabundant strength which the Great Ones have always possessed.

"But of course to reach such a harmonious condition the pupil has in the beginning to seek by an act of self-conscious will to alter the imperfect constituents of his body by transmuting them. This process often brings about a phase of very violent and painful conditions, for everything related to the past that he has himself created, is thereby stirred up to the surface. You began, of course, this process in Egypt but until now it has been more or less unconscious; having undertaken to do this work, cause and effect developed therefrom—if I may use a very inadequate term—almost automatically with very little free will apparent on the part of the personality. But now you have reached a stage when all the bodies must participate through the magic-working process of the mind under the direct guidance of the Higher Self. The clearer this guidance becomes, the quicker and more successful will these changes in your physical vehicles appear, but for a time you may apparently lose much of your present good health. This is the reason why so many occultists have sick and feeble bodies and are consequently held up to derision by those healthy materialists who have not begun to deal with the residue of the past which—did they but know it—is all accumulating in that great store-house of the subconscious mind, waiting to be dealt with later when they are capable of doing so."

My own particular efforts at transmutation during those past years certainly had manifested in unaccustomed bouts of ill-health and coupled with bad Karma in the form of financial trouble had handicapped me seriously in that occult work I had hoped to undertake. Moreover, as I found myself possessed after my intensive training was over of certain healing power, naturally I was called upon

EPILOGUE

to utilize it and was thus enabled to pay off further karmic debts from the past.

The year of which I am now writing had been a particularly busy one in this respect and, as I was not efficient as yet in dealing with my own physical vehicle, it had been inclined to give way under the strain.

It was then that someone with whom I had had great links of affection in many lives, came forward and offered to take me to the mountains to recuperate.

I felt that probably there was more behind this offer than was apparent, as by now I had acquired the habit of seeking a hidden significance behind every occurrence.

We had wasted much time trying to find a suitable place in which to stay and had been—so it seemed to us at the time—driven or lured on from one district to another, until at last we found this high valley where my last fortnight was to be spent. Here I determined to utilize to the full the air and sunshine of the heights, to seek to draw strength and healing from the earth and peace from the music of the waters, and in solitude to concentrate upon how to increase my receptivity to those specific vibrations I was striving to contact. Upon the day of our arrival my eyes were drawn to a certain mountain with precipitous grassy sides which rose through scattered trees to stony wastes. On inquiry I learned that from its summit one of the most extensive views of the district could be obtained. But for ten days thereafter it rained almost incessantly and while the weather continued unsettled it would have been madness for me, only just recovering from an illness, to have attempted to scramble up those paths turned now into rivulets; besides in any case nothing could have been seen through the veils of cloud. At all events it was a test of patience if nothing else to dwell in this realm of mists and water, watching the precious days slip rapidly away.

Then, just before my leave was up, the clouds rolled

back, revealing heights powdered with fresh snow and glittering with an ethereal beauty which no words can express; once more my eyes were turned towards that mountain and an irresistible impulse urged me to make at least one attempt to reach the summit.

It was hard going. The slopes, in may places running with water, were slippery as ice; here and there the path had disappeared. There was no shade and the heat soon became intense. Of course to anyone in training, physically fit and properly equipped, it would have been nothing at all; but at this time I was deficient in these necessities, having come to the mountains for a rest-cure, unprepared for anything more strenuous than sedate walks on moderately flat roads. It therefore put a strain upon my resources and soon my body began to send out danger signals so urgent that more than once I considered the advisability of giving up. But as each step revealed fresh glories, as peak upon peak rose into view, I became seized with that divine madness with which the devas of the mountains inspire their devotees, driving them occasionally to destruction, but often to achievements beyond their normal powers.

Besides by this time the climb had somehow become to me a kind of symbol. I was determined that nothing, so far as I was concerned, should keep me from reaching the top.

It was when I was nearing the summit that I lost my way. Some time before the path—so-called—had broken up into half a dozen tracks; I chose one I thought looked as if it led to the summit, instead of which, after taking me to the most precipitous places, it landed me in a tight corner and then disappeared.

The trouble was that, by now, my body had nearly gone on strike, so I paused to consider what I had better do. There was no chance of sitting down to rest and recover, for the slope was too steep and, moreover, running with little streams. So I had no alternative but to continue struggling up and hope that the going would improve, or to turn and slide back—it would amount to that—the way I had come. As a matter of fact I had made up my mind almost immediately that I was going on; it was really more a matter of somehow gaining sufficient strength to drive myself over this difficult patch without making one of those stupid slips or errors in judgement to which an over-strained body is liable. Such a slip, of course, might have unpleasant consequences in mountains as lonely as these; one might well lie for many an hour, a day, or even longer before one was found; but it was senseless to consider such possibilities. The thing to do now was to get my second wind; I was irritated that anyone with as much previous experience as myself should have got into such a situation, but I felt that given the choice, I would have done it again, so strong still was that inner urge somehow to reach the top. It would have been a help to have someone to give me a hand up to that next ridge, or even to shout directions and tell me what the going was like beyond and whether it was worth making the effort.

But I was alone; there was no living thing in sight; no movement even save the white shiver or a waterfall across the valley. Nothing. And suddenly I experienced one of those moments of intense awareness which come, I think, to most of us once in a lifetime, but particularly to those who find themselves facing some difficulty alone with nature. It is not actually fear, rather a sense of impotence, a recognition of your own limitations in the presence of this vastness, this power, this unfathomable mystery. You understand then what de Vigny meant when he wrote so bitterly of *l'implacable Nature*; here is Life manifesting in a thousand forms, yet each is so intensely occupied with its own activities that the death of a man, as of an ant, is of no possible significance. Mountains may fall, fire sweep away the forests, yet the processes of nature go on harmoniously, rhythmically: destruction, creation; life and death; the changing of a form matters so little in this aggregate of forms.

But to me it mattered supremely. I did not partake of this indifference. I was *Man*. Since my origin I had gone my own way, a law unto myself. I had set myself apart with deliberate intent, chosen to consider myself a special kind of creature, ignored the fact that I partook of the same elements as the rest of creation and was by that necessity their kin.

And this intense feeling of isolation now was the result of that ancient choice. This was my punishment as *Man*; that having driven myself from Eden I had lost my heritage and had become, to all appearances that separate unit which I imagined myself to be, with the fundamental weaknesses, the lack of power, the littleness in which such a cleavage from the source of Life could not but result. Yet how in *reality* could there be loneliness, isolation, for something that in its very essence was one with all life? But man had created from his illusion a thought-form of such power that it had dominated him for æons and would continue to distort his vision until, by a conscious effort of identification with the rest of life, he overcame it. Perhaps he was beginning to do so—science was showing him one way—and for the other, he must find that in himself. Had I not glimpsed it here? All about me was life, strength, healing, power. Could I but transfer into my own bodies these lavish gifts which are poured down without stint unceasingly upon all the sons of men, could I but learn to understand more of nature's laws, even the most mysterious and hidden, then nothing would be impossible. Only blind fools lost themselves on mountains; only because I was ignorant was I helpless. There was no real cleavage. I was the mountain, I was the earth, I, the sun, the waters and the snow; I, part of that same creative energy of which these were but different images.

Yet was I not even more than this? Was I not that hidden spirit which willed and which created? Yes, surely; for I alone was *conscious* of what I was and did. I alone had free will; I alone could choose the good and eschew the evil. In me—*Man*—stirred those mighty potentialities of the spirit whereby I might, in truth, become a son of God.

How often hitherto had I been told that this was my aim and my goal. I had accepted it, but it had been just an intellectual acceptance, a vicarious belief. Now suddenly I knew. Not because another told me did I acknowledge it, but because my eyes were, for that fraction of a second, unclosed. To be complete, man must indentify himself utterly with the Law of Life, sacrifice himself to it unconditionally; then does the Law give him back himself, but a self enlarged and glorified beyond belief. Now at last I thought I understood what St. Paul meant when he said that the Law will set us free. Eventually this process must be brought about through knowledge and understanding, but until we have reached that stage—the stage of the advanced occultist—is there not another way open to us? Identification through a love, a worship so intense that it becomes a burning faith? Was not that the faith which, we were told, could move mountains—not a blind faith generated from fear and ignorance, but one arising from a spiritual certainty which was not capable as yet of expressing itself in personal creative achievement?

A wave of ecstasy, of unshakable confidence passed through me. Alone? Never again, now that I knew myself in fact and in truth part of all Life. What then? If my own powers were limited and weak—the powers of that Great Life were they not inexhaustible? Could I but hold this realization—and I knew already with bitter certainty that I was not strong enough, that it would surely fade—I would in time become invulnerable. It had not faded yet.

I looked up the mountains and down. My situation had not changed, but now I was filled with a great serenity as if I had captured the spirit of those brooding heights and was partaker in their unshakable calm. I cannot hope to define this feeling more precisely than to say that I felt *secure*; nothing could happen that could be harmful to me since I knew myself in that revealing second to be inseparable from that universal Law of Love of which every activity, every manifestation was an intrinsic part.

At last I roused myself. I must go on, I couldn't stand there all day. If, as I felt at that moment so strongly, I was indeed a participator in the universal consciousness, then, despite all appearances to the contrary, my predicament was not unnoticed nor my need unknown. That was, I argued, as I began feeling my way cautiously over the slippery rock, all that ultimately mattered. So long as I manifested the requisite good will and made the best effort I could to reach the summit, the result, in a sense, was not my affair. If, for some reason I was meant to get there and was not capable of doing it alone, somehow help would come, if only through an influx of physical energy or merely in a strong impression where best to tread and in what direction to go. I had experienced that kind of help before.

It came. This is a record of sober fact, but I must admit that, for a moment, so unexpected was it and so dramatic, that I began to wonder whether I was not suffering from a stroke of the sun, or had developed a new psychic faculty and was seeing visions. For, upon the ridge above my head there appeared a few moments later the figure of a shepherd lad, strangely reminiscent of Greece with his white garments and bare legs and feet. I stared at him in amazement; but his voice reassured me. Within twenty minutes I was safely upon more solid ground and on my way to the summit.

The average man will say "coincidence". Perhaps.... Yet is it not stretching the proverbial arm of coincidence rather far? Later, on my return, I saw the boy again working with a party of harvesters down in the lower fields. Was it not strange that, in the whole vast area of desolate mountain-side, he should "by chance" have wandered at that precise moment over that precise ridge? These people are closer to nature than we, more open to the unseen forces which surround us and therefore more psychic and suggestible. To me, who have learned not to believe in "chance", it was but another proof of the existence of those influences, or intelligences which, working upon the inner planes in conjunction with the Law, are so often used to answer our need when it is sounded forth upon a vibration of faith. I am certainly prepared to believe, had I not turned to That which is greater than myself, the shepherd boy might have wandered by another track and I might have reached safety, uninjured perhaps, but would certainly not have attained my goal.

And now instead I lay entranced upon the soft turf and gazed out over this valley to those dazzling glaciers whence came the springs which had sung to us and the airs that had refreshed us and the rains that had hidden all that could be glimpsed of them below, from our sight. For only one was even visible from the valley, a small triangle of whiteness between the guardian flanks of nearer mountains. I had not known that so close these four giants brooded; I had not imagined, down there, that we were ringed about with this incredible purity and strength.

I had not known.... I had not known, for thousands of years, of those other Mighty Ones who, like these mountains, brooded over humanity in watchful and silent activity. Teachers, Adepts, Saints—name them how we will—and others too of Whom one could think only with awe; unfailing source of strength and inspiration, pouring down love and guidance upon man who knew them not, nor cared, nor sought to know. Yet now I knew; and when henceforward I was forced to walk in the shadowy valleys, when the threatening shapes of earth rose about me like the nearer mountains, illusively high because they were so close, shutting out with their rocks the vision of the white guardians, just as their shadows shut out so much of the sunlight from those who dwelt at their feet, I should still know what stood behind them, and understanding, would perhaps be able more abundantly to draw on this living energy, rejoice in it, and sometimes perhaps seek it out in its own place.

To know oneself one with Life, that was the secret, but how hard to hold this knowledge.

One cannot stay upon the heights, at any rate until one has reached that stage in evolution where time and place can be abolished by an act of will. Soon I, who was very far from this desirable stage, would have to go back. Why had I come here? Was it to obtain this glimpse that I had been impressed to climb, saved from failure—to say the least of it—by what still seemed to me definite intervention? Was it merely that I should be given this gratification of all my senses, my little personality filled with a joy and peace which I had not been able to find elsewhere? Could it be for such a personal end? I did not think so—there must be more to it than that.

It was very silent now. There was no wind, no song of water. The sun was intensely hot, yet tempered at this height by a sharpness in the air which filled one with energy and a curious mental clarity.

I placed myself in an attitude of meditation and waited. The silence grew more intense. My sensitivity increased. And gradually I became aware that the whole valley which I had imagined to be empty, was teeming with life, ranging from nature-spirits to those great devas that ensouled the mountains and seemed to float above them. But soon I began to sense other devas more remote, stupendous Beings whose auras had such amplitude that not the valley alone, but vast tracts of country were suffused by their emanations.

EPILOGUE

In glinting rainbow hues these currents flowed, widening like ripples when a stone is flung into a pool, to converge and mingle at last with the auras of other great spirits afar off. Sometimes lines of fire zig-zagged back and forth as if they were communicating and sometimes one would blaze up in a glory like a sun, glowing and expanding, until all semblance of form was lost and every spirit in the valley quivered rapturously in the repercussion of its activities.

The words "National Devas" came into my mind, and I then realized that indeed these mighty beings did appear to be in some curious way attached—if one may use such an inadequate term—to the country beneath them; but I saw, too, that the currents which they used, flowed out, regardless of man-made frontiers, to unite with those of their brothers who were the chosen guardians of other lands.

What mysterious work of fusion was in progress here? On earth all was chaotic; from below a mass of whirling, conflicting vibrations poured up to hang, dark and murky, like a fog close to the ground; thought-forms of hatred and jealousy between nations, of frontiers and tariffs, of armaments and intrigues, with fear paramount, father of them all, creating a vortex impossible for those who were in the midst of it to understand or to control.

But here above the countries, in the spacious upper airs where great Forms moved majestically and mighty Minds viewed the problems and perplexities of men by far different standards, only what was fine, only what was idealistic and noble, only thought-forms of construction, generated by love could penetrate. This was the great Sorting House of the superconscious mind of man to which he reached up for inspiration and enlightenment; for here all creative energy was garnered in, and all those men who worked for the general good were stimulated by its power.

But presently I realized that not alone the constructive efforts of man on earth were utilized by these Guardians of the Race. Destructive activities were also guided, as far as possible, into channels capable of later development, and used to break up those existing conditions which were retrograde or static, thus eventually opening the way for an influx of that energy, idealism and faith which are ever generated in an age of struggle and apparent defeat. Man's free will was untouched, but I saw very clearly now the way that Greater Will, the "Providence that shapes our end", turned all things into good. The Whole would not ultimately suffer through the stupidity and blindness of the part.

I was aware then that one approached. He stood by my side; his vibration enveloped me again in serenity and bliss. Here, in the silence, his voice spoke to my heart once more.

"Nothing is lost," he said, "nothing is wasted. It is often asked why all things must suffer, must struggle, must apparently decline and pass into obscuration. But since only through complete self-consciousness can God-consciousness be attained, it follows that those units alone that have passed through every experience both terrible and beautiful, destructive and creative, physical and spiritual, and who have gathered up into themselves innumerable aspects of the life-force, are capable of understanding the struggles of all the other units and of helping them also to develop towards the ideal.

"Today you have been made to realize as never before the underlying unity which binds all manifestations of Life together. You have perceived the work of those great National Devas which strive to bring peace, harmony and love between peoples and to destroy the barriers which pride and fear have for so long built up to separate them.

"The world is at the present time passing through what seems to be a terrible period of chaotic and apparently aimless stress. Actually nations are striving to work off their Karma and develop a truer sense of perspective and a greater understanding of the deep necessities for co-operation. For do not forget that nations follow the same method of evolution as individuals. They have their childhood, like men; their passionate and romantic age of adolescence, their maturity, their age, their decline—and their death. Sometimes, as in the lives of men, there is anarchy, sometimes defeat; sometimes what appears to be a retrograde movement takes place; sometimes will seeks to rule at the expense of Law, and reaction from previous errors in judgement manifests in fanaticism and tyranny. All natural growth is slow; and when the pace is forced too violently some form of disruption nearly always ensues. But the general trend is towards group harmony and brotherhood. Study history with an enlightened mind and you will be able to refute the assertions of those who say man has not progressed. He has within him, of course, remnants of the stages he has outgrown; he has relapses, and the more advanced in knowledge he becomes, the more terrible are the results of these relapses. But through these, too, he learns, nationally as well as individually. Seek through meditation to discover for yourself the Law of Correspondence which manifests throughout the mighty Scheme of which you are a part, and try to realize that from the smallest atom to the greatest Planetary Spirit all progress through the same cyclic movement upwards towards that state which cannot yet be known and upon which it is useless even for us to speculate."

His voice ceased. I gazed out over the mountains and contacted for a moment, it seemed, the conflicting rhythms of those multitudinous lives. How close these countries seemed with their problems, their hopes, their dreams and blind impulses! Yes, like men indeed they were; they, too, had their subconscious minds filled with ancient taboos and primitive tendencies; they, too, had that superconscious spirit which sought to guide, educate and control its body of manifestation. Yet beyond even these, faintly I sensed something more vast—some greater Life: the Planetary Lord, perhaps, of which all else here was a part. And He—was He not part of a greater Being yet? On and on . . . My mind reeled at the thought. Useless indeed was speculation! Enough for me to try and grasp the little that I had been shown, to try to solve the problems near at hand and play my part, however small, in seeking, as my teacher had once said, to bring some harmony into the turmoil of this age of Mars, the Destroyer.

His thought answered mine. "Yes," he replied, "it is practical idealists we need, not those who are apt to lose themselves in the fascinating mazes of cosmic speculations —although it helps the worker if he can realize what Powers stand behind him. We need those who can appreciate the inestimable treasures of wisdom which we have already given to mankind and re-interpret them according to the requirements of the present age.

"For the cry of the world which is experiencing that temporary disorientation inseparable from a phase when new values are being sought and old ones discarded with such rapidity, is now for new light, new guidance, new answers to those eternal problems which in one guise or another ever confront mankind. Some think there must come a fresh outpouring of wisdom; some believe in the advent of a new Messiah, others are for going back and seeking enlightenment from the religions of earlier ages. But what is most curious is that the majority still persist in ignoring that very revelation which was sent expressly to serve the modern world. Few seem to realize that mankind in general has not yet *begun* to assimilate the wisdom which was given out two thousand years ago, nor has any genuine attempt so far been made to follow out those teachings to their logical conclusion. Why then should some new teaching be expected until they do?

EPILOGUE

"I would have you consider this question: if the world had become Christian in the full meaning of the term—in other words, if every man on earth were behaving in his private life as Christ suggested he should behave, would there be any so-called 'modern problems'? Would the world be in any of the difficulties in which it finds itself today? This civilization of which some of you appear to be so proud, but which in reality is so primitive that in later incarnations you will look upon it much as you look upon that of certain native states, is the direct result of mankind's incapacity to understand and appreciate the divine promises contained in the doctrine of the Christ. For the teachings given to mankind are always synchronized to the needs of the age and race to which they are revealed; as evolution proceeds each great founder of religion repeats and amplifies previous teachings, seeking to correct those errors in interpretation which have crept in and distorted the truth. Christianity has suffered also from such errors; it has been debased and changed by men desiring to twist it to their own ends—councils of Churchmen afraid for their prestige, bigots, fanatics, and those ignorant of the enduring power of the Word. But the Word cannot be destroyed; in the end truth will prevail. The teaching of Christ was the synthesis of all that had gone before, His was the focal point, the apex of the triangle of Wisdom, turned down for an instant, like a dazzling spear-head of flame, to pierce the murk of the world. He expounded to mankind the perfect and everlasting Law, not for this age and this race alone, but for every race and for every age. 'Love God and love thy neighbour as thyself'; 'In what measure ye mete it shall be measured to you again.' Here, in two burning sentences is the Law complete. If every cult and religion were wiped out of existence and only this remained—it would be enough; for to the man who followed this Law without shadow of turning, all other things, all knowledge, all wisdom, all power and bliss would inevitably be added.

"You think now that it is impossible to *live* this law, to build a civilization upon it? I tell you it is *not* impossible. Mankind, through a multitude of bitter experiments, will come one day to the realization that life lived as Christ taught and lived it, is the only method through which happiness and harmony for the individual as well as for the race can be attained. Men talk of the Millenium—they do not realize that Christ gave them the key to that age of perfection. Let man not waste time looking for a new doctrine, nor for a new age to come upon the earth; divine gifts are not thrust into closed hands. The new age must proceed from the changed heart of each individual man and woman; the Second Coming will be the coming of the *Christ Spirit* manifesting in each body of flesh through the effort and aspiration of its owner. Before this can be, each man must first build *himself* upon the perfect pattern, for until the vessel be without a flaw how shall it hold the very Wine of Life itself?

"This is not yet understood. Men prefer to look without rather than within for revelations—it is so much easier. Yet it must be understood if humanity is to be saved from fresh disasters. Dimly the masses are aware of their desperate plight and their overwhelming need. The majority are not yet capable of rediscovering truth from that abyss of error into which it has been plunged; therefore leaders are necessary, servants of truth, lovers of humanity, yet withal men and women trained in the technique of modern methods of expression.

"Any such who are possessed at the same time of the potentialities of leadership, are now being very carefully watched by those former leaders of the Race who have stepped out of the cycle of lives and deaths and, living upon the heights, can look down on the confusions of nations and peoples, seeing the whole design with its tendencies and aims, just as you, looking down from this height, can see in what direction lead the hundreds of little paths, while to those who walk upon them only the difficulties just ahead can be perceived.

"Our work is mainly concerned with this development. But as we cannot contact directly the majority of people who are engaged in the dust of conflict and are too preoccupied, deafened and bewildered by the struggle to receive the ideas with which we would impress them, our one hope is to do so indirectly through those other men and women who are willing to become our instruments and are ready to sacrifice everything and train themselves so as to be able to correlate a knowledge of spiritual forces with those more mundane activities which their brothers are pursuing—oft-times so blindly.

"In order to facilitate this work at no great distance of time certain spiritual Centres will be founded in different places, particularly in the West. There are, scattered throughout the world, highly magnetized spots attuned to specific rates of vibration synchronized to definite epochs in the evolution of mankind. In these spots power is stored and great Beings are set to guard them, permitting access to those alone who, either consciously on the physical plane or sometimes only in their higher bodies are aware of what is to be done there. At the right moment, pupils will be sent to these places to draw upon the power and under direction of their teachers, will be shown how it is to be used. Groups will be formed and centres for meditation chosen where these pupils can work in close contact with their inner groups and teachers, undisturbed by the confusing emanations inseparable from closer contact with civilization. Scattered throughout the world these groups will constitute the links in the mystic chain destined eventually to unite mankind with its spiritual leaders and usher in a new age of peace and occult development.

'Many are already being trained to enter these groups,

but comparatively few will be capable of rising to this great opportunity unless they strive with all their will towards the goal. For very special qualifications will be demanded of them. Too many groups and movements in the past have been ruined by the lack of capacity for selfless service and the inclination to emphasize the importance of personalities which has characterized leaders and members alike. This has led to jealousy, pride and all the petty emotional manifestations of the lower self and has eventually undermined and destroyed these efforts of the Great Ones to serve humanity. Therefore this time particular care will be taken to choose only those who have been proved to be above such weaknesses. Loyalty, a just appreciation of values, harmlessness and emotional balance coupled with a desire to serve so ardent and one-pointed that it will have burned out any thought of personal achievement, will be the pre-requisites for this work.

"The need is urgent for such workers—more urgent than you know. It is essential for the salvation of humanity that all these barriers of separativeness between nation and nation, between individual and individual, should be broken down—and that soon.

"This can only be done by the enlightened. It matters not what may be their creed or race, the form their activities take or the name they give to their goal. Musicians, doctors, scientists, poets, artists, social workers of all kinds, every idealist, every dreamer who strives to make his dreams a reality, these are our co-workers, these our instruments.

"We ask, we appeal to all those who love humanity and are desirous of participating in this great work of preparation and regeneration, to make a superlative effort to prepare themselves that they may indeed be fitted to receive the baptism of the New Age.

"We say to these men and women: 'Speak peace, think peace, work unceasingly for peace. If your scope at first seems limited do not despair, begin by exerting your influence in your own immediate circle and as your power for good grows, so will the circle widen about you. Exercise self-knowledge, self-judgement, and self-control; without these no progress can be made. Think right thoughts, refuse to be caught up in the vortex of fear and hate and greed which is raging about you. Seek to bring harmony into every life that touches yours; never stir up the embers of suspicion and of jealousy. Keep a guard over your tongue and let your thoughts be always positive, helpful, and filled with love. Let each one refuse to listen to scandal or to repeat it, whether it touches personal or national life. Remember ever how mighty is the power of the word; scandalmongers stand dangerously near to the Left Hand Path and are used by the Dark Forces more often than they would care to know.

" 'Shun, therefore, the repetition of idle rumours, talk of strife and of the imminence of wars. We are doing all we can to avert another international conflagration from our side by trying to impress those who are sensitive to our influence with our foresight and wisdom. You on earth can either aid us in this work or, if you choose, aid the forces of evil which seek to bring conflict upon mankind by disseminating the poison-germs of suspicion and hatred. Learn to sift the true from the false. Be quick to recognize dangers, but do not speak of them unless it is necessary, lest the ignorant and timorous fan your sparks into flame. Be slow to judge all men but particularly other nations who, albeit by paths different from yours, are yet seeking the same goal. Remember, only temporarily are you attached to any particular national life. Those alien characteristics, faults and vices which you comdemn have been your own in the past and by that very condemnation you may be binding yourself to them in future incarnations. The life of a nation is but the reflection of certain trends of human development and these are the result of innumerable causes which must work out in specific effects on a larger scale than that of the single individual; but a nation also receives the judgement it has meted out to others, and when it is in the throes of rebirth, suffering the agonies of karmic retribution or, through lack of vision, creating anew causes for which it will have to pay in the fullness of time, it is for other nations to understand, to pity, to hold out a helping hand, to strengthen and to love—not to condemn and attack. This may seem too much to ask of mankind as it is now, but the whole can only grow through the growth of its individual members and by their example.

*Your League of Nations which the short-sighted despise because of its many imperfections (forgetting their own) is mankind's first tentative effort towards creating an ideal pattern for the future. It is the seed from which the great tree of international unity will ultimately spring, and everyone who gives it encouragement who thinks and acts with pure love in his heart is hastening that consummation; for the dreams of the idealist of today are the accepted commonplaces of the masses tomorrow.

" 'Go forward, then, remembering that there is no limit set upon achievement save the limit of individual effort, and in proportion to that effort will be the help poured down from the inexhaustible Fount of power and love. For every man achievement, liberation, power and bliss unlimited wait, the key to that door which leads from death to life is in your own hands. We say to you all, use it now, that others following in your steps may the more easily enter in.

" 'Fear nothing. There is no power in the Cosmos, no destructive force however malignant, that can touch the man who by a deliberate act of choice unites himself with the Divine Will.

* This was written before the Second World War.

"'Never yield to despair. It matters not how weak you seem to be, how dark your past has been; if the desire for service burns truly within you, it will be guarded by Those stronger than yourself, and every opportunity for development will be given you. There is no man on earth, however debased, however without a gleam of godliness, of hope, he may seem to be, who cannot climb, if he so wish, to the Gate of Liberation, who cannot escape from the Wheel of Rebirth and at last stand upright in the ranks of Those who have passed through similar sufferings and have won at last to freedom.

"'They are your Brothers; you do not strive alone. Beside you go evermore These who have sacrificed Themselves to keep that divine spark in you alive and who will breathe upon it with the breath of love until it break at last into flame, merging into the Great Flame with which They—Adepts, Saviours, Saints, Sages, and all the glorious company of the Liberated—are one.

"'Only then, O Divine Wanderer, when you, *Man*, perfected and complete, stride like a titan out of the earth's orbit to vaster planes of Cosmic activity, will the knowledge of your true destiny be unfolded. In that hour the past will appear as a night that is sped, and the future —unimaginable glory. Sphere after sphere, system after system, scheme after scheme will open out before your gaze as you pass on your way, searching still for *That* which is beyond thought or imagining, yet is forever yourself, your Source, your Existence—and your goal.'"

QUEST BOOKS
are published by
The Theosophical Society in America,
a branch of a world organization
dedicated to the promotion of brotherhood and
the encouragement of the study of religion,
philosophy, and science, to the end that man may
better understand himself and his place in
the universe. The Society stands for complete
freedom of individual search and belief.
In the Theosophical Classics Series
well-known occult works are made
available in popular editions.

THE THEOSOPHICAL PUBLISHING HOUSE

Wheaton, Ill., U.S.A.
Madras, India   London, England

Publishers of a wide range of titles on many subjects including:
Mysticism
Yoga
Meditation
Extrasensory Perception
Religions of the World
Asian Classics
Reincarnation
The Human Situation
Theosophy
Distributors for the Adyar Library Series of Sanskrit Texts, Translations and Studies

---

The Theosophical Publishing House, Wheaton, Illinois, is also the publisher of

QUEST BOOKS

Many titles from our regular clothbound list in attractive paperbound editions
For a complete list of all Quest Books write to:
QUEST BOOKS
P.O. Box 270, Wheaton, Ill. 60187